SIR FRANCIS DRAKE AND THE FAMOUS VOYAGE, 1577-1580

Published under the auspices of the
CENTER FOR MEDIEVAL AND RENAISSANCE STUDIES
University of California, Los Angeles

Contributions of the
UCLA CENTER FOR MEDIEVAL AND RENAISSANCE STUDIES

1. *Medieval Secular Literature.* William Matthews, editor (1965)

2. *Galileo Reappraised.* Carlo L. Golino, editor (1966)

3. *The Transformation of the Roman World—Gibbon's Problem after Two Centuries.* Lynn White, jr., editor (1966)

4. *Scientific Methods in Medieval Archaeology.* Rainer Berger, editor (1970)

5. *Violence and Civil Disorder in Italian Cities, 1200–1500.* Lauro Martines, editor (1972)

6. *The Darker Vision of the Renaissance.* Robert S. Kinsman, editor (1974)

7. *The Copernican Achievement.* Robert S. Westman, editor (1975)

8. *First Images of America: The Impact of the New World on the Old.* Fredi Chiappelli, editor; Michael J. B. Allen and Robert L. Benson, co-editors (1976)

9. *Friedrich Diez Centennial Lectures.* Edward F. Tuttle, editor (Supplement to *Romance Philology,* vol. XXX, no. 2, 1976)

10. *Old English Poetry: Essays on Style.* Daniel G. Calder, editor (1979)

11. *Sir Francis Drake and the Famous Voyage, 1577–1580.* Norman J. W. Thrower, editor (1984)

Portrait of Francis Drake engraved by Crispin van de Passe, from *Effigies regum ac principum*, Cologne, 1598. Courtesy of The British Library.

SIR FRANCIS DRAKE AND THE FAMOUS VOYAGE, 1577-1580

Essays commemorating the quadricentennial of Drake's circumnavigation of the Earth

EDITED BY NORMAN J. W. THROWER

UNIVERSITY OF CALIFORNIA PRESS   *Berkeley / Los Angeles / London*

The emblem of the Center for Medieval
and Renaissance Studies reproduces the imperial eagle
of the gold *augustalis* struck after 1231 by Emperor
Frederick II; Elvira and Vladimir Clain-Stefanelli,
The Beauty and Lore of Coins, Currency and Medals
(Croton-on-Hudson, 1974), fig. 130 and p. 106.

University of California Press
Berkeley and Los Angeles, California
University of California Press, Ltd.
London, England
© 1984 by
The Regents of the University of California
Printed in the United States of America

1 2 3 4 5 6 7 8 9

Library of Congress Cataloging in Publication Data
Main entry under title:

Sir Francis Drake and the famous voyage, 1577-1580.

    Bibliography: p.
    Includes index.
    1. Drake, Francis, Sir, 1540?-1596—Addresses,
essays, lectures.   2. Voyages around the world—Addresses,
essays, lectures.   I. Thrower, Norman Joseph William.
G420.D7S57   1984   910'.92'4   83-10446
ISBN   0-520-04876-8

CONTENTS

ILLUSTRATIONS

State of California
SIR FRANCIS DRAKE COMMISSION, 1975–1980

Mr. Raymond Aker
Mrs. Lalita M. Armour, *Vice President*
Mrs. Paciencia L. Balonon
Mr. John F. Barrows
Dr. Ray A. Billington[†]
Mr. Arthur L. Blum
Mrs. Ethel S. Crockett, *Vice President*
Mr. Stanton H. Delaplane
Mrs. Harriet H. Doerr
Dr. Benjamin P. Draper, *Vice President* (deceased)
Mr. Albert D. Elledge
Mr. Warren L. Hanna
Dr. James D. Hart
Mr. R. Harold Hartsough, *Treasurer* (deceased)
Dr. James S. Holliday
Mr. J. Roger Jobson
Mrs. Jule Johnson
Assemblyman John Knox
Mr. Karl Kortum
Mrs. Patricia L. Leydecker
Dr. V. Aubrey Neasham[†]
Mr. Alfred W. Newman, *Secretary*
Mr. Scott Newhall
Mr. Robert H. Power
Mr. Donald R. Thieler, *Treasurer*
Dr. Norman J. W. Thrower, *President*

[†]Deceased after the Commission had
officially completed its work in 1980.

BUCKINGHAM PALACE.

Sir Francis Drake is one of the great folk heroes of England and I know that all his admirers in his home country are happy to know that the 400th Anniversary of his landing on Californian soil is being celebrated with such enthusiasm.

Seaman, explorer, commander, administrator and statesman, Drake will never cease to inspire all those on both sides of the Atlantic who share the vigorous and enterprising heritage of one of the greatest Elizabethans.

Best wishes for a most successful and happy occasion.

Philip

June 1979

Message from His Royal Highness Prince Philip, Duke of Edinburgh, on the occasion of the quadricentennial of the landing and sojourn of Sir Francis Drake in California.

PREFACE

The quadricentennial of the first English contact with what is now the United States, through Sir Francis Drake's visit to the west coast and through the settlement sponsored by Sir Walter Raleigh on the east coast, is being celebrated in the years 1979 and 1985, respectively. In both California and North Carolina, these Elizabethan contacts merit special recognition.

Many events during a three-year period, 1977–1980, honored Drake's famous voyage of 1577–1580—the second global circumnavigation (preceded by that of Magellan), and the first from which the commander returned home. These events began in London in August 1977 with the opening of a special British Library exhibition. They continued the following month in Plymouth, with a visit by Her Majesty Queen Elizabeth II and His Royal Highness Prince Philip, Duke of Edinburgh, to the city and port from which Drake had sailed four hundred years earlier.

The California celebrations were initiated on 17 June 1973 with the approval by the Governor of California of Assembly Bill No. 253, relating to the establishment of the Sir Francis Drake Commission. The purpose of the Commission, which terminated its work on 31 December 1980, was to organize a fitting commemoration of the quadricentennial of Drake's appearance in what is now Marin County, California; his naming the surrounding country Nova Albion; and his receiving of it from the Miwok Indians on behalf of Queen Elizabeth I. By these actions, and through his diplomacy in Southeast Asia later in the voyage, Drake laid the foundation of a British commonwealth overseas which was ratified when he was knighted after his return to England.

The quadricentennial of the landing and five-week sojourn of Sir Francis Drake and the officers and crew of the *Golden Hind* in California from 17 June to 23 July 1579 was celebrated in all parts of the state, culminating in an international conference from 10 to 17 June 1979. From this conference, entitled Sir Francis Drake and the Famous Voyage, 1577–1580, this volume arose.

Among the activities in California honoring Drake's voyage were religious services, pageants, parades, exhibitions, and the publication of scholarly works. The latter included the book *Lost Harbor: The Controversy over Drake's California Anchorage,* by Warren L. Hanna (University of California Press, 1979), and two monographs, *The Plate of Brass Reexamined* (1977) and *The Plate of Brass Reexamined: A Supplementary Report* (1979), both issued by the Bancroft Library. As their titles suggest, these publications deal with two of the most vexing problems of Drake's California contact: the exact location of his anchorage and the very controversial artifact which has puzzled scholars for over forty years. Because of the timely appearance of these works their subjects are not emphasized in the present volume.

The Drake conference in California began with a reception given on Sunday 10 June 1979 by the Center for Medieval and Renaissance Studies of the University of California, Los Angeles (UCLA), co-sponsor of the conference with the Sir Francis Drake Commission. The first full day, Monday 11 June, was at the Huntington Library; the proceedings were opened by the British Consul General in Los Angeles, T. W. Aston. An exhibition, "The World that Discovered Sir Francis Drake," was viewed there. Sessions continued at UCLA; and an evening reception at the J. Paul Getty Museum in Malibu was given on 12 June by Consul General Aston. The British Embassy was represented throughout the conference by the Naval Attaché, Admiral Burgoyne. Wednesday 13 June was spent traveling to the San Francisco Bay Area, where sessions continued on 14 June at the International House in Berkeley and at the Society of California Pioneers in San Francisco. On 15 June a plaque honoring Drake was unveiled at Vista Point (at the north end of the Golden Gate Bridge) by Councillor Graham Jinks, the Lord Mayor of Plymouth, who represented Drake's home area. In the evening exhibitions were previewed and receptions held at the Asian Art Museum and at the California Academy of Sciences, both in Golden Gate Park, San Francisco. On 16 June a reenactment of Drake's landing, and of the meeting of the English sailors with California Indians, was performed at Drakes Bay in Marin County, north of the city. Here another plaque honoring Drake was unveiled by the Right Reverend and the Right Honourable Gerald A. Ellison, the Lord Bishop of London. A reconstructed Miwok Indian village was visited. Then followed a reception at the residence of British Consul General I. A. C. Kinnear in San Francisco; later there was a ball at the Sheraton Palace Hotel.

The British Library exhibition opened at the Oakland Museum on the anniversary of the landing day, Sunday 17 June. After lunch the conferees moved to the Bancroft Library in Berkeley, where an address was given by Dr. David B. Quinn, Vice President of the Hakluyt Society, London, and a Drake exhibition was viewed. The journey was then made across the bay to San Francisco, where a Special Evensong and Te Deum of Thanksgiving was held for Sir Francis

Drake—who was a deeply religious man—at Grace Cathedral on Nob Hill. A great procession, including clergy of all faiths, officials, commissioners, and members of patriotic groups both American and British, preceded the services. The lessons were read by Consul General Kinnear and by Dr. Knox Mellon, representing the Governor of California; and the sermon quoted below was given by the Lord Bishop of London. Heraldic banners of the arms of Queen Elizabeth I and Drake were presented by the Commission to the Cathedral. The final event was a banquet held at the Empire Room of the Sir Francis Drake Hotel, where an address was delivered by Dr. Helen Wallis, Map Librarian of the British Library.

During the week-long peregrination of the conference, many addresses were made to a variety of audiences. Nine papers delivered at the Huntington Library and the Berkeley and Los Angeles campuses of the University of California, along with an expanded version of Dr. Wallis's banquet address at the Sir Francis Drake Hotel, are included as chapters of this volume.

John H. Parry takes us with Drake from England to California, a story continued in later essays. In his survey "Drake and the World Encompassed," Parry puts the circumnavigation into historical perspective. The problems of navigation in Elizabethan times and those encountered by Drake in particular are considered by David W. Waters. The great danger of navigating unknown seas is graphically portrayed in this essay. The "Famous Voyage," especially in respect to the earlier source materials, is treated by David B. Quinn, who shows how dependence on incomplete and later accounts (in the absence of the original log) makes interpretation difficult. Drake in two important geographic locations during the Famous Voyage is considered by Kenneth R. Andrews and William A. Lessa. Andrews demonstrates that the true focus of the enterprise was South America. When Drake had to abandon that area, he struck boldly across the Pacific and thus reached home, as shown by Lessa. Drake's life in England's West Country is treated by Crispin Gill in "Drake and Plymouth." Drake is seen here as a child, as a married man, as mayor, as Member of Parliament, and as hero of the defeat of the Spanish Armada. James Barber, Director of the Buckland Abbey/Plymouth Art Gallery, approved the captions of photographs of the house purchased by Drake after the circumnavigation.

Literature inspired by Drake's voyage, particularly by one of his contemporaries, is the subject explored by Michael J. B. Allen, who relates these writings to other epics of navigation and discovery. W. T. Jewkes brings the literary story up to date in "Sir Francis Drake Revived." The cartography of Drake's voyage is the subject of the wide-ranging chapter by Helen Wallis, which illustrates the importance of cartography to the voyage—as well as the contribution of the voyage to cartography. The influence of Drake's pioneering circumnavigation in the Pacific on attempts to discover a passage through or around North America and unknown lands in the Southern Hemisphere in the two hundred years before James Cook is summarized in "The Aftermath," by the editor. A collection of Drake bibliographic items is also included; this was compiled by Benjamin P. Draper over many years of research in archives in different parts of the world and was prepared for publication by Frances Zeitlin, formerly the Medieval and Renaissance Bibliographer of the Research Library at the University of California, Los Angeles. Minor differences in the spelling style of the cited works are attributable to differing interpretations by the contributing scholars.

In his sermon, which he has graciously allowed us to quote, the Lord Bishop of London said, in part:

> Today we are carried back into history. We find ourselves indeed at the beginning of what historians call modern times, but in a world strangely different from anything that relates to our experience. It was a world in which the Pope could carve the New World into two pieces and allot one half to Spain and another to Portugal; a world in which the old powers of Europe could send their splendid but lumbering ships across the Atlantic to bring back the vast mineral resources they found on this side to pay for the armies and navies they needed; a world when another new power was beginning to flex its muscles and produce men of vision, courage and ambition; a world in which the cocky young sailors bred in the West Country of England were ready to sail their ships vast distances, and with a breathtaking effrontery insult the old regime and steal their great possessions from under their noses. It is a world very different from our own that we enter in this celebration. It needs much imagination to understand it.
>
> And what of the man at the center of the drama? Francis Drake was short of stature, with red hair and bright penetrating eyes. He was arrogant, self-confident, self-assured. He was fanatically religious. He was a highly skilled sailor. He was courageous and imaginative. He could be cruel. He could be courteous, thoughtful and kind. With good reason the Spaniards loathed and feared him, for almost single-handed he had challenged the might of a great empire. The name "el Draco" struck fear into their hearts. They regarded him as a pirate, a rascal, a "shameless robber who feared not God nor man."
>
> But in England he became a legend in his own lifetime. Next to the Queen he personified the hopes and the ideals of an emergent nation. He was the David challenging Goliath and laying him low. He had that charisma, that personal magnetism, which is the possession of all great leaders. He could make colossal mistakes, he could be ruthless, he could be maddening. But he created such a character for himself that men would do anything for him. And the English loved him. He had that power given to very few to imprint his personality not only on his own generation but on posterity. Men still speak with awe of Drake's Drum.
>
> But what has all this to do with us, other than a passing concern in an interesting piece of history? . . . Two considerations, one direct, one more general, can be our justification.
>
> First, it is a good thing to honour men who achieve great things and to

remember the anniversaries of their accomplishments. History is sign-posted by those geniuses who saw something that they thought worth doing and exercised their skills in achieving it. . . . We all need the inspiration of heroes, of discoverers, of inventors. Francis Drake, for his circumnavigation of the world, takes his place in the company of those who lift us out of the routine of life into the romance and wonder of the world God has given us.

But at a deeper level the life of Francis Drake illustrates, as others have done before and since, man's hunger for freedom and his determination to achieve it at whatever cost. We may vary in our judgments on what he did. Pirate or patriot? Buccaneer or hero? One thing is clear. He and his compatriots saw the world confined and restricted by power and privilege, and they were determined to break the shackles. They sailed out into the mighty oceans in order to enjoy the freedom of adventure and achievement.

The last public occasion involving the Sir Francis Drake Commission, State of California, was the unveiling of a plaque placed below the statue of Drake on Plymouth Hoe, Devon, by His Excellency, The Honorable Kingman Brewster, Jr., American Ambassador to Great Britain, 25 September 1980. This plaque, which had been brought by the Commission to Plymouth three years earlier, stands as a permanent monument to friendship between California and Devon, Drake's home county.

A great many people and institutions, a number of them named above, contributed to the 1979 Drake celebrations in California. Special acknowledgment is made to the United States National Endowment for the Humanities for a generous grant which made the Drake conference possible. Arrangements were handled efficiently by the UCLA Center for Medieval and Renaissance Studies, of which Fredi Chiappelli is director. I should also like to thank members of the Sir Francis Drake Commission, whose personal generosity in providing matching funds, other financial support, and entertainment of the participants was essential to the success of the conference.

N. J. W. T.
Pacific Palisades, California

CONTRIBUTORS

MICHAEL J. B. ALLEN, Professor of English and Associate Director, Center for Medieval and Renaissance Studies, University of California, Los Angeles, U.S.A.

KENNETH R. ANDREWS, Professor of History, University of Hull, England

BENJAMIN P. DRAPER (deceased), Professor of Communications, San Francisco State University, U.S.A.

CRISPIN GILL, formerly Editor, *The Countryman,* Burford, Oxford, England

W. T. JEWKES, Director of the Center for Programs in the Humanities and Associate Dean, College of Arts and Science, Virginia Polytechnic Institute and State University, U.S.A.

WILLIAM A. LESSA, Emeritus Professor of Anthropology, University of California, Los Angeles, U.S.A.

JOHN H. PARRY (deceased), Gardiner Professor of Oceanic History and Affairs, Harvard University, U.S.A.

DAVID B. QUINN, Andrew Geddes and John Rankin Emeritus Professor of Modern History, University of Liverpool, England

NORMAN J. W. THROWER, Professor of Geography and Director, William Andrews Clark Memorial Library and Center for Seventeenth- and Eighteenth-Century Studies, University of California, Los Angeles, U.S.A.

HELEN WALLIS, Map Librarian, Map Library, British Library, London, England

DAVID W. WATERS, Caird Fellow and formerly Deputy Director, National Maritime Museum, Greenwich, England

Drake and the World Encompassed

JOHN H. PARRY[†]

In this most famous and peerlesse gouernment of her most excellent
Maiesty, her subjects through the speciall assistance, and blessing of God,
in searching the most opposite corners and quarters of the world, and . . .
in compassing the vaste globe of the earth more then once, haue excelled
all the nations and people of the earth. For . . . who euer heard of
Englishmen at Goa before now? what English shippes did heretofore euer
anker in the mighty riuer of Plate? passe and repasse the vnpassable (in
former opinion) straight of Magellan, range along the coast of Chili, Peru
and all the backside of Noua Hispania, further then any Christian euer
passed . . . & last of al returne home most richly laden with the
commodities of China, as the subjects of this now flourishing monarchy
have done?[1]

So wrote Richard Hakluyt, that superb propagandist of overseas endeavor,
in dedicating his great work, *The principall navigations,* to his master, Sir
Francis Walsingham. Most of Hakluyt's contemporaries would have echoed his
sentiments, though they might not have equaled his sonorous prose. Allowance

†Professor Parry died 25 August 1982.

must be made, of course, for Elizabethan exaggeration. The Elizabethans, mercurial and sentimental, habitually bragged about English successes with all the strident boastfulness of the newly arrived; but they also felt the anxieties of the newly arrived. They wanted reassurance that the glories of their own time—so recent, so dramatic—were not mere sudden and temporary accidents of fortune. They wanted a pedigree of glory, an assurance of continuity, and they looked for it in a succession of heroes, past and present, real or fictitious. They flocked to see Shakespeare's historical plays, they read Hakluyt's *Voyages*; they followed the stately progression of the chronicles of Hall, Holinshed, Stow, Speed, and Camden; and they gave extravagant adulation in their own day to such men as Grenville and Sidney. After the Famous Voyage, as the circumnavigation was rightly called, Sir Francis Drake came to be included in the list of heroes. John Stow tells us that after Drake was knighted "his name and fame became admirable in all places, the people swarming daily in the streets to behold him, vowing hatred of all that durst mislike him."[2]

Yet in all this hero worship a note of reserve can be detected: Stow's account clearly implies that there *were* people who "misliked" him. Of course the coin of adulation always has its reverse side, of envy, backbiting, and malice, but many responsible people distrusted Drake for more serious reasons. His career certainly provided no pedigree of glory for the newly arrived; he was all too obviously newly arrived himself, a man of humble origin, patently a man on the make. His early activities were not reassuring. He had been engaged in smuggling, slave running, and small-scale raiding in the Spanish Caribbean. Although slaving and smuggling carried no moral opprobrium in the sixteenth century, the line between piracy and legitimate privateering was difficult to draw precisely. Drake himself always claimed that his Caribbean raids were in reprisal for injuries done him by Spanish officials at San Juan de Ulúa (see Gill, ch. 6, below) and elsewhere, but he never obtained formal letters of reprisal, and he raided without authorization in peacetime. His enemies, again according to Stow, called him "the master thief of the unknown world."[3] His last Isthmus of Panama raid, in 1573, was successful and yielded enough Spanish silver to enable him to assume the trappings and "port" of a gentleman, though this did not necessarily make him one in the eyes of his contemporaries. His liking for display offended their sense of propriety, their sense of what Shakespeare called "degree." Many of Drake's foibles—his cocksureness, his craving for popularity, his arrogant disregard of the opinions and interests of others, and perhaps most of all the smug, preachifying godliness of the man—must have irritated many of his contemporaries.

More serious still, Drake was potentially a dangerous man. His violent anti-Spanish and anti-Catholic feelings struck a popular note, especially in his native West Country; but for those who had to conduct foreign policy they were an embarrassment. So long as Drake's activities were unofficial and small in scale, they could be disavowed. Once he was recognized and publicly encouraged, however, the Crown would have to accept responsibility for his depredations.

He might then goad the Spanish to the point of war. Queen Elizabeth I and her more prudent counselors wished to avoid war if they could, and were determined in any event to postpone it as long as possible. It so happened that when Drake, already known as a bold and lucky leader, returned from the Caribbean in 1573 and received in some quarters a hero's welcome, relations with Spain were in a stage of temporary improvement. Drake's piratical success was politically unwelcome. He was warned to lie low, and for a time he found inconspicuous employment with the Earl of Essex in Ireland in a bloody and futile attempt to colonize Antrim. It was during this Irish interlude that he first met Thomas Doughty, who accompanied him on the Famous Voyage, with fatal consequences for Doughty.[4]

The Famous Voyage, despite all misgivings, proved to be the turning point of Drake's career. By means of this voyage he graduated, one might say, from slightly disreputable though successful slaver and pirate to famous privateer-explorer. He was to become a widely—if intermittently—respected admiral and ultimately a folk hero and a national legend.

To some extent the change in Drake's fortunes was due to political circumstance. During his three years' absence on the voyage, Anglo-Spanish relations again deteriorated. The Spanish seemed to be succeeding in their attempts to suppress rebellion in the Netherlands, perhaps to promote it in Ireland, and probably to unite Portugal to the Spanish Crown. Official England in consequence became more fearful and suspicious of Spain and more sympathetic to men of Drake's reputation, prejudices, and skill. Such men, it was recognized, might soon be needed. This fortuitous development had nothing directly to do with Drake, of course. His leap from slightly disreputable notoriety to national fame was more the result of the achievements of the voyage. These were indeed remarkable; the cost in men and ships was heavy, but the rewards were great. Whether from genius or fortune, the whole voyage appears as a triumph of bold and flexible opportunism, and probably its results far exceeded anything its promoters had contemplated.

There is considerable doubt as to exactly what the promoters had contemplated. The voyage was privately organized and financed. Its backers included a number of prominent men: Secretary Walsingham, a leading proponent of a "forward" policy in the New World; the Earl of Leicester, high in the Queen's favor; Sir Christopher Hatton, captain of the Queen's guard; and the Hawkins brothers, Drake's kinsmen and former employers, shipping magnates who both (but especially John, treasurer of the Queen's dockyards) had a grievance against Spain. An enterprise so sponsored would have required at least the tacit approval of the Queen, and this she appears to have given. Whether she gave more is uncertain. She would not allow royal ships to be used, but she probably made an investment of money. This participation, though it would not have been made public, would have given the whole undertaking a semi-official standing. Drake claimed at one stage in the voyage to hold a written commission from the Queen, but if such a document existed, he never showed it to his companions. The only man to whom he ever displayed what purported to be a Queen's commission was a Spanish prisoner who probably could not read English. Drake, in short, was not like Captain James Cook, a professional officer carrying out the instructions of an Admiralty or a Royal Society. He was the agent of a private, profit-making syndicate in which he himself was a substantial investor. The plans of the syndicate were kept secret, even to the extent that a false destination in the eastern Mediterranean was given out. This was done partly to deceive the Spanish, but also to deceive those of the Queen's counselors, Lord Burghley in particular, who were fearful of an open breach with Spain. Only when they were at sea, in mid-Atlantic, did Drake's companions learn that South America was their destination. Some of them took it ill; William Markham, master of the *Elizabeth,* complained later that "Master Drake hired him for Alexandria, but had he known that this [the Strait of Magellan] had been the Alexandria, he would have been hanged in England rather than have come on this voyage."[5]

The only firm documentary clue about what the fleet was supposed to do on arrival off South America is in a draft plan ascribed to the year 1577 and probably intended for Walsingham. The manuscript, in the Cottonian collection, was badly burned in an eighteenth-century fire, so that only parts of it are legible.[6] According to a plausible reconstruction of the relevant passage, it proposed that Drake should examine the Atlantic coast of southern South America, pass through the Strait, sail up the Pacific coast as far as 30°, investigate the possibilities of trade and settlement in Spanish occupied areas, and then return by the same route. Thirty degrees south is the latitude of Coquimbo in northern Chile. The draft plan did not suggest that Drake should visit the coast of Peru, or attack its harbors, and it is unlikely that Drake's final instructions, however much they may have differed from the draft plan, contained any such authorization. The promoters no doubt assumed, knowing Drake, that he would try to make the voyage pay by plundering Spanish shipping. None of them—John Hawkins least of all—would have objected to this if Drake could get away with it; but none of them, least of all the Queen, would have been so naive as to say so in writing.

All the other purposes that historians have imputed to the promoters are either inferences from the actual course of the voyage or conjecture based on knowledge of the problems that puzzled geographers of the time. Terra Australis, the supposed great southern continent, is an example of such a problem. It fascinated John Dee, the distinguished English geographer, who was consulted about most voyages of discovery in his time and was acquainted with the promoters of this one. Terra Australis appeared on many maps. The famous Ortelius world map of 1570 (the best then available), a copy of which probably accompanied Drake on the voyage, showed Tierra del Fuego as part of a great continental mass. Drake had no doubt heard and participated in discussions of this subject, but neither the surviving documents nor his conduct of the voyage give any ground for supposing that he was told to investigate it.

Another problem which engaged the attention of Dee and others was that of the Strait of Anian, the hypothetical sea passage linking Atlantic and Pacific in the north.[7] In the year before Drake sailed, Frobisher had returned from his first Arctic voyage claiming to have found the Atlantic entrance to such a passage, and he explored it further in 1577. Two of Frobisher's backers, Leicester and Walsingham, were also prominent promoters of Drake's enterprise. It was natural enough that Drake should look for a Pacific entrance to this strait while he was in the Pacific. His actual conduct suggests that he may have been so instructed, though there is no documentary evidence of it, and the draft plan would have excluded it.

Finally, there is no indication that Drake or anyone else in the early stages of the voyage contemplated a Pacific crossing, a trading visit to the Moluccas, or a circumnavigation. Lack of evidence does not, of course, amount to contrary proof. There may well have been a subsequent, amended plan, since lost, in which 30°S as the northern limit of the voyage was canceled and the Strait of Anian inserted. The Queen may well have given Drake, as he stated, private verbal instructions, or at least an assurance that she would not object to his placing a liberal interpretation on such instructions as he had. But the surviving documentary evidence reveals the purpose of the voyage only as an armed commercial reconnaissance of the southern coasts of South America. That in itself, one would think, was task enough.

Much more is known about the events of the voyage than about its aims. Official logs or reports were probably impounded and subsequently lost, but several participants later wrote their own accounts. The two most informative are of particular interest in that their authors were unsympathetic to Drake. One, John Cooke, was an adherent of the ill-fated Thomas Doughty; it was he who supplied Stow with information about the voyage. The other, Francis Fletcher, was chaplain to the expedition. Drake was given to preaching and psalm-singing. The relations between the two men perhaps illustrate the adage that two of a trade rarely agree; even so, Fletcher's narrative is full and comprehensive, illustrated with crude but useful sketches. It formed the basis, years later, of the famous book *The World Encompassed*, compiled (with discreet expurgations) by Drake's nephew and namesake, and published in 1628. These narratives are supplemented from Spanish sources by the reports of men taken prisoner by Drake and subsequently released.

The fleet sailed from Plymouth to the Cape Verde Islands, where they took their first prize, a Portuguese ship, and kidnapped her navigator, Nuno da Silva, who was familiar with the pilotage of at least part of the South American Atlantic coast. Drake made it clear that he did not need da Silva's help in navigating—indeed, he robbed him of his chart, rutter, and astrolabe. What he wanted from da Silva was information about anchorages on the coast where wood and water could be had.

They made the coast of Brazil after a slow and troublesome passage, and stood south. There was a short stay in the Rio de la Plata and a longer one in St. Julian Bay in Patagonia, that dismal, ill-omened place where Magellan had wintered more than half a century before. The first thing they saw on entering the bay was the gibbet, still standing on the foreshore, where Magellan had hanged his mutineers. Appropriately, the trial by what we would call a kangaroo court and the execution of Thomas Doughty, the gentleman-volunteer whom Drake accused of "treason," occurred here. Perhaps "insubordination" would have been a more appropriate word. Doughty, like many others at that time, found it hard to take orders from a social inferior. He was an educated man, clever, carping, essentially destructive. The sailors in the company disliked him and accused him of "conjuring": he had books in foreign languages with which, they said, he conjured up bad weather. Whether Drake believed this, who can say? Doughty was sacrificed, perhaps necessarily, to the principle of unified command—and no one thereafter questioned Drake's authority.

Although the passage of the Strait of Magellan was often enough a terrifying experience for sailing ships, Drake found favorable winds and rushed through it in sixteen days, a record for the century. But this was almost the expedition's undoing; they arrived in the Pacific at a bad time of year for weather and ran into a series of northwesterly gales that scattered the fleet, driving Drake's flagship far south of Desolation Island. There they found no land, only a wild expanse of sea. So much for the great southern continent, at least in that longitude. This was a major discovery, but because it was not made public its full import was not generally grasped until 1616, when Willem Schouten passed through Le Maire Strait and rounded Cape Horn. The wide channel between Cape Horn and Antarctica is called Drake Passage to this day.

In time the wind moderated, and Drake headed north for an appointed rendezvous with the rest of his fleet on the coast in 30°S, but there was no meeting there. Of the five ships that had left Plymouth under his command, only one remained. Da Silva's ship and two of the original fleet had been emptied and abandoned on the Atlantic side. Of the three ships that had threaded the labyrinth of the Strait of Magellan, one had disappeared in the storm off the west coast of Tierra del Fuego. Another, the *Elizabeth*, had put back into the Strait and, after waiting several weeks for a favorable wind, had returned to England "full sore against the mariners' minds,"[8] according to William Markham, though his remark suggests that they were of more than one mind. Drake's ship was alone.

There was nothing unusual about her; she was an ordinary, medium-sized armed merchantman. Her dimensions are not known, though she was probably not much more than eighty or ninety feet overall, a small vessel for so tremendous a voyage. The eighty-odd men in her, crowded though they were, must have felt an overwhelming sense of loneliness at times. On their port hand was the immense and almost unexplored Pacific—mistakenly so-called, as they already had cause to know. On their starboard hand were the labyrinthine channels and islands of the Chilean coast, equally unknown, with its frieze of high, snow-clad mountains running north and south as far as the eye could see. Drake no doubt had to employ all the devices that his personal magnetism, his bold opportunism, and his sense of the dramatic suggested to keep his men in good heart.

On the other hand, Drake had assets. The ship, though small, was seaworthy and well armed. Spanish shipping and the scattered string of Spanish settlements along the coast were virtually defenseless; until that time, their remoteness had been all the defense they needed. Drake's ship, mounting eighteen carriage guns, if she could surmount the perils of the sea, had little to fear from the enemy. Her very name gave notice to the world of Drake's intentions. She had left Plymouth as the *Pelican,* but Drake had renamed her the *Golden Hind* off Patagonia, in a gesture of shrewd bravado. A hind *trippant or* was the crest of Drake's patron and backer in the expedition, Sir Christopher Hatton, a courtier, a fighting man, and what we would now call a hawk in his attitude toward Spain and popery. By renaming the ship, Drake paid Hatton a handsome compliment, and by implication he committed Hatton to supporting the career of plunder on which the *Golden Hind* eventually embarked.

Valparaiso was the turning point of the voyage. Drake had spent many weeks in conscientious coastal reconnaissance, but he found only cold, rocky, almost uninhabited shores which offered no prospect for trade or settlement. Valparaiso itself was an insignificant place—half a dozen houses and a thatch and wattle church, hardly worth the plundering. There was a ship in the harbor, however, and Drake took her and appropriated her charts. With these to guide him, he sailed north in search of better things. After a pause for careening he put into Arica, the port for Potosí, where he took two more prizes, one carrying silver.

Then north, to the boldest stroke of the whole voyage, a lightning raid on Callao, the port of Lima, capital of the viceroyalty of Peru. Here Drake caused a fine confusion by cutting the cables of the dozen or so ships in the harbor; but as at Arica, he found no significant quantity of silver. A big consignment, he was told, had recently left for Panama in the ship *Nuestra Señora de la Concepción,* coarsely nicknamed *Cacafuego.* Drake set off in pursuit and overhauled his quarry off Cape San Francisco in what is now Colombia. Despite her nickname she was almost unarmed, and her crew surrendered after token resistance. Her cargo was enough to "make" the voyage, if only they could get it back to England. This now became their chief preoccupation.

There were three possibilities. One was to return the way they had come. The Spanish authorities evidently expected them to do this, and sent ships to the Strait of Magellan to intercept them. To Drake and his companions this probably seemed the least attractive choice. The objections included headwinds and contrary currents for several thousand miles down the South American coast, probable violent weather off the Strait, and the risk of interception. The second possibility was the hypothetical Strait of Anian. This, if it existed, would perhaps offer the shortest and most attractive route to England; the longitudinal breadth of North America was unknown (and commonly underestimated), and the discovery of a passage would be valuable. If the Strait of Anian could not be found, the third possibility remained of crossing the Pacific and returning by way of the East Indies and the Cape of Good Hope. Probably all these alternatives had been discussed in general terms even before the fleet had broken up. But now a choice had to be made, and made in light of yet another consideration, the urgent necessity of careening and refitting before undertaking another long ocean passage. This would require a sheltered anchorage remote from the possibility of Spanish pursuit. With the whole coast in an uproar, the most likely direction in which to look for such an anchorage was northwest, beyond the northern frontiers of New Spain. Hence, California. A careenage in that area would be compatible with a search for the Strait of Anian; and it could be made compatible with a Pacific crossing—but it would rule out a return to the Strait of Magellan.

This is how Nuno da Silva read Drake's mind, or rather how he explained it subsequently, in the course of questioning by the Mexican Inquisition. Probably Drake did not make up his mind until after da Silva had left him. On passage northwest he took another prize, a Spanish ship. Two of its officers had experience of the trans-Pacific passage to the Philippines, and they had charts for it, which may have swayed Drake in that direction. Shortly afterward he put into the little Mexican harbor of Guatulco, sacked it, burned the church, seized all the food he could find, took on water for fifty days, and set Nuno da Silva ashore. To leave a Portuguese in New Spain at a time when relations between Spain and Portugal tended toward war, and when the Spanish commonly suspected the Portuguese of Judaism, was hardly an act of kindness. Drake must have known this, but da Silva had no knowledge of the Pacific navigation and so Drake had no further need of him.

All this might seem to suggest that Drake intended an immediate Pacific crossing. His conduct nevertheless seems oddly inconsistent. He also released the two Pacific pilots at Guatulco, having failed to bribe or bully them into serving him. He sailed on west and north, keeping well out to sea—according to one account as far as 48°N, the latitude of Seattle and much farther than needed if he merely wanted to careen. This looks like a search for the Strait of Anian. Or perhaps he was simply filling in time to avoid arriving in the western Pacific in the cyclone season, of which his captured navigators might have warned; but this is mere conjecture. Juan de Fuca Strait, that deceptive inlet, is a little farther north than 48° but, perhaps fortunately, Drake did not find it and was probably far off shore at the time. Eventually, discouraged by the cold and thick weather, he turned south again and found the careenage he needed in the neighborhood of San Francisco Bay. The exact site cannot be identified with certainty. Drake named the agreeable country in which it lay Nova Albion and claimed it, opportunistically and a little absurdly, for the Queen.

Only one possibility now remained for the return home. As soon as the *Golden Hind* was cleaned and refitted, she set out across the broad Pacific (for a discussion of Drake in this ocean see Lessa, ch.5, below). Eventually Drake found his way to Ternate in the Moluccas, where the sultan was at loggerheads with the Portuguese and welcomed a competitive buyer of spices. Drake was able to buy six tons of cloves, and he carried back to England brave promises of that rich trade which English merchants had coveted for so long.

For many weeks after his arrival in England Drake's reception remained in doubt. News of his depredations had long ago reached Spain, and the Spanish government was clamoring for restitution and exemplary punishment. In England, official opinion—unlike popular opinion—was divided. It all depended on the Queen. She, after some hesitation, came to the conclusion that the Spanish did not intend to make Drake's adventures a *casus belli*. She decided to stand by her captain and his welcome load of treasure, rejecting the protests of the Spanish ambassador on the ground, increasingly fashionable then in northern Europe, that the sea was free to all. As for Drake's depredations, she made only token concessions. Individual Spaniards whom he had robbed were graciously allowed to sue for restitution. Few did, or could. She received Drake in private audience—one would certainly like to know what was said on that occasion—and to crown it all she visited his ship at its Deptford berth and had him knighted on his own quarterdeck. The British today have grown accustomed to thinking of knighthood as the routine reward of successful businessmen, civil servants nearing retirement, popular entertainers, and the mayors of county boroughs, but in Elizabeth's day knighthood was an honor not lightly bestowed. That such a man as Drake, of humble origin and with a slightly disreputable early history, should be admitted to this coveted standing was almost unprecedented. It gave a whole new glamour and respectability to the seaman's trade.

Drake was a seaman first and foremost, a superb ship handler and a superb navigator. Though not an innovator, he was an expert, accurate and up to date. For this we have the testimony of Nuno da Silva, who had seen him at work day after day, and, more significantly, that of John Davis and Pedro Sarmiento de Gamboa, the most distinguished English and Spanish navigators, respectively, of their time. He was a superb leader, careful of his men. One of the most striking features of the Famous Voyage was the low rate of sickness; nearly all the *Golden Hind*'s company returned safe to England. This was a rare accomplishment in those days, and it reflected Drake's attention to the details of diet and hygiene. In contrast, of Magellan's fleet only eighteen men survived the voyage.[9] As an admiral and commander of fleets Drake was somewhat less than superb. His old pirate habits died hard, and he was always more interested in taking prizes than in destroying the enemy's fleet. It was Lord Admiral Howard, not Drake, who effectively directed the operations against the Armada. Drake was a difficult colleague, at times an unreliable second. There were episodes in his later career of insubordination and disgrace, notably over the Cadiz affair in 1589, and his life ended in a moment of failure.

The Famous Voyage, in fact, was not simply the turning point of Drake's career, it was the climax, the most significant thing he ever did—not because of the loot, not because of the scare he gave the Spanish in their Pacific sanctuary, not even because of his geographical discoveries, which though important were not followed up, but because of the tradition, the pattern of comradeship and command, which he established. One recalls the speech he made to his ship's company after Doughty's death:

Wherefore we must have these mutinies and discords that are grown amongst us redressed; for by the life of God it doth even take my wits from me to think on it. Here is such controversy between the sailors and the gentlemen, and such stomaching between the gentlemen and sailors, that it doth even make me mad to hear it. But, my masters, I must have it left, for I must have the gentlemen to haul and draw with the mariner, and the mariner with the gentleman. What, let us show ourselves all to be of a company, and let us not give occasion to the enemy to rejoice at our decay and overthrow. I would know him that would refuse to set his hand to a rope, but I know there is not any such here; and as gentlemen are very necessary for government's sake in the voyage, so I have shipped them for that, and to some further intent; and yet though I know sailors to be the most envious people of the world, and so unruly without government, yet may I not be without them.[10]

In Drake's day, command was traditionally the prerogative of a gentleman, of a man of gentle birth and appropriate training in manners and in arms. Doughty had presumed, on his social standing as Drake's equal or superior, to claim to be his equal in command as well; so off a dangerous shore, far from home, Drake had him beheaded. Other commanders, Edward Fenton for example, failed to grasp this nettle. Their voyages ended, as often as not, in quarrelsome disaster. Drake's speech did not plead for democracy or equality, as some have pretended. Sixteenth-century Englishmen had no use for equality, and there is no place for democracy in a ship. What Drake was saying is that a ship, above all a fighting ship, must be a fighting unit under a unified command, and not merely a device to transport fighting men. The handling of ships is a highly skilled profession, deserving of respect in its own right. The right to command must depend, therefore, not on social standing, as in those days it commonly did ashore, but on professional standing and training. If social and professional standing happened to coincide, so much the better.

Drake was no leveler. He insisted that fighting ships must be commanded by fighting seamen, and not by gentlemen of the sword who happened to find themselves at sea. In his day this was a new and revolutionary notion. The English and the Dutch were the first Europeans to grasp this apparently simple principle, and to this, more than anything else, they owed their extraordinary naval success for more than three hundred years. The Queen herself sanctioned the principle when she had Drake knighted, though in her day it was far from generally accepted. It gained acceptance rapidly in the seventeenth century under the impetus of the Dutch wars. The Articles of War, which have been for three hundred years the charter of the Royal Navy, were from their promulgation the charter of a professional navy, at least so far as its officers were concerned. Their preamble states roundly: that it is upon the Navy, "under the good Providence of God, the Wealth, Safety, and Strength of the Kingdom chiefly depend." The navy about which such a statement could be made had come a long way, in two or three generations, from the miscellaneous collection of ships, mostly privately owned and largely manned by part-time pirates, which had fought Queen Elizabeth's wars.

NOTES

1. Richard Hakluyt, *The principall navigations, voiages and discoveries of the English nation,* facsimile ed. (Cambridge, Hakluyt Society and the Peabody Museum of Salem, 1965), "Epistle Dedicatorie," p. 2v.

2. John Stow, *The Annales or General Chronicle of England* (London, 1615), p. 807.

3. Ibid.

4. Doughty, a gentleman, scholar, and soldier, also served under Essex but fell from his favor. Doughty was still accepted at court, however, where he introduced Drake to one of Queen Elizabeth's favorites, Christopher Hatton (knighted in 1578 and appointed Lord Chancellor in 1587). Thomas Doughty and his younger brother, John, accompanied Drake on the Famous Voyage, but although both were involved, only Thomas was accused of "treason" and executed. On his return to England, John Doughty prosecuted Drake on a charge of murdering his brother, but the case was eventually dropped.

5. Report of John Winter of 2 June 1579, British Library Lansdowne MS 100, no. 2. See E. G. R. Taylor, "More Light on Drake," *Mariner's Mirror,* 16 (1930) 150.

6. British Library Cotton MS Otho E. VIII, fols. 8–9. (The library departments of the British Museum were transferred to a newly founded institution, The British Library, in 1973.) See also E. G. R. Taylor, "The Missing Draft Project of Drake's Voyage of 1577–80," *Geographical Journal,* 75 (1930) 44–47, in which part of this document is reproduced.

7. Because of the problem of determining longitude, the continent of North America was believed to be much narrower than it actually turned out to be. Thus the supposed passage through it was thought to be relatively short. Anian, the name first used by Marco Polo for a kingdom in northern Asia, was located on most sixteenth-century maps in northwest America. The existence of this northern sea passage to the Indies was finally disproved by the land journeys of Alexander Mackenzie and the maritime explorations of Captains James Cook and George Vancouver in the second half of the eighteenth century (see Thrower, ch. 10, below).

8. See Edward Cliffe's report of John Winter's voyage in W. S. W. Vaux, ed., *The World Encompassed,* Hakluyt Society, 1st ser. 16 (London, 1854), p. 281.

9. Magellan himself was killed in a skirmish with the natives in the Philippines on 27 April 1521 during the first global circumnavigation (1519–1522). Of the five ships that started out, only the *Victoria* returned to Spain, with Juan Sebastian de Elcano as captain and seventeen others. Some years later other members of the expedition made their way back to Spain after having been imprisoned by the Portuguese in the East Indies.

10. John Cooke's narrative (British Library Harleian MS 540, fols. 93r–110v), reprinted in Vaux, *The World Encompassed,* p. 213.

11. N. A. M Roger, The Articles of War (Havant, Kenneth Mason, 1982). The wording of "An Act to make Provision for the Discipline of the Navy," Victoria 1866, which is similar to the wording of Charles II 1661, pp. 13, 35.

Elizabethan Navigation

DAVID W. WATERS

How did seamen in the age of Drake find their way about inshore waters and the wide oceans "where only water and heauen may be seene"?[1] Once at sea, seamen avoid the shore, a place of hazards. Today, as in Drake's day, the prudent seaman stays as far from the shore as feasible and gives himself as much searoom as he can get, and he does both as soon as possible. The sea is treacherous, and the land is unyielding to a ship unsuspectingly embayed on a lee shore. The coast is a fine sight in good weather but a dreadful sight in a storm. Then, wind and sea can drive a ship to destruction on fanged reefs, against towering cliffs, or on the sands of hidden shoals.

The mariner's England of Elizabeth I and Francis Drake is perhaps best delineated in the "General Carte, & Description of the Sea Coastes of Europe and Navigation," in the English translation of Lucas Waghenaer's *The Mariners Mirrour* of 1588 (fig. 2:1). It shows England—with Scotland, another realm, to the north and Ireland, still in the turmoil of conquest, to the west—strategically placed off the northwest coast of Europe, where she flanks the Channel that links all of Europe and all the lands overseas with England and northern Europe.

A chart in the same "waggoner" (a book of engraved sea charts with accompanying printed sailing directions) best shows the significance of Land's End and the importance of the Lizard as the point of departure and the landfall for all mariners of the Channel (fig. 2:2). It also shows particularly well what a shipmaster in coastal waters expected of his chart: that it should show the

2.1 Title page of Anthony Ashley's English translation of Lucas Waghenaer's *Spieghel der Zeevaerdt*, Leyden, 1584–85. The English translation came out in London in 1588 as *The Mariners Mirrour,* with re-engraved title page, plates, and charts.

The navigational instruments of the time are illustrated. They are, from top to bottom and left to right: sea quadrant, celestial globe, terrestrial globe, another sea quadrant; on both sides, sandglasses and cross staves, with mariners in the center in English dress holding sounding leads and lines, compasses (dividers) and sea compasses. On board ship, one seaman is sounding, another takes a sight with a sea astrolabe. Courtesy of the Trustees of the National Maritime Museum, Greenwich.

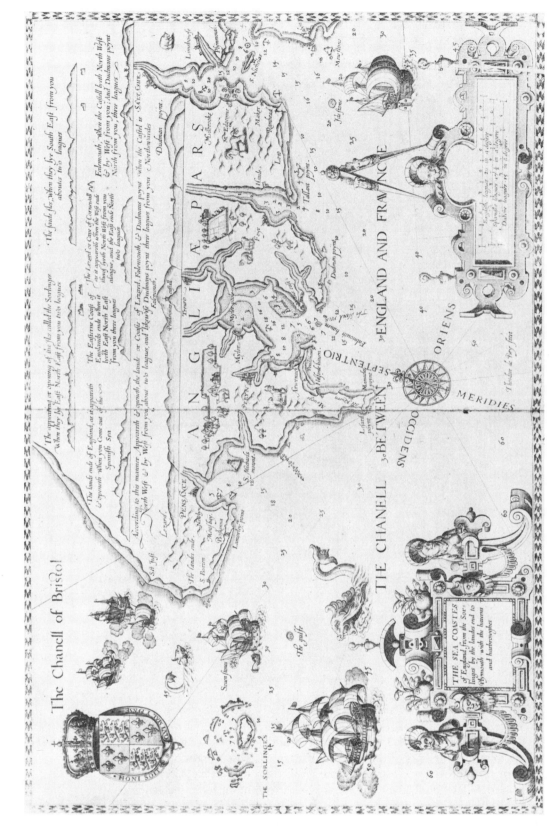

2.2 Land's End and the Lizard, from Anthony Ashley's translation *The Mariners Mirrour*, 1588, of Lucas Waghenaer's *Spieghel der Zeevaerdt*, Leyden, 1584–85. Courtesy of the Trustees of the National Maritime Museum.

general appearance of a harbor in a plan view, including the fairway (indicated by a line of soundings showing the depth of the water in fathoms (a fathom equals six feet), and the safest anchorage (indicated by an anchor). He was not concerned with the coast between harbors, which he shunned, but with the harbors themselves, so that the chart exaggerated a harbor's size in relation to the coastline. He was concerned with the appearance from seaward of the land around the approaches to harbors, however, so the charts included coastal elevations. There were no lines of latitude or longitude in these detailed charts, but there was a scale of miles—though clearly, in practice, it was of little value. Thus, these charts were essentially for pilotage, for entering or leaving port—unlike the general navigational chart, with its scales of distance, latitude and longitude, and network of rhumb or directional lines from which to take off the courses between places.

The most important thing a pilot must know is that he has sufficient depth of water under his vessel to keep her afloat. His most important instrument has always been, as it was in Drake's day, his lead and line for sounding the depth of water. The lead could also be "armed" with tallow placed in a recess in its base, which could be used to bring up a sample of the seabed, revealing whether it was of sand, shells, pebbles, mud, or rock (when the tallow was merely dented). Knowledge of the depth of the water and the nature of the seabed enabled the experienced mariner to determine more precisely where he was when he was in "soundings," that is, at sea over the continental shelf, where the land continues under the sea surface for some distance before abruptly dropping down into the ocean bed hundreds and thousands of fathoms. The edge of the continental shelf comes at about one hundred fathoms, or six hundred feet, of water, the depth beyond which it was not practical to sound with a hand lead and line. When a navigator who was approaching land from the ocean found bottom by sounding, he knew he had reached the edge of the continental shelf and was approaching the hazards of the shore, where he would need all his skill of pilotage. The continental shelf and its soundings in the English Channel and the western approaches are clearly shown in a manuscript chart of 1596 by Thomas Hood, one of the first English hydrographers (fig. 2:3).

The fairway into and out of a harbor was often buoyed to help the shipmaster keep to the deepwater channel. Buoys were made like barrels, of wooden staves and iron bands, and were either tun-shaped like barrels floating on their sides or conical with a mooring ring at the submerged, pointed end. Although a rope cable was attached to the buoy and an anchor kept it in position, buoys often broke adrift in storms.

Landmarks and wooden beacons were also used to warn of dangers in and around fairways and to act as leading marks with which to keep ships in the channel. One of the novel features of *The Mariners Mirrour* was the inclusion of such symbols in the introductory text. Buoys were particularly necessary in the waters of northern Europe because of the nature of the tides and tidal streams there. The Elizabethans did not know the cause of the tides, though they correctly associated the phenomenon with the phases of the moon. In most

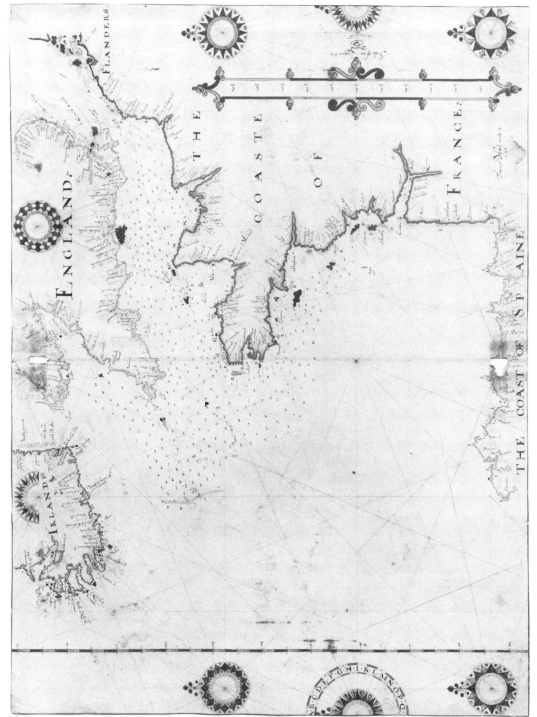

2.3 Manuscript plane chart of the Bay of Biscay and the English Channel, Thomas Hood, 1596. Courtesy of the Trustees of the National Maritime Museum.

places in England the tides occur twice daily (they can differ as much as thirty feet in the Bristol Channel) and are accompanied by fast-flowing flood and ebb tidal streams. The pilot's sailing directions, which in Drake's day were usually contained in a printed rutter (derived from the French *routier*, a route book), gave the direction of the tidal streams off various important places according to the phase of the moon. They also contained a tide table listing the times of high water (H.W.; full sea) at various ports on days when the moon was new or full. This was known as the establishment of the port. With the aid of an annual almanac, the pilot could find the age of the moon on any day of the year and then calculate the times of high or low water at the port and the time and direction of the flood and ebb streams. He might also use a small chart on which lines from various ports of similar establishments were drawn linking them to a point on a compass rose which represented an hour on a clock face, the hour of high water on days of full and change. An accompanying circular diagram for each point with numbers from one to thirty enabled the pilot to find out the times of high (or low) water at intermediate stages of the moon's cycle and so to avoid the labor of calculation.

The tides of course determined the times at which a ship could enter or leave harbor. Often the strength and direction of the tidal streams forced a ship with an unfavorable wind to anchor until the current reversed. If she then weighed anchor she would go with the tide—"tide over"—until it was necessary to anchor again. Thus it was that Drake's nonchalance on Plymouth Hoe in 1588, when the first sighting of the Spanish Armada was reported to him, showed his mastery of the situation and of men and their emotions; in other words, his leadership. He knew the tides, and he also knew that before the ebb began, when he could get out of the sound, he had plenty of time to finish his game of bowls.

Besides knowing the depth of the water and the direction of the tidal stream, the navigator must know the direction in which his ship is steering. The Elizabethans used a magnetic sea compass (fig. 2:4) for this purpose. The sea compass was a wooden box in which was pivoted a card with the thirty-two points of the compass drawn on it, attached to a needle. When the needle had been "fed," the compass pointed to magnetic north; because the needle was made of soft iron, it would lose its magnetism in time and the pilot would feed it with a lodestone (a lump of magnetic iron ore), one of his most prized possessions (fig. 2:5).

At sea, the pilot plotted his ship's position and progress on a chart, usually a portulan chart—that is, one drawn geometrically on sheepskin, using magnetic compass directions and estimated distances to delineate the coastline. The chart included a scale of miles and was covered with a network of interlacing directional lines. In the absence of parallel rulers, which were not invented until the 1580s and were not brought to sea until much later, these lines enabled the pilot to measure off with a pair of dividers the direction between places, also the distance sailed or to be sailed. He estimated his speed with the aid of a sandglass which measured half-hour intervals; from the 1570s, the English also used a log

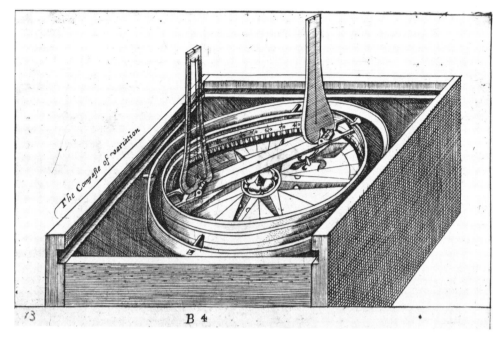

2.4 A compass of variation, in W. Barlow, *The Navigator's Supply*, London, 1597. Courtesy of the Trustees of the National Maritime Museum.

and line, in conjunction with a half-minute glass. The length of the log line run out in half a minute was measured off in fathoms and then converted into miles sailed per hour. Cast every hour, the log line was a great help in estimating progress. It is likely that, by the end of the century, fathom lengths equivalent to sea miles were being marked on the log line with knots, as they were early in the next century; from this practice springs the seaman's use of the term knots to express speed.

The English had been interested in the possibility of a northwest passage around America to the Orient since the end of the fifteenth century, when John Cabot, under a charter from Henry VII, discovered Newfoundland. He was accompanied by his son Sebastian, who later became *Piloto-mayor,* or Pilot-major, of Spain, and was thus privy to all the navigational lore and skill of the Spaniards and to their commerce with the Indies. In the late 1540s, after the death of Henry VIII, the English bribed Sebastian Cabot to return to England and teach their seamen the art of ocean navigation. The English, with an economic crisis on their hands, rightly believed that they had to find markets overseas. Cabot organized a training ship, had twenty seamen trained as navigators within two years, and advised the Privy Council on setting up the first chartered overseas trading company, the Muscovy Company, which brought Russia into direct contact with Europe as a result of English voyages initiated to the northeast.

On Cabot's death in 1557, the Privy Council saw to it that a successor was

2.5 A sixteenth-century lodestone.
Courtesy of the Trustees of the National
Maritime Museum.

appointed: a Welsh mathematician, Dr. John Dee, who had been educated at Louvain University, the leading cartographic and scientific instrument center of Europe. When Dee had returned to England in 1547, he had brought with him the latest globes by Gerard Mercator, the leading globe maker of the day, sea compasses, and "exquisitely made instruments Mathematical,"[2] which he gave to Trinity College, Cambridge. Dee had developed mathematical navigation in the 1560s, and he instructed such Elizabethan sea captains as Frobisher and Davis on arctic navigation for their voyages in search of a northwest passage in the 1570s and later.

One of the problems of arctic navigation was connected with chart work: in such high latitudes, drawing a chart on a plane surface results in great errors and distortions. The advantage of a globe is that it truly represents the earth's surface in miniature—unlike a chart, with its flat surface—and so avoids the distortions that are found in charts constructed as if the curved surface of the earth were flat. In northern navigation, the distortions inherent in that assumption are gross because the convergence of the meridians upon the pole is pronounced. One solution provided by Dee was a circumpolar chart, but this is not an easy projection for a navigator to work with. Hydrographers knew, of course, that the meridians on a globe converge until they meet at a point at each pole; but none knew how to represent this correctly on a plane surface, such as a chart, so that directions and distances could be represented and measured off accurately. As early as 1569, Mercator had published a large engraved world chart on which, by means which he did not explain, he had expanded the distance apart of the parallels of latitude in approximate proportion to the expansion of the meridians of longitude, which resulted in their being drawn parallel. As he explained, for the first time, compass directions drawn on this chart were correct, as were distances if they were measured off from the latitude scale. But in practice, the scale of the world chart was too small for navigational use.

Only when the Cambridge mathematician Edward Wright (who voyaged into the Atlantic in 1589 to gain navigational experience) published his *Certaine Errors in Navigation detected and corrected* in 1599 did the mathematical explanation of Mercator's projection, as it came to be known, and Wright's table of meridional parts for constructing it, become generally available. Wright accompanied his book with a large engraved chart of the Azores—the first detailed "Mercator's" navigational chart published. The next year he published an engraved world chart on this projection, which was long known as Mr. Wright's projection. The chart is notable also because it includes only the known coastlines. It is found in many copies of Hakluyt's *The principal navigations,* from which a typical logbook of the period, that of Drake's contemporary John Davis, is illustrated here (fig. 2:6).

The rhumb, or directional line, had been a problem for navigators since they had begun oceanic navigation. These lines were not understood for a long time, and not until 1537 did Portugal's chief pilot, Pedro Nunes, explain their nature. He was the first to point out that because a rhumb line cuts a meridian at a constant angle, and because meridians converge on the poles, rhumb lines are spiral lines. Once this was understood, it became possible to represent directional lines on globes and thereby make them useful to navigators. Mercator did this on his notable terrestrial globe of 1541, a copy of which Dee no doubt brought back with him from Louvain, but it was fifty years before an English globe was published for navigational use. The globe was financed by the merchant William Sanderson and made by Emery Molyneux, and the gores were engraved by Jodocus Hondius of Amsterdam, then a fugitive in England. This was the largest globe yet made: it was twenty-five inches (sixty-two mm) in diameter and included the tracks of Drake's (1577–1580) and Cavendish's (1586–1588) voyages of circumnavigation and, of course, rhumb lines. A matching celestial globe was produced at the same time. These globes must have been too large for shipboard use, for the great cabin of an Elizabethan ship was a very restricted space.

Magnetic variation bedeviled the Elizabethan navigator's sense of direction. The cause of the error was not known, but its effect was to deflect the north-seeking point of the magnetic compass needle to the right or left of true north, the direction toward the earth's pole. Seamen had been aware of variation since the mid-fifteenth century, and since about 1505 various instruments had been invented to enable the pilot to measure it. The most successful variation measuring instrument was the compass of variation, invented by William Barlow and described and illustrated by him in *The Navigators Supply* of 1597. This instrument continued in use, virtually unchanged, for two centuries. In Eliz-

Moneth Iuly.	Dayes	Houres	Course	Leagues	Elevation of the pole Deg	Min	The winde	THE DISCOVRSE.
	31	24	S.by W.	27	62		N.W.	This 31 at noone, comming close by a terciano or great cape, we fell into a mighty rase, where an island of ice was carried by the force of the current as east as our barke could saile with him wind. all sailes bearing. This cape as it was the most Southerly limit of the gulfe which we passed over the 30 day of this moneth, so was it the North promontory or first beginning of another very great inlet, whose South limit at this present wee saw not. Which inlet or gulfe this afternoone, and in the night, we passed over: where to our great admiration we saw the sea falling down into the gulfe with a mighty overfal, and roring, and with divers circular motions like whirlepooles, in such sort as forcible streames passe thorow the arches of bridges.
August								
Noone the	1	24	S.E.by S.	16	61	10	W.S.W.	The true course, &c. This first of August we fell with the promontory of the sayd gulfe or second passage, having coasted by divers courses for our saueguard, a great banke of the ice driven out of that gulfe.
Noone the	3	48	S.S.E.	16	60	26	Variable.	
Noone the	6	72	S.E. Southerly.	22	59	35	Variable to calme.	The true course, &c.
	7	24	S.S.E.	22	58	40	W.S.W.	The true course, &c.
	8	24	S.E.	12	58	12	W. fog.	The true course, &c.
	9	24	S.by W.	13	57	20	Variable & calme.	The true course, &c.
	10	24	S.S.E.	17	56	40	S.W.by W.	The true course, &c.
	11	24	S.E. easterly.	40	55	13	W.N.W.	The true course, &c.
	12	24	S.E. easterly.	20	54	22	W.S.W.	The true course, &c.
	13	24	S.S.E.	4	54		N.W.	This day seeking for our ships that went to fish, we strooke on a roche, being among many iles, and had a great leake.
Noone the 14		24	S.S.E.	28	52	40	N.W.	This day we stopped our leake in a storme. The 15 of August at noon, being in the latitude of 52 degrees 12.min. and 16 leagues from the shore, we shaped our course for England, in Gods name, as followeth *
*Noone ye 15					52	12	S.S.W.	The true latitude.
	16	20	S.s.e. halfe point s.	50	51		S.W.	The true course, &c.
	17	24	E.by S.	30	50	40	S.	The true course, &c. This day upon the Banke we met a Biscaine bound either for the Grand bay or for the passage. He chased vs.
	18	24	E. by N. northerly.	49	51	18	W.	The true course, &c.
	19	24	E halfe point north.	51	51	35	Variable W. & S.	The true course, &c.
	20	24	E.S.E.	31	50	50	S.W.	The true course, &c.
Noone the 22		48	E.by N.	68	51	20	S.S.W.	The true course, &c.
	23	24	E.by N. Northerly	33	51	52	S.	The true course, &c.
	24	24	E.by N.	31	52	10	Variable.	The true course, &c. This 24 of August observing the variation, I found the compasse to vary towards the East, from the true Meridian, one degree.
Noone the 27		72	E. Northerly.	40	52	22	Variable & calme.	The true course, &c. for 72 houres.
Noone the 29		18	E.S.E.	47	51	28	Variable W. & N	The true course, &c.
Noone the 31		48	S.e by e. Easterly.	14	51	0	Variable.	The true course, &c.
September	2	48	E. Southerly	65	51		N.W.	The true course, &c.
	3	24	E.by S. Easterly.	24	50	50	W.N.W.	The true course, &c.
	4	24	S.E.by E.	20	50	21	N.N.E.	The true course, &c.
	5	24	S.E.by E.	18	49	48	N.N.E.	The true course, &c. Now we supposed our selves to be 55 leagues from Sillie
	6	24	E.by S.	15	49	40	N.	The true course, &c.
	7	24	E.S.E.	20	49	15	N.N.W.	The true course, &c.
	8	24	N.E.	18	49	40		
	9	24	W.S.W.	7	49	42		
	10	24	S.E.by E.	8	49	28	Variable	
	11	24	N.E.by E.	10	49	45	Variable	
	12	24	N.W.by W.	6	50		N.E.	
	13	24	E by S. Southerly	15	49	47	N.E.	
	15							This 15 of September 1587 we arrived at Dartmouth.

Vnder the title of the *houres,* where any number exceedeth 24, it is the summe or casting vp of so many other dayes and parts of dayes going next before, as conteine the foresayd summe.

Arepo

2.6 Page of a logbook of the 1580s, from Richard Hakluyt, *The principal navigations,* London, 1598–1600. Courtesy of the Trustees of the National Maritime Museum.

abethan days its practical value was that it enabled the true direction both of a ship's course and of a coastline to be determined to within one or two degrees, so a major source of navigational and hydrographic error could be avoided. Some logbooks of the period included a column for recording the variation observed and another column for true course made good.

From early in the sixteenth century the Portuguese had made a practice of observing and recording magnetic variation experienced at sea. They had attempted to use their knowledge of this variation to determine more precisely their position at sea, particularly their east-west position. They were not aware that, because of an annual change of variation, the variation at any one place changes measurably within a few years.

The Dutch, like the English, were anxious to exploit the wealth of the Indies, having mastered the art of oceanic navigation in the 1590s with the help of English navigators. In 1599 they collected and published tables of variation experienced at sea. These were translated and published that year by Edward Wright as *The Haven Finding Art* and were no doubt used by Captain John Davis, who sailed under the command of James Lancaster in 1601 on the first voyage of the East India Company to the Orient.

The following year a table was published in Thomas Blundeville's *The Theoriques of the Seven Planets* which gave magnetic dip, calculated by Henry Briggs for every degree of latitude, in an attempt to assist navigators to determine their position in a north-south direction. Magnetic dip was the discovery of the compass maker Robert Norman, who first described it in *The Newe Attractive,* published in 1581. The hope by 1600 was that "sea-men" would be able "to find out thereby the latitude of any place upon the sea or land, in the darkest night, that is without the helpe of Sunne, Moone, or Starre"[3] with the aid of a dip-needle, an instrument invented by Norman for measuring magnetic dip. The hope was vain, but it is interesting to reflect that the pioneering of these Englishmen in magnetism not only inspired William Gilbert's pregnant researches into magnetism (his *De magnete* was published in 1600) but ultimately led to radio direction finding and to radar in the twentieth century.

How, aside from the instruction of Cabot and his protégés, did the Elizabethans learn navigation? Some picked it up from renegade Portuguese and Spanish pilots, or from Frenchmen who had acquired it from Portuguese, Spanish, or Italian navigators. During Elizabeth's reign, most learned it by apprenticeship to English masters, who increasingly gained their knowledge and skill from books related to the art of navigation. More and more such books were written by Englishmen, and in the latter part of Elizabeth's reign, waggoners from Holland added to the material available.

The most important of all the navigational books was undoubtedly Richard Eden's translation of Martín Cortés' *Breve compendio de la sphera y de la arte de Navegar,* published in Seville in 1551 and 1556, and translated into English and issued in London in 1561 as *The Arte of Navigation* (fig. 2:7). This became one of the great formative books of the English nation; it was still being

and lykewyſe the Roſe, that it decline not to one parte
oʒ other. And yf it be quicker then it ought to be, then
make the poynt that it goeth vpon ſomewhat blunter.

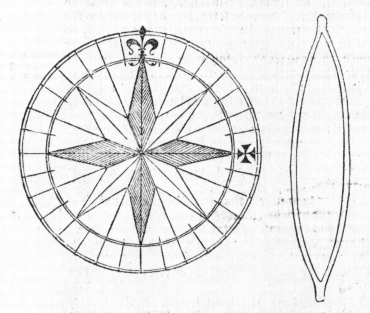

❡ The. v. Chapiter, of the effecte

oʒ pʒopertie that the compaſſe hath to
Noʒtheaſtyng, oʒ Noʒthweſting
wherby is knowen the
variation of the
compaſſe.

Any and diuers are the opinions that
I haue harde, and also read in certein
wʒyters of later dayes, as touchynge
the Noʒtheaſtyng, and Noʒthweſting
of the compaſſe. And yet mee ſee-
meth that none doeth touche the
pʒicke, and fewe the whyte. They
call it Noʒtheaſtynge , when the
needle

2.7 Compass card and needle, from Richard Eden's translation *The Arte of Navigation*, London, 1561, of Martín Cortés' *Breve compendio de la sphera y de la arte de
navegar*, Seville, 1551. Courtesy of the Trustees of the National Maritime Museum.

A Regiment for the Sea, containing

verie neeeſſarie matters for all ſorts of men and *Seamen.*

trauailers, wher vnto is added an Hidrographicall diſcourſe
touching the fiue ſeuerall paſſages into Cattay, written by
william Borne.

𝕹ewly co𝔯𝔯ected and amended by Thomas Hood, D.in 𝕻hiſicke, who hath added a new Regiment, and Table of declination.

𝖂hereunto is alſo adioyned the Mariners guide, with a perfect
Sea Carde by the ſaid Thomas Hood.

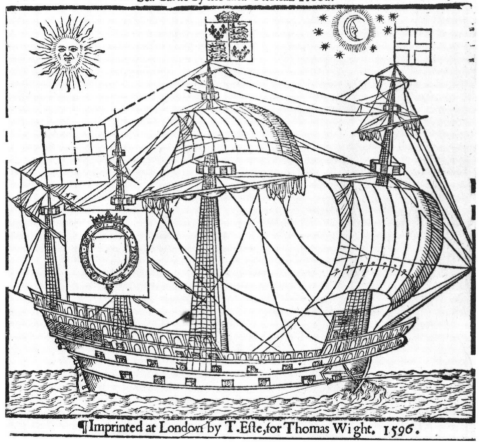

¶ Imprinted at London by T. Eſte, for Thomas Wight. 1596.

2.8 Title page of William Bourne's *A Regiment for the Sea*, London, 1596, seventh edition; the first edition was published in 1574. Courtesy of the Trustees of the National Maritime Museum.

published in the 1630s, seventy years later and long after the English had acquired the reputation of being great seadogs. A few years after its appearance, the first navigational manual written by an Englishman was published in 1574: William Bourne's *A Regiment for the Sea,* which contained the first reference in English to the log and line (fig. 2:8). Although these two books provided virtually all the theory and practice needed by the aspiring navigator, a further one appeared in 1581. John Frampton's translation of another great Spanish navigation manual, Pedro de Medina's *Arte de Navegar* of 1545, was published in London that year and reprinted in 1595; it had already been published in French and Italian and was about to appear in Dutch.

There is no question that many of Europe's seamen learned to navigate through works first published in Spanish. In Cortés' *Arte,* a compass card and needle were first illustrated and directions for making a sea compass were first given. From this book, too, the seamen learned how to navigate the Atlantic using the techniques of nautical astronomy developed by the Portuguese in the latter half of the fifteenth century. When unknown marine currents had affected the reckoning of the Portuguese on the oceans, their astronomers had advised them to use the altitude of the Pole Star above the horizon to check their estimates of distance sailed in a north-south direction. From this had been developed the latitude navigation which the Elizabethans now learned and practiced: to measure the altitude of the Pole Star above the horizon and apply a correction to it so that the elevation would equal the elevation of the North Pole above the horizon—which in turn equals the latitude of the place of observation. The angular distance of the observer north or south of the equator was being measured, in effect, from the center of the earth. Because there are difficulties in observing the Pole Star and because it is not visible in the Southern Hemisphere, the Portuguese had also developed the art of observing the altitude of the sun when it was on the meridian at midday (fig. 2:9). Their astronomers had provided them with tables of the sun's declination—that is, its angular distance north or south of the celestial equator on each day of the year—and with rules that taught them how to apply declination to measure the true elevation of the sun. This elevation subtracted from ninety degrees gave them their observed latitude. The theory of this latitude navigation was clearly explained in Eden's *Arte of Navigation* and in Frampton's translation, which also contained declination tables and rules for applying the corrections.

Cortés' work described how to make the necessary instruments for taking these observations. The one used most was the sea astrolabe, a wheel-like instrument six to eight inches in diameter, made of cast brass. The astrolabe was graduated on its circumference from zero to ninety degrees and had an axially mounted alidade with sight vanes affixed to it, and it was suspended by a thumb ring. In use, the alidade was adjusted so that at noon, when the sun was at maximum altitude, its rays passed through both pinholes in the sighting vanes. Then the sun's altitude, or zenith distance, was read off to within one-quarter to one-half degrees where the alidade cut the scale. Another Portuguese invention was an instrument then in use: the three-foot-long cross-staff. This wooden

ORIZONTE

~~~~~~~~~~~~~~~~~~~~~~~~~~~~~

Libro segundo del altura del Sol.

2.9 Taking a meridian altitude observation of the sun with an astrolabe. Folio xv(b) of Medina's *Regimiento de Navegaciō*, Seville, 1563. Courtesy of the Trustees of the National Maritime Museum.

staff had an angular scale on it and a sliding crosspiece. The observer at midday raised the cross-staff to his eye, placing the butt of the staff against his cheek, then slid the cross along the staff until the lower edge grazed the horizon and the upper edge covered the disc of the sun. When the maximum altitude was observed, it was read off from the scale at the position where it was met by the cross.

It was not long before the English had improved on both instruments. In the 1590s Captain John Davis (after whom the Davis Strait between Greenland and Labrador is named) invented the back-staff, for taking observations of the sun at sea (fig. 2:10). With this instrument the navigator measured the shadow cast by the sun by standing with his back to the sun; he would observe the horizon through an eye vane and a horizon slit and, at the same time, the shadow cast on the horizon vane by a shadow vane. The back-staff, often called Davis' quadrant, replaced the sea astrolabe in the next twenty-five years or so; along with the cross-staff, it became the navigator's principal instrument for measuring altitude until the mid-eighteenth century, when both were superseded by Hadley's reflecting quadrant.

Although these noonday observations enabled the navigator to measure latitude to within fifteen to thirty miles, he had no means of measuring longitude, that is, his angular progress in an east-west direction, other than by estimation (fig. 2:11). This was because longitude is calculated by measuring the difference in time between places, and no accurate means of measuring time had yet evolved. Indeed, it would be some two centuries before the navigator could figure out longitude scientifically. This meant that he could not account for the effect of ocean currents on his estimate of the easting or westing of his ship. As a consequence, it was common that a ship's position would err in longitude by as much as ten degrees—equivalent on the equator to six hundred miles—in the course of a long voyage. This was true of sailing in the eighteenth as in the sixteenth century. The navigator was therefore thrown back upon the only method that afforded any security: he could measure the latitude of places, so he sailed to the latitude of his intended landfall and aimed at a point some two or three hundred miles east or west of it. Then he turned toward his landfall, proceeding cautiously until soundings or sightings of the coast warned him that he had reached it. From there he could sail to his intended port of call. It was thus that Drake pursued his course around the world.

Drake's skill and good fortune as a navigator are reflected in the charts and maps of South America made after his return. In Ortelius' famous atlas *Theatrum orbis terrarum*, first published in 1570, the Pacific shores of South America are grossly distorted toward the south, as they are in Mercator's maps of a decade or more later. The cartographers had received conflicting delineations of the coastline from their Spanish sources which had arisen from errors in estimating its longitude. The hydrographers had chosen the more westerly of the coastlines and hence had given the southwest coast of South America a considerable bulge to the west. Drake, it will be recalled, sailed the entire length of the Pacific coast of South America, and the results of his (now lost) surveys were

t:ween page 248 and 249.

2.10 Davis quadrant or back-staff, from Jonas Moore, *A New Systeme of the Mathematicks*, London, 1681. Courtesy of the Trustees of the National Maritime Museum.

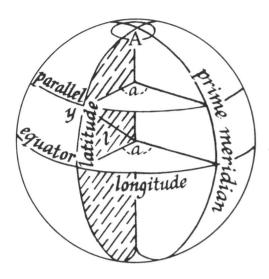

The angular relationship of latitude and longitude to the Globe

2.11 The angular relation of latitude and longitude to the globe.

incorporated into later charts and maps, notably, and relatively quickly, into the map of America contained in Richard Hakluyt's edition of Peter Martyr's *Decades,* published in Paris in 1587 (see Wallis, ch. 9, below).

Just as the first tutoring of English seamen in ocean navigation was carefully organized, so in due course provision was made, through the farsighted munificence of the great City of London merchant Sir Thomas Gresham, for the continuance of instruction and the improvement of the art for the benefit of Elizabethan seamen. Under Gresham's will, drawn up in 1575, after his and his wife's deaths his house was to become a college, housing seven professors, including one of astronomy and one of geometry. The professors were strictly enjoined to lecture publicly in English on the art of navigation according to the capacity of their audience, which, they were reminded, would be merchants and other citizens. The college, a pioneering establishment in research and education, was opened in 1598. Sir Thomas put into effect with his college the hopes and desires of several generations of Elizabethan seamen, merchants, and scholars who were aware of the benefits that would accrue to the nation when Englishmen could navigate their own ships, laden with merchandise for trade in far lands and consumption in their own, safely across the oceans.

Another such farsighted Elizabethan was Sir Walter Raleigh. On the death in 1583 of his half-brother, Sir Humphrey Gilbert, Raleigh took over Gilbert's plans for colonizing North America. To help realize these plans, he took into his service the brilliant young mathematician Thomas Hariot, whose task was to improve the art of navigation—but only for the sea captains in Raleigh's employ. This he did, introducing improvements comparable to those being made at the same time, unknown to him by Edward Wright. Unlike Wright's results, which were ultimately published as *Certaine Errors in Navigation detected and corrected*, Hariot's were kept secret from other seamen and have come to light only in the past twenty-five years. Nevertheless, there was a general improvement in the practice of navigation in Elizabethan times which was quite notable—consider Davis with his back-staff and Bourne and the log and line. By 1610, only seven years after Queen Elizabeth's death, Edward Wright could claim that "in our time the whole Arte of Navigation has groune to much greater perfection, than ever it had in any former ages." Thus Robert Norman's versifying "In Commendation of the painfull Seaman" of the 1580s rings true:

If pylots painfull toyle be lifted then alofte,
For using of his Arte according to his kinde:
What fame is due to them that first this Arte outsought,
And first instructions gave to them that were but blinde."[4]

Francis Drake's voyage of circumnavigation demonstrated to the world, among other things, that the English were second to none as navigators. In 1579 Drake himself claimed, according to the Chief Alcalde of Guatulco, Gaspar de Vargas, "that there was no one in the world who understood better the art of sailing than he did," to which Vargas added, "from what they [the prisoners] saw of him during the two days of their imprisonment, they understand that he must be a good sailor."[5] Nuno da Silva, the Portuguese pilot who was Drake's prisoner for fifteen months, later testified to the Spanish authorities that "he is a very skilful mariner."[6]

Gaspar de Vargas, in his report of April 1579, also told the Viceroy, Martín Enríquez, that, "'Francisco Drac' boasts of being . . . a good sailor 'and so learned.'"[7] In fact, completing his voyage vindicated Drake's claim to be master mariner of the globe. Not the beginning of this great venture, but the completion by his own navigational skill and mastery as a mariner is what yielded him true glory. Certainly he picked the brains of the Portuguese and Spanish pilots who had skills or knowledge he needed to acquire, and he did so by seizing them, their charts, and their instruments and, before releasing them, consulting with them "about matters concerning navigation";[8] even so, these men assessed him as a very capable navigator.

Shortly after Drake's return from his great voyage of circumnavigation and his knighting at Greenwich, he was approached by Richard Hakluyt, as Hakluyt explained in his *Diverse voyages* of 1582, to set up a lectureship in London on navigation as "a matter of great consequence and importance for the sauing of many mens liues and goods, which nowe, through grosse ignorance are dayly in great hazerd, to the no small detriment of the whole realme."[9] Sir Francis, on being asked if he "woulde do this honour to himselfe and benefite to his countriey to bee at the cost to erect such a lecture . . . in most bountifull maner . . . answered, that he liked so well of the motion, that he would giue twentie poundes by the yeere standing, and twentie pounds more before hand to a learned man, to furnish him with instruments and maps, that would take this thing vpon him."[10]

The lectureship did not materialize because the most suitable man chosen by Hakluyt demanded twice as much income as Sir Francis offered. Nevertheless, "the worthy and good knight" promised to be "as good as his worde" if his offer were matched by another to raise the forty pounds a year "to make this lecture a competent living for a learned man," that "the whole realme . . . might reape no small benefite thereby."[11] Drake appears here in a different guise, as the would-be patron of learning—a role that shows that the great circum-navigator was not jealous of his art of navigation. Far from it: instead, he sought to further it for the benefit of his countrymen. Although for reasons of state the ways and means by which Drake navigated are not known in detail, and only the memory of the voyage remains, it is possible—as attempted here—to recon-stitute the books, charts, and instruments he used with such unprecedented skill and to such great effect.

It is a curious and perhaps consoling fact that Drake's last voyage, to the West Indies, during which he faced disaster and met death, ended by stimulating navigational research; for not only did Hawkins and Drake die on that ill-fated expedition of 1595–96, but so did Drake's chief pilot, Abraham Kendall. A navigational manuscript was found among Kendall's effects when they were returned to England. The manuscript was referred to the Earl of Cumberland (whose pilot Kendall had been on a voyage of 1594 to Guiana) in the belief that it was an original work by Kendall. Cumberland sent it on to Edward Wright for his opinion, and Wright immediately, and indignantly, identified it as an unauthorized copy of his as yet unpublished *Certaine Errors in Navigation.* Perhaps Sir Francis Drake, who had been careful to insure the identification of landfalls in the Caribbean by obtaining the services before sailing of two Por-tuguese pilots, had been equally careful (though not overly scrupulous in the means adopted) to ensure that navigation of the ocean passage to the Caribbean should be no less reliable. However that may be, it was in great part due to this disclosure and to the use by others of the fruits of his research that Wright resolved to put *Certaine Errors* into print and brought it out as a book in 1599. It could have been otherwise; his manuscript might well have remained, like Thomas Hariot's, which was of equal brilliance, unpublished and unknown, to the impoverishment of navigational knowledge and skill among English seamen. As it was, Drake's last voyage contributed to the realization of Wright's hopes for the perfection of navigation: to the founding of the Royal Obser-vatory at Greenwich, where the buildings and instruments now form a part of the National Maritime Museum, "for rectifying the tables of the motions of the heavens, and the places of the fixed stars, so as to find out the so-much desired longitude of places for perfecting the art of navigation."[12]

NOTES

1. Martín Cortés, *The Arte of Navigation,* trans. Richard Eden (London, 1561), A3v, "The Epistle Dedicatorie. . . ."

2. John Dee, "The Compendious Rehersal of John Dee, November 9, 1592," in E. G. R. Taylor, *Tudor Geography* (London, 1930), p. 256.

3. Thomas Blundeville, *The theoriques of the Seven Planets . . . where unto is added . . . two . . . instruments for sea-men* (London, 1602), title page.

4. Robert Norman, *Safeguard of Sailors* (London, 1587), "In Commendation of the painfull Sea-man," p. 3.

5. Printed in Henry R. Wagner, *Sir Francis Drake's Voyage around the World* (San Francisco, 1926), p. 381. Original deposition in archives in Seville.

6. Ibid., p. 348.

7. Ibid., p. 381.

8. Ibid., p. 346.

9. Richard Hakluyt, *Divers voyages touching the discoverie of America . . . , London, 1582* (London, 1850), p. 16.

10. Ibid.

11. Ibid., p. 17.

12. Royal Warrant, 4 March 1674/5, appointing John Flamsteed (Astronomer Royal) "Astronomical Observator," in E. G. Forbes, *Greenwich Observatory,* vol. 1: *Origins and Early History (1675–1835)* (London, 1975), p. 19. Original in State Papers Dom. 44. p. 10.

Early Accounts of the

Famous Voyage

DAVID B. QUINN

"The famous voyage of Sir Francis Drake into the South Sea, and there hence about the whole globe of the Earth, begun in the yeere of our Lord, 1577," as published in 1589 by Richard Hakluyt, is the earliest account of the circumnavigation. As such, it has received much critical attention and has inspired much speculation. What Hakluyt says about his plans for a narrative in his address to the reader prefacing *The principall navigations*[1] may or may not be precisely true. He writes that he is able to print an account of Thomas Cavendish's recently concluded circumnavigation, which gives fuller details on the Far East and St. Helena than are extant for Drake's voyages—which proves that he possessed a narrative of that voyage. But Cavendish alone may not satisfy his reader, Hakluyt says, so he makes a somewhat lame excuse for not printing an account of Drake's voyage:

> I must confesse to haue taken more then ordinairie paines, meaning to haue inserted it in this worke: but being of late (contrary to my expectation) seriously delt withall, not to anticipate or preuent another mans paines and charge in drawing all the seruices of that worthie Knight into one volume, I haue yeelded vnto those my freindes which pressed me in the matter, referring the further knowledge of his proceedinges, to those intended discourses.

In spite of all this, Hakluyt did manage to insert the narrative we know as "The Famous Voyage" into his volume. He did so after everything had been printed but before the book was in public circulation. A six-leaf gathering, the first three leaves signed Mmm 4–6, the remainder unsigned, and without page numbers, was inserted between pages 643 and 644, and the correct catchword was added at the foot of the last page.[2] It has been argued that the insertion was made later, perhaps in 1594 or 1595,[3] but this is not so. The vast majority of the surviving copies of *The principall navigations*[4] have the Drake leaves, and a certain limited number of them have been established as strictly contemporary; so the insertion was made at the end of 1589 or the beginning of 1590 (it is not known precisely when the book appeared).[5] It is clear too, from internal evidence, that Hakluyt received a substantially longer narrative and pared it down, possibly with the help of one or more of his assistants, to a size which would be possible to insert. This editing was done masterfully, for the account of the voyage is very complete, and it retains throughout a relaxed and personal tone. Hakluyt reprinted it in 1600 with hardly any changes.[6] It has remained since 1589 the basic authority for the voyage, however much *The World Encompassed* (1628) and materials from manuscripts in England and Spain have supplemented it.

This section, which is written in the third person and refers throughout to Drake as "our Generall," has the character of a continuous narrative by a single hand. We know that this was not the case, as will be indicated below. It could not, therefore, unless our analysis is hopelessly at fault, have been by a man who accompanied Drake on his voyage. Hakluyt had taught himself to transform written material from crude data to coherent and personal narrative. The Reverend Philip Jones, who assisted him in putting together *The principall navigations* (and who may have had a larger share in the task than the evidence shows)[7] had demonstrated that he could translate a Latin text in an easy, flowing style: he had by then completed Albertus Meierus' *Methodus describendi regiones* (1587) as *Certaine briefe, and speciall instructions for gentlemen, merchants, students, souldiers, mariners, &c. employed in services abroad* (1589).[8] He had, indeed, dedicated the translation to Drake and in it had commended Hakluyt to him, but this was in January 1589, before Drake had gone to Portugal (Jones used the calendar dating, not the legal dating, on the dedication: 24 January 1589). Jones could have done the conflation and contraction of documentary material in a hurry if Hakluyt had been too fully engaged in other matters connected with his large book. But I like to think that the compression and its carefully balanced selection of events was in some ways indicative of Hakluyt's special skills, which he demonstrated more fully in the second edition and in some of the narratives he handed on to Samuel Purchas. Indeed, clergymen, when they were not intent on theological argument among themselves, were accustomed to putting across complex theological or moral precepts to their congregations in their sermons and were particularly suited for this kind of high-grade journalism. "The Famous Voyage" indeed shows what they (or he, if it was Hakluyt alone) could do in this regard, at great speed and with an absolute limit on length.

There is no clear evidence about the original text that was delivered to Hakluyt, which he kept and did not print, except that he was asked, he said, not to print it so as not to forestall the efforts of another would-be author working on a book on Drake. Neither is there direct evidence about the origin of the text which Hakluyt actually printed as "The Famous Voyage," though there are indications that sources extant in other versions were employed in some way in it. In the absence of evidence, all we can do is either say we do not know the answers or make some hypotheses about both texts which can form a basis for discussion.

One overriding fact must be kept in mind. Hakluyt compiled *The principall navigations* when he was in the employ of Sir Francis Walsingham, Queen Elizabeth's principal secretary of state.[9] Clearly, he owed a number of documentary items to this association. He was, moreover, under Walsingham's orders regarding what he could and could not print. The corrector or censor, Dr. John James, was appointed by Walsingham; the book was dedicated to Walsingham; and, very exceptionally, Walsingham himself certified it to the Company of Stationers for publication. When Walsingham found that the account of Sir Jerome Bowes, which had been passed by him or by the censor, was considered by the Muscovy Company as likely to prejudice their future trading relations in Russia, it was removed from the earliest printed copies and a somewhat milder version was substituted. Walsingham was also in a position to tell Hakluyt what to print and what not to print about Sir Francis Drake.

It seems likely that Walsingham, not some competing author, was the source of the omission of the original narrative which Hakluyt possessed about the circumnavigation.[10] It is clear that Walsingham had a dossier on Drake's activities during the circumnavigation as a necessary part of his official duty to investigate Drake's actions on the voyage and afterward. However, with the dispersal of the Walsingham archive and the loss of much of its content (the residue among the State Papers in the Public Record Office is far from complete), we cannot particularize it in any great detail.[11] Walsingham was therefore in a position to provide Hakluyt with at least some of his materials when it had finally been decided, with the book already printed, to add "The Famous Voyage" to it—though it is too much to say that it can be *proved* that he supplied such material. What is clear is that in November 1589 *The principall navigations* was planned to appear without any account of the most famous English expedition made to date. It was also to appear without any narrative (or with only an incidental reference to one small part of it) of the almost equally flamboyant West Indian voyage of 1585–86; perhaps the publishers of *Sir Francis Drakes West Indian voyage* were unwilling to release it for reprinting.

Any discussion of the publication of materials on Drake's voyages in *The principall navigations* must take into consideration Drake's position at the time of the work's compilation and publication. In June 1589 Drake returned from his voyage to Portugal in disgrace. An investigation established to the satisfaction of the Queen and her ministers that his inaction at crucial stages had prejudiced the success of the expedition—the greatest single force sent against Spain during the whole course of the war.[12] Whether or not Drake was a principal cause of the failure, from the summer of 1589 until 1593 he lived as a private gentleman in the West Country and was excluded from state affairs—as Raleigh was, but for very different reasons, during part of the same period. To publish anything about Drake, especially anything laudatory, was likely to have political implications because his public popularity was as great as his official disgrace was unqualified. The less said about him the better. The suppression of the original narrative given to Hakluyt about the circumnavigation was therefore most likely to have been an official measure of Walsingham's. The omission of an account of the 1585–86 voyage can be explained along similar lines, though this cannot be demonstrated because Hakluyt made no claim to have possessed a narrative of this voyage which he had withdrawn.

One of Drake's possible lines of defense, and a line of publicity which might have helped toward his rehabilitation, would have been to prepare narratives of the positive services he had done for the state before the Portugal voyage. There is evidence that he did this, but it is not yet clear when he began—perhaps soon after his return to the West Country. A possible hypothesis is that Drake, or someone he employed for this purpose, was the author of the suppressed version of the circumnavigation which Hakluyt withdrew (under pressure from Walsingham). At some time between 1589 and 1595 Drake employed the Reverend Philip Nichols to compile narratives of some of his voyages. We know of Nichols from the small book on the Isthmus voyage of 1572–73, *Sir Francis Drake revived,* which did not appear until 1626.[13] This book is said to have been based on the reminiscences of a number of seamen and to have been revised and supplemented by Drake himself. It was therefore completed well before Drake left on his last voyage in 1595, and it could have been in progress some years earlier.

The other volume which is likely to have been put together by Nichols with Drake's aid, though we have no direct evidence on this point, is the longer narrative of the circumnavigation, *The World Encompassed,* issued in 1628 and, like *Sir Francis Drake revived,* published by Sir Francis Drake, Bart., Drake's nephew.[14] This volume claimed as its base the journal of the Reverend Francis Fletcher (chaplain on the circumnavigation), supplemented by narratives of other participants. It is a reasonable assumption, though one which does not seem to have been made until now, that *The World Encompassed* was also put together under Drake's auspices before 1595. This work may have been the basis for the discarded account of 1589, and it may even have been used in the account of the later part of the voyage in "The Famous Voyage" narrative. These claims cannot, except for the last, be made with any certainty, but they can be used to explain much that is otherwise inexplicable.

There is no doubt whatever that Drake intended to publish under his own name a narrative of all his voyages up to and including the Portugal one as a means of convincing the Queen of the extent of his services to England. He wrote a preface to this effect addressed to her and dated 1 January 1592.[15] The English legal year began on 25 March, so this would be 1593 by our reckoning. But it could have been 1592. Hakluyt, for example, often and confusingly used calendar dating instead of what was known as English style, just as we have seen Philip Jones do. In this preface, Drake complained that writing came hard to him. Indeed, we do not have any example of his narrative style, or even of his relaxed epistolary style; his surviving letters are brief, on immediate matters of business. It is almost certain that he did not complete any such narrative. If the date was 1593 he would not have had time to do so, for he was soon after that gradually taken back into the confidence of the higher officials and eventually the Queen.

How then, in light of the draft preface, can the thesis expounded above be explained regarding the material in *Sir Francis Drake revived* and *The World Encompassed*? The explanation would be that Drake's early plan was to obtain the services of others better qualified at writing than he to write up successive narratives of his voyages from his own material, together with whatever his assistants could glean from survivors of the voyages and his own recollections and documents, so that a full, clear, and exculpatory narrative could be put together. The Reverend Philip Nichols would be perfectly capable of doing this in the manner stated on the 1626 title page: "out of the report of Master Christopher Ceely, Ellis Hixom and others who were in the same voyage with him . . . and much holpen and enlarged by divers notes, with his own hand [Drake's] here and there inserted." This is excellent evidence that the narrative was composed and completed under Drake's own eyes. There is much less specific evidence about *The World Encompassed*, which was said to have been "carefully collected out of the notes of Master Francis Fletcher Preacher in this employment, and divers others his followers in the same." There is no doubt that Fletcher's narrative was used extensively in this book; the only copy of the journal itself, the first part (extending to 25 November 1578), dated 1677, establishes this clearly.[16]

We are left then with two alternatives: first, that in 1589 Drake was having Philip Nichols and possibly someone else write up the materials so far as he could assemble them or, second, that narratives of the circumnavigation (and possibly also the account of the 1572–73 voyage) were already in existence before the end of 1589. The publication of the circumnavigation was stopped; or it could have been, as Hakluyt stated, "withdrawn." Drake's collection of voyages would therefore, at this time, have been a series of narratives published as having been compiled by another man (Philip Nichols?) but backed secretly by Drake's authority. The publication of "The Famous Voyage" did at least give Drake public recognition, and this may have satisfied him for a time, but it can be argued that by the end of 1592, at the latest, he was taking on a different task. He would revise and rewrite, in his own hand and in his own style, the narratives already compiled for him and present them to Elizabeth. This, and perhaps this alone, can explain the mysterious preface of 1 January 1593. "Madam," he said,

> Seeing divers have diversely reported and written of these voyages and ac-
> tions which I have attempted and made, every one endeavouring to bring

to light whatsoever inklings of conjectures they have had; whereby many untruths have been published, and the certain truth concealed, as I have thought it necessary myself, as in a card to prick the principal points of the counsel taken, attempts made and success had, during the whole course of my employment in these services against the Spaniard.

He denied that he was apologizing for anything he had done, but said rather that he was merely trying to put the record straight in order that he should not be excluded from service in future, "not as setting sail for maintaining my reputation in mens judgement, but only as sitting at helm, if occasion shall be, for conducting the like action hereafter." He wrote for later ages, he claimed, so "that posterity be not deprived of such help as may happily be gained hereby, and our present age, at least, may be satisfied in the rightfulness of these actions, which hitherto have been silenced." He hoped his labor would not be lost because it had not been easy—"also in writing the report thereof, a work to him no less troublesome."[17]

This document has every indication of authenticity, and it very much contains the flavor of a seaman's bold writing. But why should Drake write such a preface if he had not completed anything substantial himself? The answer could be that he had already had both the 1572–73 and 1577–80 voyages written up for him by a professional hand or hands, and that he was engaged not in writing them from the beginning but in revising them with touches of his own in order to make it appear that he had written the whole series himself. This argument implies that Philip Nichols, and possibly others, had originally been employed to write on their own account voyage narratives that they could publish under their own names, but that well before 1 January 1593 Drake had decided to use them instead as his ghost writers and to base his own final narrative on the work they had done for him. This scheme was not followed, it is suggested, because in 1593 Drake saw signs that he would eventually be rehabilitated, and he therefore consigned to limbo among his papers the two narratives already discussed, together with the preface and whatever original notes and papers he had retained. These arguments are not conclusive and cannot be so in default of new evidence, but they are worth putting forward as part of the context within which "The Famous Voyage" was conceived and executed.

There are a few further significant facts. First, there is no evidence that Drake was able to retain the log of the circumnavigation. He surrendered his illustrated journal, written by himself and his relative John Drake, to the Queen, who subsequently suppressed it. It is now lost. The Queen probably demanded and impounded his log: if he had to depend on Fletcher's journal and other narratives for *The World Encompassed* (if in fact it was written before 1595), he cannot have had the log in his possession. On the other hand, it is highly probable, indeed almost certain, that he impounded Fletcher's journal on or before his return in 1580 together with as many of the unofficial journals of his men as he could get hold of, since none have survived in their original state.

Nothing was heard of the Fletcher journal except in *The World Encompassed*—when it was presumably still in the Drake archive—until one John Conyers, now identified as a well-known London pharmacist, copied the first part of it in 1677, nearly a century after its compilation, without naming its location. But no body of papers deriving from Drake survive in the Drake family archives, so it must be concluded that most or all were dispersed during the civil struggles of the mid-seventeenth century.

The World Encompassed, apart from the initial paragraphs perhaps added by Drake's nephew, is a clear, straightforward narrative of the whole voyage. It differs from *Sir Francis Drake revived* in that the latter is written in the third person, whereas *The World Encompassed* is written in the first person, though it does not purport to be Drake's own narration. His nephew writes in his dedication to the Earl of Warwick as if it were: "I rather choose to say nothing, rather than too little, in praise of the deceased author." Henry R. Wagner thought the 1628 volume was the work of the compiler of the 1626 volume, but he considered both roughly contemporary with their dates of publication, and he insisted that *The World Encompassed* contained much padding, which he thought of as seventeenth-century additions. On the contrary, the narrative is fluid and coherent, with only the occasional moralizing and comment on fauna and flora that the 1677 copy of the first part of Fletcher's narrative contains. Wagner does make some good points, notably that the compiler used Edward Cliffe's narrative of John Winter's portion of the voyage (Hakluyt printed it in 1600), and this seems highly probable. There is no reason why it should not have been available to Drake after his return; Drake would doubtless have demanded full details of Winter's voyage before and after he left him. Otherwise most of *The World Encompassed* is Fletcher, but Fletcher purified of any adverse comments on Drake (at least in the part where we have the full journal and can compare the two).

There is no doubt that the second part of the voyage also largely depended on the part of the Fletcher journal of which the full version is missing. No doubt this part, too, was purged of comments on Drake which were not to his credit. Even for the first part of the voyage, the compiler had available other sources than Fletcher. With some version of this narrative already existing in 1589, there seems no reason why it too should not have been put in its present form by Philip Nichols. No doubt it benefited from "the notes of . . . divers others his followers in the same" from Fletcher's journal, and certainly from Drake's memory and any miscellaneous notes he had managed to salvage.

We are now in a position to say something about the manuscript Hakluyt received, as has been proposed, either from Drake or from his assistant (Philip Nichols appears the obvious candidate). The manuscript was almost certainly favorable to Drake and had some of the modifications in Fletcher's journal noted above. This alone could have made it unacceptable to Walsingham or his censor. But Hakluyt evidently retained his copy even when he was not allowed to print it. He says of the Cavendish narrative, "in relation of the Philippinaes, Iapon, China, and the Isle of S. Helena it is more particular, and exact; and therfore the want of the first made by Sir Frauncis Drake will be the lesse." It is not certain whether he is speaking of the voyage made by Drake or the narrative made by him.

Wagner has traced, as far as possible, the surviving sources from which it can be deduced that "The Famous Voyage" (as printed) was derived. Wagner establishes that much of the earlier parts of "The Famous Voyage" derived from John Cooke's narrative (B. L. Harley 540, ff. 93–100ʳ)[18] and that what can be termed its middle course derived from the "Anonymous Narrative" (B. L. Harley 280, ff. 83–90).[19] Internal evidence suggests that both these documents in their existing form were written after Drake's return, probably some time after, and that they were based on journals kept during the voyage and are not those journals themselves. Both are critical of and sometimes biased against Drake, but both contain significant information on the voyage which is not obtainable from Fletcher's journal for the first part of the voyage or from *The World Encompassed* for the later stages. We cannot be certain where Hakluyt obtained them, but it is reasonable to assume that if Walsingham (or his censor) was responsible for suppressing the first version supplied to Hakluyt, then Walsingham was the source of these and probably other items from which "The Famous Voyage" was finally put together.

Wagner stresses that for the first part of the Hakluyt narrative there is no definite trace of the use of Fletcher or any derivative of Fletcher, though he gives one or two instances where such a use might have been possible. The "Anonymous Narrative" is only some three thousand words in length, and it concentrates mostly on that part of the voyage between the Island of Mocha, off Chile, and Guatulco, Mexico. Wagner is obliged to concede that, thereafter, Hakluyt appears to depend on Fletcher. By this he means the version attributed to Fletcher and others in *The World Encompassed*, for we have no text of Fletcher's journal for this part and there are few discrepancies in Hakluyt (though there is much compression) from what was printed in 1628. This would indicate that Hakluyt had recourse to a version of this text written before the end of 1589.

It is unlikely that Hakluyt had Fletcher's journal; if he had, he would almost certainly have either used it in 1600 or else bequeathed it to Purchas, who would at least have referred to it in his *Pilgrimes* of 1625, where he relies on "The Famous Voyage." The probable explanation is that for the first two stages of the voyage, up to the departure from the Spanish settlements at Guatulco, Cooke and the "Anonymous Narrative" were sufficient to give a balanced picture, even in the small scale to which they were being reduced; but for the later stages (the California one and the trans-Pacific and homeward ones), Hakluyt was driven back on the original narrative which had been suppressed. Because it is not likely to have contained such controversial matter about Drake as Fletcher's original account of the Doughty affair had included, using the original would not lead him into trouble with Walsingham and the censor, who are likely to have objected to a pro-Drake version of the Doughty episode and other controversial incidents on the outward voyage. That Hakluyt had kept this version is sufficiently indicated in his remarks already quoted.

The argument, then, is that the first narrative was suppressed as giving too much credit to Drake for certain episodes, and that it was replaced almost certainly from official (Walsingham) sources when it was finally realized that to omit the circumnavigation entirely would distort the picture of English overseas enterprise. Hakluyt and his associates were then able to use parts of the original version, which was basically Fletcher as modified in *The World Encompassed*, to round off and balance the latter part of his narrative. This again brings us back to the point that what emerged as *Sir Francis Drake revived* and *The World Encompassed*, in 1626 and 1628, respectively, were compiled for and partly by Drake with the assistance of the Reverend Philip Nichols between the summer of 1589 and the end of 1592 (or perhaps 1591). Further, *The World Encompassed* was in existence in some form before November 1589—it was excluded from *The principall navigations* at that point, yet partly resuscitated by Hakluyt when he had to hastily put together "The Famous Voyage" a month or two afterward. There is a great deal of conjecture in all this, and it is not possible to support firmly many of the points made here, but it seems desirable to attempt an hypothesis or series of hypotheses which would put "The Famous Voyage," and with it the principal English sources for Drake's circum-navigation, into a reasonable perspective. As for the Reverend Francis Fletcher, there is nothing to say. He disappears in September 1580, leaving nothing but his journal—in Drake's hands, to use or misuse, as he thought fit.

"The Famous Voyage" is, in its contracted state, only about fourteen thousand words long, yet it contains a clear, coherent, and basically complete account of the voyage. As such it is a considerable achievement in compression and elucidation. A good many of the criticisms which have been levied against it, notably by Wagner, have been somewhat misconceived. It does contain mistakes, and it does not cover all the episodes of the voyage fully. But it must be remembered that the only other complete account of the voyage, *The World Encompassed*, is almost precisely three times as long and therefore has space for much more incident than Hakluyt could afford. The 1677 Fletcher journal of roughly one-fifth of the voyage is some twenty-four thousand words in length; the complete Fletcher journal would have run to some seventy or eighty thousand words at least if it had been continued on the same scale. (Of course, parts of the later sections of the journal are used in *The World Encompassed*, but almost certainly not the whole of it.) Even John Cooke's narrative (which again covers only the first part of the voyage), with its "Anonymous Narrative" of the final two-thirds, is over twelve thousand words in length. Edmund Cliffe's account of this stage of the voyage out and of Winter's return is also on a modest scale, under seven thousand words.[20]

The question of length must be taken into account in any evaluation of "The Famous Voyage." Compression—and hasty compression at that—was bound to leave gaps and almost certain to produce mistakes and ambiguities in detail. It is remarkable that no more weaknesses of this sort show. The most out-standing feature of the narrative is that it reads freshly, like the account of a participant in the voyage; and indeed, it does contain some statements in the first person. It is therefore a major achievement on the part of Hakluyt and his assistant or assistants to have turned a composite account into this simple, direct, first-person narrative. If this reading is correct, Hakluyt's skills as an editor, long before he tried himself at greater length and scope in the second edition of *The principall navigations,* were well developed.

At the same time, there are signs here and there that the compression was done in haste. It can be argued that too much space is given to some comparatively minor episodes and too little to some major ones. Altogether very little light is thrown on the methods and personality of Francis Drake himself, except perhaps in his dealings with the ship *Cacafuego* and with the California Indians. The early stage of the voyage is treated, perhaps, in too leisurely a fashion in view of the compression needed later. Most readers are inclined to complain that far too little is said about the Doughty affair; but not only was it still very much a controversial matter in 1589, it was in fact a minor episode in the geographic picture which Drake's voyage drew for Englishmen for the first time.

Drake's primary objective—the exploration of Patagonia and of the Chilean coast—is, after all, well covered, as is his voyage through the Strait of Magellan. Insufficiently described are his violent struggles with the westerlies after he had emerged into the Pacific, as well as his discovery that Tierra del Fuego was an archipelago, not a solid land mass extending to the South Pole. The main facts of the robberies of the Spanish ships are given as effectively, if in less detail, as in Cooke's narrative and *The World Encompassed.* The stay in New Albion is given disproportionate emphasis because of Hakluyt's view that North America was the proper field for English imperial enterprises and colonization. If the crossing of the Pacific is skimped like the crossing from Africa to Brazil, this accorded with Hakluyt's later practice of cutting down open sea passages as boringly repetitive for his readers. His detail on the Moluccas is firm and precise: again, English contacts with the Spice Islands were part of his, and even more his elder cousin's, program for English commerce. The final voyage home is also skimped, and the abortive call at the African coast north of the Cape of Good Hope is denied.[21]

The overall impression is of a narrative that picks up a great deal of what was novel about the voyage and, especially, what was likely to be important for future English voyagers. Clearly, Hakluyt saw in the Drake material which he could print in 1589 a close complement to what he could reveal on the much more recent circumnavigation of Thomas Cavendish. All in all, "The Famous Voyage" deserves its fame as the best short account of the circumnavigation. Indeed, in many respects it is an outstanding account. But to say this is not to deny its shortcomings and errors, which are mostly venial, the results of its hasty preparation and compression.

In his second edition, where he was not under the same pressure as when he added "The Famous Voyage" to the first edition, Hakluyt remained satisfied with the narrative—perhaps too satisfied. His customary improvement of the forms of place names and addition of side notes was characteristic of his dealing with other texts of 1589. He removed a nonsensical sentence, the intended meaning of which he could, indeed, have supplied by revision.[22] He also added a brief paragraph on the voyage along the South American coast which is paralleled in a series of notes evidently made shortly after 1582, now in B. L. Harley MS 280, fol. 81.[23] The mistakes on the depth of water in the Plate estuary point conclusively to a direct relation between John Cooke's narrative and Hakluyt's 1589 version.[24] His alteration from 55°20 to 57°20 of the southernmost latitude that was reached on the voyage can be ascribed to his use of material from Nuno da Silva, though he may also have had other evidence,[25] and his alteration of the latitude at which the California coast was reached from 42° to 43° may have been similarly based.[26] His removal of the mention of snow on the coasts of western North America,[27] which reappears in *The World Encompassed,* is likely to have come from conversations with persons who had been with Drake—or perhaps because he thought the incident improbable. The fact that Hakluyt supplemented "The Famous Voyage" only with a narrative from Nuno da Silva[28] and Edward Cliffe's[29] account of Winter's phase of the voyage (taken from Linschoten, as published in English in 1598) perhaps signifies his satisfaction with the account as it stood. He also added a list of the kings of Java and a brief vocabulary of Javanese words, obviously obtained from someone who had been on the voyage.[30] It would seem that direct contact between him and Fletcher can be ruled out.

The conclusion must be that, even though Hakluyt felt that "The Famous Voyage" could be supplemented in certain particulars, as above, it was still as authoritative as he could make it. The fact that it was retained in the second edition shows that he was not in contact with the Drake family and its archive. Walsingham had died in 1590 and his papers were not available. Hakluyt's failure to include further critical material on Drake would, perhaps, follow naturally from the reticence he showed with regard to dead heroes and his desire not to revive old controversies; his deletion from the 1589 version of some personal remarks in Luke Ward's narrative of the Fenton voyage of 1582 is a case in point.[31] If the volumes published in 1626 and 1628 still cause difficulties (perhaps resolved above), they nevertheless greatly increased the available material on Drake. The revelation of the British Library version of Cooke, the edition of "Anonymous Narrative" by Vaux in 1854 (even if inaccurately transcribed), and the meticulous work of Zelia Nuttall and H. R. Wagner in English and Spanish repositories have revealed materials which can be used both to enlarge greatly "The Famous Voyage" and to call into question some of its details.[32] But the narrative remains basic, and it contains celebrated and vivid passages without which our knowledge of the circumnavigation would be much the poorer. What Hakluyt can be especially criticized for is having failed to use the material on the maps, manuscript and printed, which he had seen (see Wallis, ch. 9, below).[33]

Hakluyt was cautious, as he had to be, in regard to the more controversial aspects of the circumnavigation. He ignores many of John Cooke's critical remarks, and he makes his account of the Doughty controversy as neutral as possible, but he neither glorifies nor denigrates Drake. Throughout, he concentrates on the voyage rather than the man. This is characteristic of his treatment in both editions of his great collection. Biography, not Hakluyt's primary concern, emerges from voyage narrative only as incidental to action; he sticks firmly to the "nauigations, voiages and discoueries" of his title page. Samuel Purchas, his successor, shows much more interest in the personality of his characters.

Given the tightrope Hakluyt was obliged to walk, his "Famous Voyage" is both comprehensive and fair, and it reflects great credit on his capacity to present a complex pattern of sea voyaging concisely, on the whole accurately, and in a style which conveys something of its excitement and novelty. Along with the narrative of "N. H." on the Cavendish circumnavigation,[34] as well as some other materials about that voyage, the 1589 edition of *The principall navigations* gave Englishmen, for the first time, direct evidence from English sources of expeditions which multiplied substantially the areas covered by earlier attempts and which strongly reinforced Hakluyt's propagandist purpose: to stress that by this time Englishmen had the resources and knowledge to penetrate any part of the oceanic world, if only they had the will and the capital resources necessary. "The Famous Voyage" narrative played an important part in making the coverage of English maritime activities truly worldwide.

APPENDIX

The biographies of Philip Nichols and Francis Fletcher are crucial to the arguments put forward in the preceding pages, though it cannot be claimed that all the suggestions made here can be fully established from what is known at present. As both men attended Cambridge University, the main secondary authority, which does not cite sources, is John Venn and J. A. Venn, *Alumni Cantabrigiensis,* pt. 1, vol. I (Cambridge, Eng., 1922), henceforth cited as Venn.

There are no great lacunae in what we know of the life of Philip Nichols "of Lincoln," who matriculated in 1569 and was a member of Corpus Christi College, proceeding to the B.A. degree in 1573-74, the M.A. in 1577, and a fellowship at his college from 1576 to 1583. He was ordained deacon and priest in the diocese of Lincoln on 31 May 1576, and in 1579 he was incorporated as a member of Oxford University. He disappears from sight for some years after 1583, having possibly married and or become a chaplain at sea or in a noble household. Nichols would seem to have been available to enter Drake's service on the latter's return from Lisbon in June 1589, and to have been available to prepare the first (rejected) draft of "The Famous Voyage" for Hakluyt in 1589; and he is likely then or shortly thereafter to have written up for Drake the account of the 1572-73 voyage which we know as *Sir Francis Drake revived.* In the fair copy of this work which Sir Francis Drake, Bart., the younger, prepared for publication in 1626 (and which is now in the British Library, Sloane MS 301) the title is simply: "A Relation of the rare occurrances in a third voyage made by Sir Francis Drake into the West Indies in the years 72: and 73, when Nombre de Dios by him and 52 others only in his company surprised. Faithfully taken out of yᵉ Reports of Mʳ Christopher Ceelie, Ellis Hixom and others who were in the same voyages with him by Phillip Nicholls Preacher. Reviewed also by yᵉ same Sir Francis Drake, and much holpen and enlarged by divers notes with his own hand here and there inserted." The published title contained this information but was preceded by the more flamboyant title *Sir Francis Drake revived: calling upon this dull or effeminate age to follow in his noble steps of gold and silver*. In the absence of other evidence, the title can tentatively be attributed to the publisher, Nicholas Bourne. Bourne went on to print the other work, which Nichols may have had a major part in compiling, based largely on Fletcher's journal: *The world encompassed by Sir Francis Drake, being his next voyage to that to Nombre de Dios formerly imprinted; carefully collected out of the notes of Master Francis Fletcher preacher in this imployment, and diuers others his followers in the same: offered now at last to publique view, both for the honour of the actor, but especially for the stirring vp of heroick spirits, to benefit their countrie, and eternize their names by like noble attempt*. It is worth noting that both these books were published during a renewed war with Spain and that they took the nationalistic slogans on their title pages from the war fever of the time; so they themselves became war propaganda against Spain by reviving the achievements of Francis Drake more than half a century before.

Whether through Drake's influence or not, Nichols spent the rest of his ecclesiastical career in the West Country. He was briefly vicar of Stoke Climsland, near Falmouth, in 1591 and rector of Mylor, within easy reach of Plymouth by water, from 28 November 1591 to May 1592; so he could have remained closely in touch with Drake during the years when Drake was (we think) contemplating turning the narrative which Nichols had written for him into direct speech as his own accounts of his ventures. Nichols moved, later in 1592, to be rector of Wembworthy, in central Devonshire, the living of which he held until 1606 (he was made a prebendary of Exeter Cathedral in 1599 and held his canonry until 1606). He then moved to the rich rectory of Honiton, in the east of the county, where he remained until his death in 1614. Venn is incorrect in saying that he died in 1606; W. H. Wilkins, "The Rectors of Honiton, 1505–1907," *Transactions of the Devonshire Association*, 66 (1937) 406, gives a valuable summary; his will, and the administration, were destroyed in the Exeter Probate Registry in 1942, but they are noted in E. D. Fry, ed., *Wills and Administrations Relating to . . . Devon and Cornwall* (London, 1903), p. 131; there was a contest over his property outside the diocese of Exeter in the Prerogative Court of Canterbury, and letters of administration were given first to his sister, Dorothy Gredicot (née Nicholls), and then revoked and reissued to his widow, Joan Nicholls (née Beaumont), Public Record Office, London, PROB 6/8, fol. 140.

Venn admits that the ground for Francis Fletcher is much less sure. Fletcher can probably be identified with a man of that name who entered Pembroke College in 1564 but did not take a degree. Though record of his ordination has not been found, he must surely be the rector of St. Mary Magdalene, Milk Lane, London, who, after holding the preferment for a short time, resigned in July

1576 to join Drake in his preparations (see George Hennessy, *Novam reper-torium ecclesiasticum Londonense* [London, 1898], p. 268). Venn believes that Fletcher was next the rector of Bradenham, Buckinghamshire, between 1579 and 1592 (the first date covers the period when Drake's Francis Fletcher was still at sea). But in fact, the rector of Bradenham from 1575 until at least 1581, when he became one of the Queen's chaplains, was Richard Fletcher, on his way to high episcopal office. If Francis Fletcher served at Bradenham (and he may indeed have been placed there at some point as the result of some relationship) it was as curate or vicar. From Venn it then appears that in 1593 Francis Fletcher became vicar of Tickhill, Yorkshire, but he does not appear in the Public Record Office, Certificates of Institutions to Benefices (E331) or in the Composition Books (E334). But he was certainly vicar of that parish when, in 1605, he married Margaret Gallard, a widow of the parish (*Yorkshire Archae-ological Journal,* 101 (1891) 215), and his benefice was filled by another in 1619. His will has not been found. For reasons indicated above, it does not appear that he retained his valuable journal of the circumnavigation, but surrendered it to Drake in 1580; nor has any further contact between them been discovered. The surviving transcript of the first part of the journal was made by John Conyers, "Pharmacopolist," in 1677 (British Library, Sloane MS 61) and is more likely to have come from a Drake source than from Fletcher's papers. There seems little doubt that his journal was used by Drake, probably through the agency of Philip Nichols, at various times between 1589 and 1594, and that it appeared in a form which had Drake's approval as *The World Encompassed* in 1628.

NOTES

1. *The principall navigations* (London, 1589), sig. *4v.

2. These are reprinted in the facsimile edition, ed. D. B. Quinn and R. A. Skelton, of Richard Hakluyt, *The principall navigations* (1589), 2 vols. (Cambridge, Eng., 1965). In the modern index by Alison Quinn, the notation 643A to 643L has been used for material from them (II, 836).

3. H. R. Wagner, *Sir Francis Drake's Voyage Around the World* (San Francisco, 1926), p. 238.

4. See the discussion in D. B. Quinn, ed., *The Hakluyt Handbook*, 2 vols. (London, 1974), II, 477–489. A total of 121 copies is listed, but there are some duplicates. All but 10 have the Drake leaves, which were never reprinted for later insertion. This proves that the copies which went out in 1590 had the Drake leaves already inserted (except, possibly, a small number), but there is no clear correlation with the Bowes leaves; many of the unsophisticated copies have these in the second state, as we should expect (9 of 13 copies in Oxford and Cambridge, pp. 481–482), but the equally unsophisticated Weld-Blundell copy (p. 488) has the Drake leaves with Bowes in the first state.

5. *The principall navigations*, 1589, I (1965), xxii–xxiii.

6. *The principal navigations,* III (1600), 730–742; he had also printed the California portion earlier (III, 440–442) to stress the English claim on the west coast of North America.

7. *The principall navigations,* 1589 (1965), xviii–xx.

8. First published at Helmstadt in 1587. The English translation is Short Title Catalogue (S.T.C.) 12003.

9. *The principall navigations* (1589), I (1965), xx–xxi.

10. If this is so, some modification should be made of the statement in ibid., p. xxi, that the substitution of the Bowes leaves is our only indication of censorship.

11. Walsingham's involvement in the Drake affair is well brought out in documents in Wagner, *Sir Francis Drake's Voyage*, pp. 442–443 (from Public Record Office, London, SP94/1, fol. 57), and in Zelia Nuttall, *New Light on Drake* (London, 1914), pp. 420–428 (from P.R.O., SP12/143, 30, and SP12/1/444, 17), as well as (in my opinion) in the notes in British Library Harley MS 280, fol. 81 (printed in W. S. W. Vaux, ed., *The World Encompassed* [London, 1854], pp. 175–177), of which Hakluyt made use in 1600.

12. For the disastrous Portugal voyage see K. R. Andrews, *Drake's Voyages* (London, 1967), pp. 135–146, and for Drake's long period of disgrace Sir Julian Corbett, *Drake and the Tudor Navy*, 2 vols. (London, 1898), II, 334–374.

13. S.T.C. 18544, under Philip Nichols as author; no. 18545 is another edition of 1628. The title is a translation of the Latin title of a Dutch tract, *Franciscus Dracus redivivus* (Amsterdam, 1596), upholding Drake and Cavendish as champions of Protestantism in the struggle of the United Provinces and England against Spain. It is reprinted in I. A. Wright, ed., *Documents Concerning English Voyages to the Spanish Main, 1569–1580* (London, 1932), pp. 245–396.

14. S.T.C. 7161, under Sir Francis Drake the younger; no. 7612 is another edition published in 1635.

15. Prefixed to *Francis Drake revived*, sig. A3.

16. This can be seen in N. M. Penzer, ed., *The World Encompassed* (London, 1926), where the 1677 copy is printed in full except for some of the crudely copied sketches, all of which are in Wagner, *Sir Francis Drake's Voyage*. This account indicates Fletcher's basic hostility to Drake, which came to a head later in his voyage and explains the lack of any further contact between them. The Fletcher text was considerably modified to Drake's advantage for the first part of the 1628 edition of *The World Encompassed*, and presumably comparable modifications were made to the lost portion of the original.

17. *The World Encompassed*, sig. 4v.

18. This is a copy made by John Stow some time before he completed the 1592 edition of *The annales of England from the first inhabitation vntill 1592* (1592: S.T.C. 23334). The heading of the document is "For Francis Drake. Anno Domini 1577" and is ambiguous. It could, indeed, mean that it was presented at some point to Drake, but in the context it must merely be Stow's indication that he intended to use it for his chronicle of the year 1577, which he did. It is difficult to accept its citations of speeches as containing the exact words spoken at the time; and it was probably written in its present form to support the case of John Doughty in his charges against Drake, though much has a ring of authenticity.

19. This is in a contemporary hand but bears no indication of its origin or author. It is certainly a redaction of an earlier journal because it records, e.g., news of the sending back to Spain of Nuno da Silva, Drake's former pilot (put ashore by him at Guatulco), which took place in 1582, thus making the narrative later than this year.

20. *The principal navigations*, III (1600), 748–753.

21. The "Anonymous Narrative" says they entered a great bay to the west of the Cape of Good Hope, but finding no water had to go to sea again, where they obtained enough water from a rainstorm to carry them forward. But "The Famous Voyage" insists that "the Cape of Good Hope, which was the first land we fel withall: neither did we touch with it, or any other land, vntill we came to Sierra Leana." Either the text Hakluyt was using differed from the Cooke text we now have, or in compression of his sources Hakluyt slipped on this point.

22. Sig. 3M6r. "Wee had by proofe in this place, as also at the furthermost Islands, that the sunne being at the least 8. degrees from the Tropike of Capricorne, the night was but two howers long, and scant that, so that we perceiued that when the sunne should be in the Tropike, there would be no night at all." (See Wagner, *Drake's Voyage*, p. 263.)

23. See n. 11 above, associating the document with Walsingham. It is a series of supplementary answers by one of Drake's men to an interrogation, the major parts of which do not appear to be extant.

24. Hakluyt turned the Cooke narrative's "54 and 3½ fathoms" into "54 and 53½ fathoms" of fresh water. (This is brought out by *The principal navigations,* III (1600), p. 744.)

25. *The principal navigations,* III (1600), p. 744, where Nuno da Silva says "seven and fiftie degrees."

26. Ibid., p. 737. Compare *The principall navigations,* sig. 3M7r. "in 42. degrees."

27. "Lowe plaine land, & clad and couered ouer with snow."

28. In Jan Huygen van Linschoten, *Jan Huygen van Linschoten his discours of voyages into the Easte and Weste Indies* [trans. W. Phillip] (London, 1598; S.T.C. 15691), printed in *The principal navigations,* III (1600), 742–748. In order to be able to include some English material in his section on western North America, Hakluyt printed separately the portion of "The Famous Voyage" relating to Drake's California visit (III, 440–442), with a long heading stressing his taking possession of New Albion. (This is the only instance of Hakluyt's duplication of part of a narrative.) Here he made the change, noted above, to 43° as in the main narrative; but he also took the opportunity (which he did not do in "The Famous Voyage") of setting the sequence right in placing the cleaning and caulking of the ship at the island of Caño before instead of after the raid on Guatulco. He was always uncertain whether to stress potential mineral resources where there was no clear evidence for them. He did draw attention to the "great shewe of rich minerall matter" to be found in New Albion, though he could not make up his mind how to express this in the text. In 1589 (sig. 3M8r.) it appeared as "There is no part of earth here to be taken vp, wherein there is not a reasonable quantitie of gold or silver". In the main narrative in 1600 this becomes "There is no part of earth here to bee taken vp, wherein there is not some speciall likelihood of gold, and silver" (III, 442), whereas in the subsidiary version (III, 738) it is "There is no part of earth heere to bee taken vp, wherein there is not some probable shew of gold or siluer." We have no indication from what source he obtained this information because it does not appear in other extant document sources. Perhaps Drake himself was the source, noting the possibility of bullion (rather than its proved existence) to attract future English expeditions to the place.

29. *The principal navigations,* III (1600), 748–755.

30. Ibid., p. 742.

31. *The principall navigations* (1589), I (1965), i.

32. Zelia Nuttall, ed., *New Light on Drake* (1914), provided the greatest addition we have on the circumnavigation through her researches in Spain and Mexico; H. R. Wagner, *Drake's Voyage* (1926) added translations of a few additional Spanish documents and much commentary on earlier materials. E. G. R. Taylor, "More Light on Drake," *The Mariner's Mirror,* 16 (1920), 134–151, added the draft plan of 1577, the fragmentary character of which has caused much difficulty in interpretation (see also John Hampden, *Francis Drake Privateer* [London, 1972], pp. 111–113), and John Winter's brief outlines of his voyage (British Library Lansdowne MS, 100, no. 2), written on 2 June 1579 (a modern version is in Hampden, pp. 239–243). There is some tendency in Wagner to expect Hakluyt to have put much more into "The Famous Voyage" than was physically possible; this arises from failure to take into account the limitation of the narrative to a bare twelve pages.

33. See British Library, *Sir Francis Drake: An Exhibition to Commemorate Francis Drake's Voyage around the World, 1577–1580,* ed. Helen Wallis (London, 1977).

34. *The principall navigations* (1589), pp. 809–815: Hakluyt replaced this with a fuller account in the second edition.

Drake and South America

KENNETH R. ANDREWS

South America, I believe, was the area that Drake and his partners were primarily concerned with: more specifically, that part of the South American continent which lay to the south of the then existing Spanish and Portuguese conquests and settlements. This was no passing whim or fancy of 1577, nor even simply a convenient cover for a raid of plunder on Spanish shipping. For about a decade an important group of Englishmen was seriously interested in the commercial and colonial potential of this region, which became for a short while a major focus of English overseas ambition. I am prepared to concede, however, that Drake also visited the northwest part of the New World, and that this visit has given rise to a great deal of speculation in more recent times. So I propose to consider this aspect of the venture first, though not, I hasten to add, to deal with Drake's landfall.

There are two good reasons for thinking that Drake and company might have had this northern part of the world in mind from the outset. In the first place, Martin Frobisher had gone out to Baffin Island the previous year, 1576, and had returned with a painted globe suspended from his bowsprit, loudly boasting that he had found the Northwest Passage. The fact that it consisted of a not very large, landlocked bay is beside the point. What matters is that the next year, when Drake was to sail, London was agog with speculation about Frobisher's second expedition, in which he was expected to follow the passage through to the South Sea. Furthermore, Frobisher's most exalted backers in 1577 were Queen Elizabeth, the Earl of Leicester, and Sir Francis Walsingham, who were at the same time Drake's chief sponsors. Is it not reasonable to suggest that in sending Drake to the South Sea these people wanted him to explore the western approach to the passage? For one of the doubts that still worried Frobisher's friends and supporters was whether his strait had a western outlet. Did the sea north of America join the Pacific Ocean, or was America linked by land to the Far East? In 1577 this was a matter of some concern, and its solution could markedly affect English hopes of participating in the world's richest trade.

In the second place, the idea of approaching the Northwest Passage via the Strait of Magellan and what Englishmen liked to call the backside of America, meaning California, had already been mooted. As early as the 1520s two Englishmen had set out for the South Sea on Magellan's route in order to collect information about a northern passage from the Pacific to the Atlantic, but they got no further than the River Plate. Nevertheless, a similar idea was expounded at length in a discourse written by Richard Grenville probably in 1575.[1] Grenville had earlier proposed to the government a southern project—"A discovery of lands beyond the equinoctial"—with his specific target the most southerly triangle of the South American continent, not yet occupied by Christians.[2] This project had nothing whatever to do with the northern hemisphere. It was only when Grenville, under pressure, was forced to give up his venture that he belatedly came out with a new argument in favor of the southern voyage: it would provide a better approach to the Northwest Passage than the approach being urged by Frobisher.

The relevance of Grenville's northwest discourse to Drake's Famous Voyage must be handled with care. On the one hand, the connection between Grenville's southward scheme and Drake's enterprise cannot be denied. Indeed, it has hardly been stressed enough. In fact, Drake and company virtually took over Grenville's basic plan and carried it out. On the other hand, it must be remembered that the Northwest Passage approach was not an integral part of Grenville's project but an afterthought, principally to provide an argument or excuse for the southerly voyage. And although we may now see some sense in saying that it was easier to reach the Strait of Anian by way of the Strait of Magellan than by a direct course west, the argument would not have been convincing at that time, when optimism about the Atlantic approach was rising. Two years later, in 1577, Frobisher was riding a crest of confidence, and it seems most unlikely that at this euphoric moment his sponsors would have backed a rival. So long as Frobisher's efforts promised imminent success, the alternative proposal must have looked too laborious and hazardous to attract the necessary funds, given the well-known scepticism of merchants and courtiers about northern passage schemes. Taking the relevant considerations into account, therefore, I find that although the Northwest Passage was a matter of great interest in 1577, the idea of sending a fleet out to the Pacific to look for the back end of it was unlikely to gain support at that particular juncture.

Leaving aside such questions of likelihood and coming closer to the realities, is there any evidence that Drake or his promoters intended the voyage to include a reconnaissance of the Strait of Anian? The short answer is no: there is no such evidence. Furthermore, the only extant evidence of their intentions—the draft plan of the voyage[3]—says plainly that Drake was not expected to go anywhere near the Strait of Anian. On the contrary, the plan was for him to return through the Strait of Magellan without proceeding north of latitude 30° S. According to the plan, therefore, Drake's instructions would have specifically precluded any approach to the northwest coast of America. This is decisive, in the absence of any evidence that the plan was changed or of any reason for changing it. Unlike the vast majority of people, Drake did not go to California because he wanted to: he was looking for a way home, having realized that his instruction to return via the Strait of Magellan was little short of an invitation to suicide.

So let us consider the deep south of the New World, the region that interested not only Drake, but Grenville before him. In the original petition outlining his project Grenville was deliberately vague and cryptic about the lands he proposed to explore for purposes of trade and settlement, but his objective can be clearly discerned in spite of this. "In the places already subdued and inhabited by the Spaniard or Portingal," he wrote, "we seek no possession nor interest. But if occasion be free and friendly, traffic with them and their subjects." This suggests territories near or even adjacent to Iberian colonies. Again, the emphatic denial of any intention to trespass is accompanied by equally strong assertion of a right to settle unoccupied lands: "Beside that not only traffic, but also possession, planting of people and habitation hath been already judged lawful for other nations in such places as the Spaniards have not already added to their possession." He instances Florida and the French attempt in Brazil, evidently thinking in terms of America. He describes the territory of interest as beyond the torrid zone and "lying in the temper of England and other parts of Europe." Again, "the countries that we seek so lie that the course continueth not near the line but, crossing the same, still hasteth directly to the temper of our regions." That is, you cross the equator and go on south until you come to temperate lands, and Grenville finally identified these explicitly as American: "since Portugal hath attained one part of the new found world to the East, the Spaniard another to the West, the French the third to the North: now the fourth to the South is by god's providence left for England."

John Oxenham and his companions, captured by the Spaniards, translated all this into plain English: "A gentleman named Grenville," said one, "had asked for a licence to settle on the River Plate." He understood the colony was to be "on the coast of the North Sea, towards the River Plate, in a country of which they had reports, from some Portuguese, that it was very rich." Oxenham said Grenville had tried many times to persuade him to join his expedition the-purpose of which was to establish settlements "on the coast of the North Sea, or in the Strait of Magellan, or on the coast of the South Sea." And he added that Francis Drake had often said to him that if the Queen granted him a license "he would pass through the Strait of Magellan and found settlements over here in some good country." The phrase "over here" (*por acá*), uttered in Lima, must have meant the west coast of South America and implied that part of it to the south of Spain's dominion. The witnesses also declared that the Queen revoked her license to Grenville because she learned that the Spaniards had settlements beyond the Strait, and she feared that Grenville "might do harm in the possessions of her brother King Philip." Again, one can hardly avoid inferring Peru and Chile.[4]

Oxenham and his companions knew Grenville and they knew Drake. Although one of them claimed not to know Drake's intentions, the other two admitted that Drake would carry out Grenville's scheme if given the chance. In 1577 he was given the chance, and he took it: that is the heart of the matter, and it is the essential message of the draft plan, which was a plan for the reconnoitering of the east coast of South America from the southern edge of Portuguese settlement in Brazil southward, through the strait, and then northward on the west coast to the fringe of Spanish power, roughly reckoned to be toward the thirtieth parallel. This the draft plan, though fragmentary, sufficiently conveys; and this construction of it has been adequately explained elsewhere and accepted by the best authorities, so that in the present context this part of the argument can be taken as read.[5]

The similarity of the Grenville and Drake plans is striking. Of course there were certain differences in presentation, political in origin. Grenville talked vaguely of the Southern Hemisphere in general and devoted a great deal of space to repudiating any suggestion that he might offend the Iberian powers. This was because, at the time when he submitted his petition, amicable relations between those powers and England had recently been restored. Elizabeth meant to keep the peace, which also explains why she suppressed the project. In 1577 the situation changed sharply. Don John of Austria suddenly took up an aggressive stance in the Netherlands in July, and Elizabeth at once turned acid. The draft plan, which proposed to commit her directly as a partner to an implicitly anti-Spanish venture, was presumably submitted after Don John's breach of the peace; there would have been little point in opening the matter to the Queen before then, in view of her rejection of Grenville's plan. Consequently, the author or authors could afford to be more explicit about the objective than Grenville had been and could take far less trouble to justify the scheme. The Drake plan does not argue a case, for the case is already known. It lays down tersely a course of action and the means requisite thereto in a manner strongly reminiscent of John Hawkins' State Paper plans for later naval expeditions. The Queen's support is obviously expected—and it is of course obtained. The difference between the two documents thus serves only to underline their common ground and purpose.

English interest in this part of America, therefore, was no mere flash in the pan. It embodied serious ambitions which persisted for a decade, from the early seventies to the early eighties. These ambitions were commercial and colonial as well as predatory, and they were comparable in importance to English ambitions in North America. If this idea sounds strange, it is because our minds have been influenced by subsequent events. At the time, however, the English had almost no experience of any part of America, and they formed their impressions of this land of opportunity chiefly from reports of the Spanish and Portuguese colonies there. It was the success and wealth of those holdings which, more than anything else, inspired English interest in the New World. In earlier decades the central regions of America had been the main attraction, but English trade met increasing difficulties there during the sixties. Petty plunder continued in the seventies, but as the prospects of conquest, settlement, or steady trade grew dim, attention shifted elsewhere.

Peru was now the great magnet. Direct trade with the Spaniards there could mean enormous profits, returned in silver. And adjacent parts of the mainland like Chile might yield precious metals as abundantly as Peru. Thus Grenville noted "the likelihood of bringing in great treasure of gold, silver and pearl into this realm from those countries, as other princes have out of like regions." The temperate climate implied a potential native market for English cloth and encouraged thoughts of planting. Some of the people there, notably the Araucanians, were bitter enemies of the Spanish and might welcome the English as allies. Spain's shipping on these coasts was defenseless: what a chance to combine trade, planting, and plunder. Above all, if one wished to damage Spanish power, here was the place to do so with minimum risk and maximum profit. The idea of an Elizabethan conquest of Peru, outlandish as it may appear to us, was already buzzing in young Richard Hakluyt's head in 1579, and it is unlikely that the idea originated there. It may well have been floating about elsewhere since the early seventies.

But the Atlantic side of the continent was the initial concern, perhaps because, as we are told, certain Portuguese talked about a rich country near the River Plate, perhaps because the English had been learning from the French, who had a longstanding and currently active interest in Brazil and its region.[6] Probably both influences were at work. In any case, the Grenville petition shows that some of the men who were expected to take part in his enterprise had already voyaged to Brazil, presumably in the service of the Hawkins brothers. The elder brother, William, born in 1519, was Grenville's partner in the South Sea project, and he was old enough to have played some part in his father's Brazil ventures in the reign of Henry VIII. The last known of these occurred in 1540, when William was twenty-one, and if he did not actually sail on this occasion, he would probably have been involved as the heir apparent to the family business. No doubt on an earlier occasion, as a boy of twelve or so, he had gained a vivid impression of Brazilian man when his father brought back an Indian chief to present at court, "at the sight of whom the king and all the nobility did not a little marvel, and not without cause," as Hakluyt wrote later.[7]

Whatever the reason, William Hawkins was one of the key figures in the revival of English interest in Brazil in the 1570s, and his brother John was probably the brain behind Drake's voyage and author of the draft plan. The Hawkins interest of course included Drake. They were ship-owning and mercantile magnates, and he was their most successful captain. In fact, since the battle of San Juan de Ulúa in 1568, Drake had taken over John Hawkins' role as the group's leading commander, as a private admiral, in effect. This position was more important for Drake in the seventies than was the somewhat remote benevolence of Leicester, Lincoln, Walsingham, Hatton, or even Queen Elizabeth, and it is also more important for our understanding of the project. Drake had to have the blessing of those great men, and finally of that great lady, but the Famous Voyage was essentially a Hawkins venture, and it has the Hawkins trademark stamped all over it.

That trademark should have been something like a pair of culverins crossed over a bag of merchandise, symbolizing the interdependence of trade and plunder. How can a voyage of trade, or of commercial reconnaissance, be deliberately and of malice aforethought piratical from beginning to end, as Drake's incontestably was? To explain this now would take too long, but the fact is fundamental. Failure to grasp the intimate relation between trade and plunder has been a major factor in the misunderstanding and misinterpretation of Drake's circumnavigation on the part of historians and geographers for the past fifty years. Drake's pillage of Spanish shipping and settlements on the Pacific shores of America was clearly not displeasing to his promoters. To suggest that the Hawkins brothers, who had launched Drake's raids on Panama, or that Leicester, who had sponsored a similar raid by Andrew Barker as recently as 1576, or that the Winters, likewise men of war, expected Drake to make a peaceful voyage is to fly in the face not only of the documents but also of common sense. The *Golden Hind,* like Grenville's intended flagship the *Castle of Comfort,* was a ship fit and fitted for privateering, as efficient a predator as any of her size at that time. But none of this means that the draft plan for the commercial reconnaissance of those southern coasts was pure wool to pull over Elizabeth's innocent eyes. The commercial intent, and the colonial intent behind it, were perfectly serious and genuine. "wch viage by godes favor is to be performed in xiii month. all thowghe he shold spend v monthes in taryenge uppon the coaste to get knowle[dge] of the prynces and cowmptres ther."[8]

In these five months Drake was "to find out places meet to have traffic for the venting of commodities of these her Majesty's realms. . . . so there is great hope of gold, silver, spices, drugs, cochineal, and divers other special commodities such as may enrich her highness' dominions and also set shipping awork greatly." Actually, Drake spent over nine months ranging the shores south of thirty degrees on either side, and eight months of this period had passed before he took any action against Spanish property. It is true that he had no success in finding suitable places of trade. The population proved more often hostile than friendly and—what was worse—sparse and poor, showing no sign of having anything worth buying.

Mocha Island on the west coast looked promising, and the chaplain, Fletcher, waxed eloquent about the colonial prospects there: "This island is most rich in gold and silver and it aboundeth in many good things necessary for the maintenance of God's good people. Flourishing with trees and fruit continually, wanting nothing but a people fearing God to enjoy it."[9] He compared it to the Isle of Wight because it lay like a "door-bar" to the land, "a most golden province of the world named Valdivia." He thought that if both the mainland and the island were possessed by one prince, they would be invincible. But the natives of Mocha took the English for Spaniards, and bloodshed resulted. The work of reconnaissance which Drake seems to have carried out conscientiously was not encouraging, but this was by no means the end of the matter.

John Winter, the captain of the *Elizabeth*, who turned back from the Strait of Magellan, spent four months on the east coast of South America before returning home. The main reason for this loitering was that his ship and crew were run-down. He particularly needed fresh victuals. At St. Vincent, the most southerly Portuguese port, he found the Englishman John Whithall. Whithall was an important person there, son-in-law of the richest sugar planter, and he had written to London asking for direct trade, explaining in businesslike detail what was needed and how matters should be arranged.[10] In this letter, dated June 1578, he wrote: "they have discovered certain mines of silver and gold, and look every day for masters to come to open the said mines: which when they be opened will enrich this country very much." John Winter talked to Whithall, as he explained, because "I would understand the state of the country and disposition of the people."[11]

This was no idle curiosity. When Winter reached England in June 1579, St. Vincent and neighboring Santos became a new focus of English attention. The young Hakluyt interviewed Winter's men and promptly entered the arena of grand strategy: "the island of St. Vincent is easily to be won. . . . it is able to victual infinite multitudes of people." It should be annexed, while English pirates seize the Strait of Magellan and people it with *cimarrones* from Panama and a select company of both sexes from English jails. "There is no doubt," Hakluyt opined, "but that we shall make subject to England all the golden mines of Peru and all the coast and tract of that firm of America upon the sea of Sur. And work the like effect on the hither side of that firm."[12] It would be rash to conclude from this excited utterance that Hakluyt when young was a southern man altogether, but he seems to have considered the deep south of the New World highly important for England's future as a commercial and colonial power.

At about the same time, the Hawkins brothers were preparing to follow up the St. Vincent contact in their characteristic style. In January 1580 the Spanish ambassador reported that John Hawkins was fitting out three ships, "the pretence being that they are taking merchandise to the coast of Brazil." In fact, he added, they were actually taking trade goods. Next month he again referred to the venture, specifying St. Vincent as the destination.[13] Further light is shed upon this project by a state paper endorsed as "draft of a commission for Master William Hawkins being sent to discover new trades."[14] Drafted between January and October 1580, this royal patent would have given Hawkins certain rights and powers in connection with a voyage "which he intendeth with the favour of almighty God to make unto the coasts of Africa and America to the south and southwestwards, for the better discovery of all trades of merchandises in the said coasts." Hawkins was also permitted to serve "Don Anthony, King of Portugal, against any his enemies" and to make free with the proceeds of any such action—all of which of course amounted to a privateering license against

Spanish shipping, ports, and goods. So once again there is this combination of trade and plunder, and once again William Hawkins is the protagonist of the southward drive. But evidently larger interests were involved, for Walsingham literally applied his hand to the document, and (to judge from deleted passages in the manuscript) there is some question that either the Privy Council or the Muscovy Company may have drawn up instructions for the voyage.

This voyage was postponed, however, because, according to the Spanish Ambassador Bernardino de Mendoza, Drake's return in September led to a decision to enlarge the expedition and to go to the East Indies as well as Brazil. But the *Minion* of London did depart in October, dispatched by London merchants on a trading venture to St. Vincent and carrying as purser one Thomas Griggs, who had been steward in Winter's *Elizabeth* and Hakluyt's chief informant on Brazil. As Griggs reported later, the *Minion* was not a happy ship; and commercially the voyage was unpromising, with a lot of trouble between ship and shore. But it looks as though the English—or some of them at least—were interested in other possibilities as well as Brazil trade, notably the overland routes to Peru, the unexploited mines of Brazil, and the savages of the interior fighting against the Spanish. All of these figure in Griggs's report of the voyage.[15]

In effect, John Winter's return did a good deal to quicken English interest in American lands beyond the equator. Drake's return complicated the issue, however. The Hawkins-Drake group remained primarily concerned, it would appear, with South American prospects. But the new contact with the East Indies naturally influenced government policy, and some of the leading Muscovy merchants brought their weight to bear in favor of a Far Eastern expedition. The result was a good deal of confusion, both at the time and among historians since. The emergence of Dom Antonio as Pretender to the Portuguese throne in 1580 seemed to offer Spain's enemies various opportunities of trade, plunder, or even conquest in Portuguese spheres of influence, notably the Azores, the East Indies, and Brazil. All this came to nothing in the event, but for a few years there was much scheming in the dark and even a few ineffectual skirmishes. Upon one corner of this obscure scene it is now possible to throw a little light.

Shortly after his return, Drake submitted to the crown (presumably through Walsingham because the document is in Walsingham's hand) "a project for a corporation of such as shall venture unto such dominions and countries situate beyond the equinoctial line." The new company, headed by Drake, was to have monopoly rights in "such dominions as are situated beyond the equinoctial line . . . in the late notable discovery made by Francis Drake." The Queen was to receive one-fifth of the profits of any gold and silver mines that might be discovered, provided they were not lawfully possessed by any other Christian prince, and she was asked to set up a Casa de Contratación on the Spanish model to regulate the new trade.[16] This last clause caused Conyers Read to conclude that this was a plan for an East India Company, and Read's view is, I believe, generally accepted.[17] But the island of Ternate, where Drake is said to have reached a commercial understanding with the Sultan, and its neighbors, constituting the group then called the Moluccas, lay in fact north of the equator and were so indicated on contemporary maps.[18] Furthermore, Drake can hardly have claimed to be their discoverer, nor was there any prospect of mining precious metals there. The East Indies at this stage were seen as a potential sphere of trade, not as suitable lands for conquest and direct exploitation. As the phrase Casa de Contratación suggests, it was the Spanish-American type of specifically colonial exploitation that the author of this document envisaged, and the only region beyond the equinoctial line towards the South Pole that Drake could be considered to have "discovered" was actually the same intriguing triangle of the South American continent which he had been appointed to explore in 1577.

Drake's first intention, therefore, on returning from the Famous Voyage, was evidently to pursue and develop the work for which he had originally been dispatched: trade and settlement in the South American lands adjoining those of Spain and Portugal. He no doubt had in mind another South American expedition which might cover the promoters' expenses as handsomely as the first had done and by similar means.[19] Given the real purposes of the 1577 expedition, this was, after all, the logical sequel, and the reason why this pattern of events has not been discerned before is that Edward Fenton's voyage, expressly for the East Indies, was the actual sequel. It is noteworthy, however, that Drake and the Hawkins brothers took little part in that ill-starred expedition. Some of their men, including a younger Drake and a younger Hawkins, did go with Fenton, but the heads of the group preferred to follow their own chosen course of trade and plunder beyond the equinoctial.

It appears that William Hawkins eventually set out for Brazil around the end of 1582. The promoters, calling themselves "the company of discovery"—a significant echo of those 1580 phrases—were William and John Hawkins and Francis Drake. Drake's corporation thus appears to have given way to a partnership in the earlier scheme proposed by William Hawkins. It was a strong expedition of four ships, well fitted for warlike action, judging from the cost account, but also laden with merchandise. It did not in fact reach Brazil but went to the Caribbean instead, and one of the reasons given for the change of course, which was decided at the Cape Verde Islands on the way out, was "fear of 5 armados, set to guard Brazil, as a prize advised."[20] Thus the hopes of Drake and the Hawkins brothers, originating in Grenville's project, implemented by the 1577 voyage, and nurtured from the time of Winter's return in 1579, now fell to the ground, and with them any prospect of substantial success for the English in the region.

The main reason for this downfall was the Spanish reaction to the English threat. Briefly, this was expressed in the instructions to Don Diego Flores de Valdés for his great southward expedition of 1582. He carried a contingent of settlers to occupy the River Plate estuary and so to preempt the large continental gate through which Drake had cast a hasty glance in 1578. He also carried a small army under Don Alonso de Sotomayor which was intended to step up the Araucanian war and secure Chile against would-be invaders. His third task was to take Don Pedro Sarmiento de Gamboa and another force to the Strait of Magellan, which they were to fortify and garrison. This triple reply to Drake's attack shows that the Spanish understood very well the thrust of English ambition at this juncture. Although the efforts of Diego Flores, Don Alonso, and Pedro Sarmiento met with many grave troubles, they were sufficient to deter the English. Edward Fenton was obviously very interested in Brazil, and he thought about seizing St. Vincent as well as about passing the Strait of Magellan, but the Spanish presence on the eastern shores of South America at the time dispelled these notions.

Indeed, a certain lack of resolution on the part of the English interlopers is evident at this point, a certain lack of commitment which clearly contributed to the result. William Hawkins was content to change course for the West Indies and make a profitable trade there rather than risk serious opposition on the Brazilian coast. The London-Brazil trade petered out within a few years, largely because neither side trusted the other, but perhaps also because the English lacked the single-minded determination of the Dutch to share the sugar trade. English activity on these coasts continued intermittently for the rest of the century, but the visitors' attitude remained, as it had been from the beginning, somewhat ambiguous, tentative, and opportunist.

In America at this stage the English were probing, reconnoitering, seeking the most promising and least difficult spheres of profitable activity. Ventures commonly had more than one function, or they had alternative functions: on the northwest route to Cathay, for example, one might hope to sell English cloth to the Eskimo, and one might eventually turn to mining for gold instead. Venturers like the Southampton merchant Edward Cotton, Hakluyt's informant about earlier Brazil expeditions, were prepared to take what they could find. Cotton sent out a River Plate expedition in 1583, instructing his men to combine trade at St. Vincent with seal hunting and dredging for pearls in the Plate estuary, and he expected them to bring back information and specimens of all potentially profitable South American products.[21] Circumstances and the timing of events exercised a selective influence on the geography of English enterprise in the Western Hemisphere. The pioneers' energies were not persistently applied in a particular direction but were easily deflected, so that the channel they eventually found depended on the historical conjuncture. The years of the Fenton and Hawkins expeditions, 1582 and 1583, can thus be seen on reflection as a turning point at which South American hopes faded and North American ambitions began to gather strength—a significant shift of focus in the prehistory of the British Empire.

NOTES

1. Roger Barlow and Henry Patmer sailed with Sebastian Cabot in 1526. Grenville's discourse is in British Library (B.L.) Lansdowne MSS, 100, no. 4. Printed in R. Collinson, ed., *The Three Voyages of Martin Frobisher* (London, 1867), pp. 8–12.

2. B.L. Lansdowne MSS, 100, fols. 142–146. Printed in *Collinson, The Three Voyages,* pp. 4–8.

3. B.L. Cotton MSS Otho E. VIII, fols. 8–9. Printed in John Hampden, ed., *Francis Drake, Privateer* (London, 1972), pp. 111–113.

4. Zelia Nuttall, ed., *New Light on Drake* (London, 1914), pp. 5–12.

5. K. R. Andrews, "The Aims of Drake's Expedition of 1577–1580," *American Historical Review,* 73 (1968), 724–741.

6. In 1568 an English translation appeared of André Thevet's *Les singularitez de la France antarctique* (Paris, 1557) under the title *The New found worlde, Or Antarctike* (Short Title Catalog [S.T.C.] 23950). It spoke of silver mines found in the neighborhood of the River Plate and dwelt at some length on the hostile relations between the Iberians and the natives.

7. Richard Hakluyt, ed., *The Principal Navigations,* III (1600), 700–701.

8. Hampden, *Francis Drake,* p. 118.

9. N. M. Penzer, ed., *The World Encompassed and Analogous Contemporary Documents* (London, 1926), p. 141.

10. *The Principal Navigations,* III (1600), 701–703.

11. Nuttall, *New Light on Drake,* p. 389.

12. E. G. R. Taylor, ed., *The Original Writings and Correspondence of the Two Richard Hakluyts* (London, 1935), p. 142.

13. *Calendar of State Papers, Spanish,* III (London, 1896), pp. 3, 8.

14. Public Record Office, London, SP 12/142/44.

15. *The Principal Navigations,* III (1600), 704–706.

16. P.R.O., SP 12/144/44. Printed in Nuttall, *New Light on Drake,* p. 430. The one-fifth share was an idea derived from the Spanish *quinto real.*

17. C. Read, *Mr. Secretary Walsingham and the Policy of Queen Elizabeth* (Oxford, 1925), III, 396–397.

18. It is only since Drake's time that the term "Moluccas" has come to embrace a wider area.

19. It is relevant that in February 1581 an English translation appeared of Agustín Zárate's history of the discovery and conquest of Peru, entitled *The Discoverie and Conquest of the Provinces of Peru* (S.T.C 6123), with a dedication praising Drake for his Famous Voyage. The book dwelt upon the mines of Potosí, even dragging them into the title.

20. B.L. Harleian MSS, 267, fols. 101–102.

21. *The Principal Navigations,* II (1599), ii, 110–112; III (1600), 701.

Drake in the South Seas

WILLIAM A. LESSA

The geographic area of Drake's suspenseful adventures in the South Seas is a wide one, for within it are included not only Micronesia and the Philippines but also the culture area known to anthropologists as Indonesia. At the time of Drake's visit, Indonesia was a sophisticated world only recently Islamized, but before that it had belonged to the powerful Brahmanistic empire of Madjapahit and before that to the ancient Buddhistic empire of Shrivijaya—a far cry indeed from the simple food-gathering Coast Miwok of California and the Patagonians of Argentina, also encountered by Drake.

Any discourse on Drake's great voyage around the world must concede that the available documentary sources are greatly flawed and do not include the captain's journal or his chart, given to Queen Elizabeth and presumably lost to posterity. The approach in this chapter must perforce be a composite derived from various sources, and it must reflect a certain amount of judgment in the selection of materials so as to reconcile discrepancies and eliminate the numerous biases and falsifications that plague the investigator.[1]

The chief sources used here are "The Famous Voyage"[2] and *The World Encompassed*,[3] both apparently based mostly on a manuscript prepared by Francis Fletcher, Drake's sea chaplain, but never published as intended. To these sources can be added two depositions made by John Drake, the captain's young cousin, before the Tribunal of the Spanish Inquisition while he was a prisoner of the Spaniards.[4] The Moluccan portion of the circumnavigation is rounded out by some valuable Spanish sources and the "Anonymous Narrative."[5]

When Drake left the barren Farallon Islands off the coast of California on 25 July 1579, he intended to follow roughly the route taken by Saavedra in 1527, Villalobos in 1542, Lopéz de Legaspi in 1564, and subsequent Manila-bound galleons. This route began at Acapulco, in latitude 15°51′N, and dropped to somewhere between the tenth and fourteenth parallels, where the northeast trade wind was picked up. The Spanish course followed this safe and serene zone westward in a straight line until the southernmost Marianas were near, whereupon it rose slowly to 13° so that the galleons could reach Guam or Saipan.

By a stroke of good luck Drake had with him some charts and sailing directions he had taken four months before from Alonso Sánchez Colchero, one of two pilots of a small bark captured while bound for Panama with a cargo of sarsaparilla, lard, honey, and maize. More important, Colchero had been on the way to meet the new governor of the Philippines and to pilot him to those islands. Drake tried to bribe Colchero into escorting him across the Pacific. That failed. He tried to intimidate him, but the courageous Spaniard stood fast. Drake could not break his spirit even when he hung him by the neck until he was unconscious—this for Colchero's refusal to pilot him into a small port that he intended to destroy. This was not the English captain's shining hour; nevertheless, he now had a readymade route to follow before he sailed north to California to await the right season to cross the Pacific.

The track of the *Golden Hind* across the sea is imperfectly known, but I am deeply indebted to Raymond Aker of the Drake Navigators Guild for a well-reasoned reconstruction detailed in a letter and chart sent to me in 1975. According to Aker, Drake had intended to deviate from the usual route taken by the galleons by sailing southwest to 1°30′N and then west along that parallel to Halmahera and the Moluccas. (The Spanish route was farther north, because it terminated in the Philippines.) But upon encountering the equatorial counter-current mentioned in John Drake's second deposition, and wishing to avoid crossing the southern limit of the northeast trade winds (which would have caused him to enter the doldrum belt), Drake gave up the plan to drop so close to the equator. Instead, he directed his course northwest toward "China," meaning the general direction of the Philippines. In so doing he regained the established Spanish route from Acapulco to Manila. He passed north, not south, of the Marshalls and eastern Carolines and then fell in with the "Island of Thieves" at about 8°N (fig. 5:1).[6]

This was the first land seen by Drake since he had left New Albion; it took him sixty-eight days to reach it, for he arrived on 30 September 1579. Documentary sources say that about a hundred canoes, carrying what can be estimated as about eight hundred men, came out to meet the *Golden Hind*. The canoes are described as double-outriggered with bamboo floats. They had twin endpieces that rose high up from the hull and curved inward in a semicircle. The canoes were of one piece, red, and highly polished. They were decorated with festoons of white cowrie shells which dangled from cords and gave an animated appearance, glistening in the light and swaying with the undulations of the sea. The islanders were completely nude; they had jet black teeth, long fingernails,

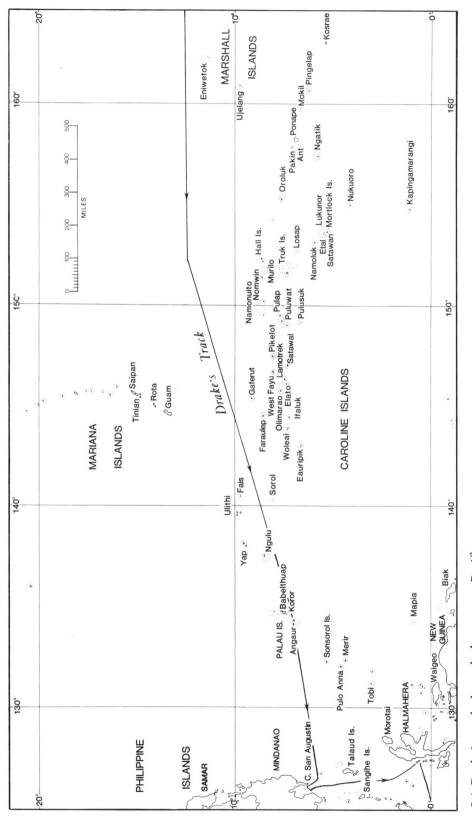

5.1 Drake's track through the western Pacific.

and greatly elongated earlobes, and they chewed betel nut (fig. 5:2).

At first the natives were eager to trade coconuts, potatoes,[7] certain fruits, and fish for beads and other trifles, though they coveted iron most of all. But their initial agreeability was ephemeral. The exchanges became so one-sided on the part of the English that they stopped trading. This profoundly enraged the islanders, who got back into their canoes and assailed the *Golden Hind* with stones, a common weapon in the Caroline Islands. Drake reacted to this hostility by firing a piece of artillery to frighten them. The islanders retreated to shore, but soon new groups began paddling to the vessel. Pretending to be docile and willing to trade fairly, they again boarded the ship but at once began to steal whatever they could lay hands on. Drake ordered his men to fire at them, and twenty were killed. Thereupon the English decided to leave, calling the place the Island of Thieves[8] so that later European sailors would be warned against these ingrates. If nothing else, Drake had proved that Stone Age weapons were no match for English guns.

This portrayal of events has glaring discrepancies which must be reconciled. In the Carolines one absolutely never finds certain of the canoe traits mentioned in the English records: double-outriggered boats, bamboo floats, and endpieces that rise high and curve inward. These traits are distinctly Indonesian, never Carolinian; the canoes of the Carolines are single-outriggered with wooden floats, and their endpieces curve outward if they curve at all. The canoes described in the documents are twin-ended; this is a trait of the Carolines but not of Indonesia, where double-outriggers obviate the need for twin ends because boats are always tacked, never shunted. Micronesian canoes, on the other hand, with their boomed, lateen-type sails, are shunted from one tack to the other by changing ends and reversing direction, requiring that the ends be identical (fig. 5:3).

There has been no speculation on these discrepancies in the accounts, to the best of my knowledge, by students of Drake's voyage. But the contradictions can be attributed to errors in the records resulting from faulty memory, which caused Fletcher and others to blend Indonesian canoe traits, seen over a period of almost five months, with Carolinian features, seen earlier for only three days at the Island of Thieves.

Having decided that Drake's island or islands were in the Carolines, we must select one of the six places there variously championed by navigators, historians, geographers, and anthropologists. Four are atolls—Ngulu, Ulithi, Sorol, and Woleai—and all have to be eliminated. Some are too far north of the equator, and none had a population of twenty-two hundred, which I estimate would have been necessary to send out a hundred canoes containing approximately eight hundred men. Moreover, atolls cannot grow the betel nut palm except as a rarity because of the coralline nature of their soil. There are other clues, too, which are not satisfied by the atolls.

This leaves the two high islands of Yap and Palau. Yap does not satisfy the geographic, demographic, and ethnographic criteria as well as Palau does, so Palau is where my research has led me. If my conclusions are correct, then Drake

Kadou,

habitant des îles Carolines.

5.2 Kadu, a Woleaian (from the Carolines), from Louis Choris, *Voyage pittoresque autour du monde,* Paris, 1822, pl. 22. Courtesy of Special Collections, University of California, Los Angeles, Library.

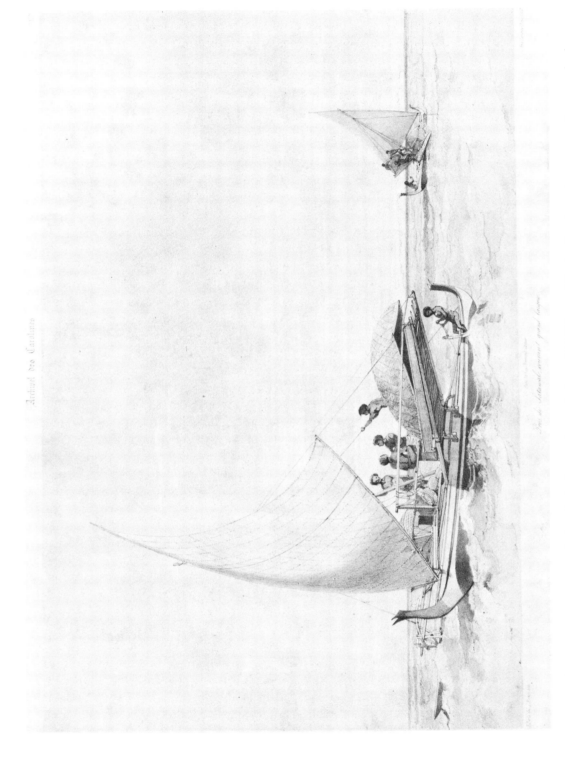

5.3 Carolinian canoes, twin-ended and single-outriggered, from [F.] Edmond Paris, *Essai sur la construction navale des peuples extra-Europeéns*, 2 vols., Paris [1843], II, pl. 107. Courtesy of Special Collections, University of California, Los Angeles, Library.

in 1579, rather than Francisco Padilla in 1710, was the first to discover the Palau Islands. Of course, the problem of identification would be greatly lessened if in Elizabethan times it had been possible to determine longitude with any degree of accuracy; but that could not be done until 1761, when John Harrison's chronometer was put to use successfully on an English vessel bound for Jamaica.

A few years ago the suggestion was made that Drake's first landfall after leaving California was really the northeast coast of the Philippine island of Mindanao.[9] Although this suggestion is fascinating and has much to commend it, it must be rejected for a variety of reasons (fig. 5:4). One is that the coast there at about 8°N is inhospitable and sparsely settled, as I observed when I made a chartered flight over the area in 1966 to test this conjecture. Another is that Philippine canoes, except for tiny dugouts, do not have the twin ends or the decorative shells mentioned by Fletcher. There is also much doubt that in the Philippines one would have found nudity, long fingernails, and the use of slings.

An even more startling suggestion regarding the Island of Thieves has been made by Robert Silverberg, who maintains that Drake never saw such a place at all and that the whole episode is a figment of the imagination inserted into the record for some ulterior motive.[10] This suggestion has more merit than might meet the eye. For one thing, Antonio Pigafetta had already described Magellan's "islands of thieves," the Islas de los Ladrones, in terms which seem to be echoed by Drake historians. This would not be the first time English accounts had pilfered from Pigafetta: witness Fletcher's description of the monstrous-looking Patagonians. Moreover, the English may have wanted to establish territorial or navigational claims which might enable them to compete with the Spaniards. This is what seems to have happened with one of their documentary sources, which alleges that the *Golden Hind* reached a latitude of 48°N off the coast of what is now the state of Washington, farther north than any Spaniards, and that the crew encountered bitter cold and saw snow on the low hills in June![11] Another argument against the reality of Drake's Island of Thieves lies in the contradictory ethnographic features mentioned in both "The Famous Voyage" and *The World Encompassed,* where Micronesian and Indonesian traits are hopelessly jumbled. Finally, of the early Drake maps, neither that of Nicola van Sype (ca. 1583) nor that of Jodocus Hondius (ca. 1595) depicts an "island of thieves." Although three others do show the track of Drake's voyage touching on or near the "Ins. Latronum" or some similar label, they appear to refer to Magellan's islands, not Drake's.[12]

Standing in the way of accepting my make-believe skepticism are the two depositions made by young John Drake before the Spanish tribunal, the first in 1584 at Santa Fe in what is now Argentina and the other in 1587 at Lima, Peru. In these depositions, made from memory, he gives some of the details supplied by Fletcher but adds a few of his own, particularly that Francis Drake's guns killed twenty of the thievish "Indians," who were naked and had arrived in a hundred canoes.[13]

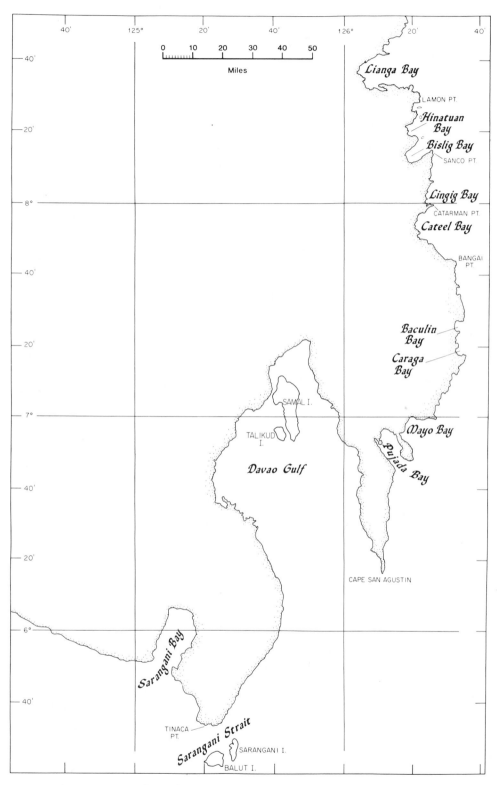

5.4 Mindanao: east and south coasts.

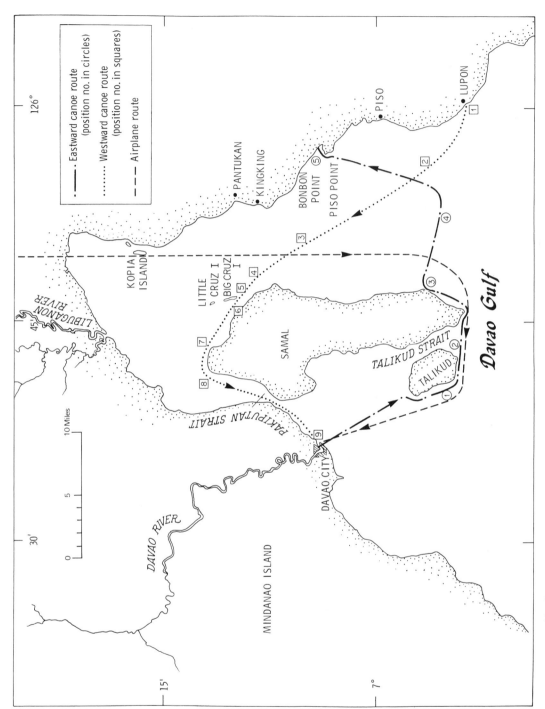

5.5 Davao Gulf: the author's canoe and plane routes.

Young John had set out with Edward Fenton on a voyage intended to raid Spanish ships and then proceed to Ternate to facilitate the clove trade in accordance with an agreement Drake had made with Babullah (Babu), the sultan of that spice island. The young man had detached his vessel, the *Francis*, from Fenton's fleet of four vessels, and he was captured in the Rio de la Plata. The time of his capture is important. He had returned to England from the circumnavigation on 26 September 1580 while he was still quite young—having set out with his "cousin," Captain Drake, when he was only about fifteen years of age. He remained in England only about nineteen months before leaving on 1 May 1582 for South America. During this brief time in England young John was probably not privy to any scheme to rewrite history, and in any event he would have had nothing to gain by lying to his captors about the Island of Thieves. If anything, he was taking the risk of infuriating his inquisitors by describing this episode in Drake's great voyage.[14]

Three days after his arrival in Palau, or the Island of Thieves, Drake sailed west until he came upon what was reported as "foure ilands." At the given latitude of 7°5′N, there are no four islands in this part of the Pacific. In reality, I maintain, he had entered Davao Gulf of Mindanao, the most southerly of the major islands of the Philippines. Although he saw two islands named Samal and Talikud within the upper reaches of the large gulf, he mistook the eastern and western peninsulas bordering this body of water for two more islands. We need not speculate on how such a mistake could be made, for we know that as late as 1767 Philip Carteret thought the two peninsulas were islands.[15] His confusion was instigated by a two-centuries-old belief that a nonexistent St. John's Island was located off the northeast coast of Mindanao. One might wonder how two peninsulas could be mistaken for two islands, but the answer is simple: at the southern latitudes of Samal and Talikud, Drake could not see the land uniting the two peninsulas at the head of the gulf. To test this suggestion, I reconnoitered the gulf in 1966 and discovered that when crossing it eastward from one peninsula to the other in a motor-driven double-outrigger, one cannot see the connecting terrain in the background (fig. 5:5). Crossing the gulf again the next day in the opposite direction, this time at an even more northerly latitude, I observed that one still cannot see the connecting coast until one has almost reached the northern part of Samal.[16]

Sea level is not the same as mast level. I therefore also scouted the gulf in a small plane at a generous height of about a hundred feet, following a course due south from the connecting land. Looking backward constantly from the plane, I found that the coast uniting the two peninsulas disappeared from sight at a latitude even farther north than the one reached by Drake in the gulf. The day was cloudless, and it was close to the time of year when Drake sighted the "foure ilands."[17] Interestingly, *The World Encompassed* said that the fourth of these islands was Mindanao, as indeed it was—but so were the other three islands of this second largest of all the Philippine Islands.

No reports of human contact in the gulf are contained in the records, but this need not disturb us. Alonso de Arellano, who had detached his vessel, the *San*

Lucas, from López de Legaspi's fleet on the way to the Philippines, arrived in Davao Gulf in 1565 and reported seeing no signs of life until the next day, when two or three natives came down from the mountains on the eastern peninsula and then retired, to be followed later by thirty or forty men and their chief. Arellano saw no canoes until some appeared days later from the northern reaches of the gulf.[18] We know from early Spanish accounts that Mindanao was sparsely settled in those days, especially on the shores. This is undoubtedly why the English make no mention of contact with indigenes.

Leaving Davao Gulf, Drake headed south for the Moluccas, and on 22 October his vessel passed between the islands of Sarangani and Balut off the southernmost tip of Mindanao. There he saw his first natives since leaving the Palaus. They were in two canoes, and they wanted to talk to the Englishmen, who could not respond because of a strong wind which forced the *Golden Hind* away from the two little boats.

Drake was now entering Indonesian waters. He passed several small islands bordering the eastern Celebes Sea, but for the most part their identity has never been fully established. Meeting a Portuguese trading vessel whose captain attempted to befriend Drake in the belief that his vessel was Spanish and off course, the English captain angrily waved him off. The galleon went on its way, with Drake tailing it in the hope that it would lead him to the Moluccas—for, after all, he was lost. Upon overtaking the Portuguese ship he ordered it to surrender, but its captain would not be intimidated and prepared instead to fight the English "Lutherans," as Drake had loudly proclaimed they were. The *Golden Hind* fired a culverin at the galleon and then sped off to the southeast before the Portuguese could reply.[19] Drake's ship held a huge booty of silver, gold, and other goods captured from the *Nuestra Señora de la Concepción* off Punta de la Galera just north of Cabo San Francisco, so discretion rather than bravado was called for.

Near the small island of Siau, Drake was fortunate in picking up two men, fishing in canoes, who consented to guide the *Golden Hind* to the Spice Islands. He negotiated the Molucca Passage and on 4 or 5 November 1579 came in sight of the famed Moluccas, a name originally given only to four or five islands off the western coast of Halmahera, where cloves and other spices were grown and traded at fantastically high prices.

Having learned that the people of the powerful little island of Ternate were at odds with the Portuguese, whom they had recently expelled, Drake decided to anchor there rather than at neighboring Tidore, Ternate's great rival, where the Portuguese were entrenched. His choice was the right one (fig. 5:6).

The English accounts of Drake's reception and brief stay at Ternate characterize it as friendly and euphoric. As soon as messengers had been exchanged from both sides, Babullah, the sultan, came to greet the *Golden Hind* with his greatest personages, all bedecked in their finest garments. Music and other sounds filled the tropical air. The rowers in four Moluccan canoes (fig. 5:7), who propelled their boats with great skill and swiftness, kept time to a simulta-

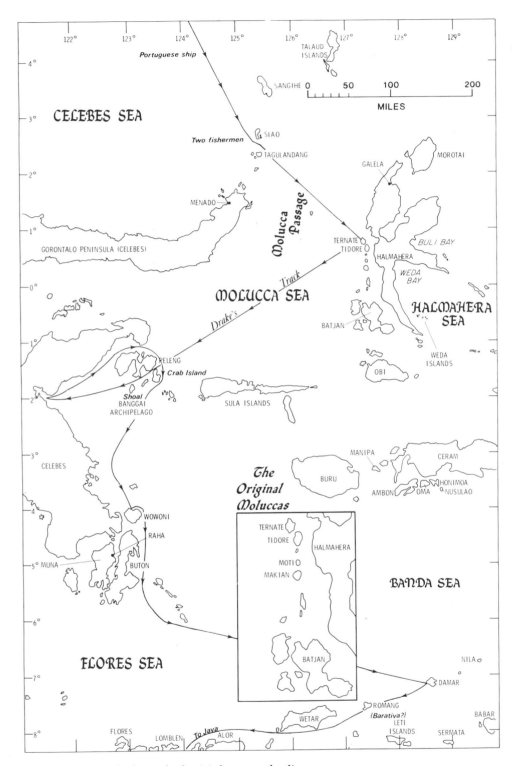

5.6 Drake's track through the Molucca and adjacent seas.

5.7 Royal canoes from Ternate and Tidore with crescent and helicoid profiles, from F. Valentijn, *Oud en nieuw Oost-Indiën,* 5 vols., Dordrecht and Amsterdam, 1724–26, I, 363. Courtesy of the Huntington Library, San Marino, California.

neous beat produced by two men in each canoe, one striking a small drum and the other a piece of brass. The rowers ended each stroke with a song. In response to the sultan's formal salute to the visitors from his canoe, the English thundered their ordnance to the accompaniment of trumpets and drums, followed by instruments of sweet music. This "musical paradise" so delighted the sultan that he requested that the English musicians be put in the *Golden Hind's* boat, and he enjoyed their music for an hour as he towed the ship into the harbor.

When the *Golden Hind* had been hauled to a safe anchorage, Babullah promised to visit the ship the following day, but he did not do so. This made the English uneasy. When later in the day Drake sent his officers ashore to make an official visit he did not go with them, as the sultan had requested through his own brother. Babullah had sent large quantities of sago, rice, hens, a kind of liquid sugar, bananas, and coconuts to Drake's vessel, however.

One can easily understand Drake's trepidation. His small ship was heavily laden with plunder. The Moluccas were in a delicate political condition, and although Babullah wanted to give the English exclusive trade with Ternate, he wanted them in turn to attack the Portuguese on the nearby island of Tidore. The sultan was a devout Moslem of strong personality, and his considerable talents had expanded his country's sovereignty far beyond its traditional control over northern Halmahera and the eastern Celebes. The English were greatly impressed by his popularity with his people, who were at that time zealously observing the worship and proscriptions of the Islamic month of Ramadan.

As a result of all this there was more tension and disagreement than English sources have hinted, and Spanish accounts give a truer picture of the situation. Drake arrogantly and deliberately tried to trade for cloves without paying Babullah's export duty of ten percent, and for this the sultan had ordered him to be put to death. Drake was forced to appease Babullah by sending him presents, not only to ensure his goodwill but to gain his consent to be received ashore for conferences. After this irenic gesture, the two leaders met and came to a verbal agreement regarding friendship between their respective nations and the establishment of factories at Ternate, in return for which Drake promised arms and protection for the sultan's provinces. This provided the basis for Fenton's later unsuccessful expedition to reach the Moluccas.

After remaining a mere five days at Ternate and taking on a cargo of perhaps six tons of cloves, Drake departed on 9 November 1579, undoubtedly because of some uneasiness regarding his new allies, with whom he had not really established a firm political relationship. He was anxious to find some obscure island where he could careen his vessel, and he soon reached an uninhabited isle to the south.

This small wooded place came to be called Crab Island because of the large, delicious robber crabs the crew found there. The true identity of the spot has never been established, but it seems likely that it was in the Banggai Archipelago off the northeast coast of Celebes. Drake erected a stockade to protect the *Golden Hind* as she was being cleaned of barnacles and caulked and tarred. Around the stockade he placed his cannon, and within it he pitched tents and deposited the ship's cargo. On 12 December Drake sailed from Crab Island after twenty-six days of repairs and recuperation. Because of the long voyage home that lay ahead he left behind some of his cannon and anything else considered superfluous. This included three blacks, one of them a slave girl named Maria. Maria, who had been taken from Don Francisco de Zárate when Drake had captured a Spanish vessel off the coast of Nicaragua in April, was now in an advanced stage of pregnancy.[20]

When the *Golden Hind* left Crab Island she was a happy ship. Everyone aboard was looking forward to the voyage back to England. But for four weeks they had to pick their way carefully to avoid the numerous reefs and shoals encountered as Drake attempted to round the southern end of the strangely convoluted island of Celebes, with its tentacle-like peninsulas.

Then, in early January, the ship ran aground on a steep-sided reef.[21] Nothing Drake could do would float her off, and there was danger that she would be stranded for good. Maintaining an outward semblance of calm and confidence, the captain had the crew kneel while he led them in prayer, beseeching Almighty God to extend His mercy to them in the name of His son, Jesus Christ. The night was filled with anguish. When daylight finally appeared, new attempts were made to find an anchor hold, without success. Drake then issued orders to lighten the ship of three tons of its cloves, eight pieces of ordnance, and certain meal (cassava?) and beans, but none of the silver and gold, possibly because the bullion was stored in ballast. All this was to no avail.

There was nothing to do but express despair and recrimination while awaiting what seemed an inevitable doom. Mr. Fletcher preached a sermon, and all received Communion together. Scholars have speculated that the minister surprised everyone by dwelling not on the ways of God and the hope for an everlasting life, but on the need for repentance of their sins, especially the execution of Thomas Doughty at Port St. Julian and the depredations on the western coast of South America.

Suddenly, in mid-afternoon of 10 January 1580, the wind which had pinioned the *Golden Hind* against the reef changed to port, and a gale drove the vessel into the deep sea again. The crew became "glad men," and they "gave God such praise and thanks as so great a benefite required."

I cannot tell from the records whether Drake had a comedic mind, but a remarkable manifestation of black humor followed at the expense of Parson Fletcher. Some have viewed it as a playful reaction to the terrible tension that Drake had felt while his ship was in the deadly grasp of the shoal. But this was no mere jest; it was a malicious prank to retaliate for Fletcher's probable defiance and accusations in his sermon when all seemed to be at an end.

Drake fixed a chain to a hatch in the forecastle of the ship and fastened the chaplain's leg to it with a lock. The captain, seated cross-legged on a chest and holding a pair of slippers, surrounded himself with the ship's company and announced: "Francis Fletcher, I do here excommunicate thee out of the Church of God, and from all the graces thereof, and I denounce thee to the devil and all his angels." Then he charged Fletcher on pain of death never to come before the mast, swearing that if he did he would be hanged. He had a posy, or legend, written and bound about Fletcher's arm with the admonition that it must not be taken off on pain of hanging. The legend read, "Francis Fletcher the falsest knave that liveth."[22]

All Drake's subsequent wanderings throughout the Moluccan and Banda Seas, trying to find a way to break out of his island-walled prison, need not be traced here.[23] Most of the numerous islands he encountered have not been identified. However, one of them, Barativa, stands out because of the delightfully sensual experiences it afforded the ship's company.

The *Golden Hind* was led there by two friendly canoes. The natives of

Barativa were attractive, both in appearance and because of their civil behavior. The men were nude except for their heads and private parts. The record keepers apparently could not bring themselves to say that the women were bare-breasted and merely stated that they were "covered from the middle to the foot"; but it was noted that on their bare arms they wore numerous bracelets made mostly of horn and brass. The island was rich in gold, silver, copper, tin, and sulphur. The "fruits" (*sic*) were diverse and plentiful, including nutmegs, ginger, long peppers, lemons, cucumbers, coconuts, bananas, and sago. One can imagine the thrill of savoring spices that in England could be afforded only by the wealthy. Since they had left home, the records state, the visitors had nowhere found greater comfort and better refreshment, except at Ternate. After two paradisal days spent here, the *Golden Hind* continued her probing way toward Java.

The last outstanding event experienced by the men sailing under the cross of St. George took place not in the Pacific or the passages leading into it but in the Indian Ocean. Having penetrated the Lesser Sundas at Ombai Strait north of Timor, Drake on 11 March put in at a good harbor generally identified as Tjilatjap (Cilacap) on the southern coast of west-central Java. Drake socialized with several rajahs there. One can imagine the refinements of food, dress, cloth, weapons, dwellings, and music which prevailed. After all, this island had once been the center of powerful Hinduistic and Buddhistic empires.

Although Drake was anxious to finish servicing his ship and to set out straight for the Cape of Good Hope, his departure was precipitated when a Portuguese spy in disguise was apprehended on board the *Golden Hind*. From this or another source Drake learned of the imminent arrival of three European ships. On 26 March Drake hurriedly hoisted sail, leaving the last port he would enter before arriving at plague-ridden Plymouth on 26 September 1580, eleven weeks short of three years since he had set out on his historic voyage.

A favorite pastime is to list Drake's "firsts" during the circumnavigation. This is not altogether easy for the South Seas, as spoilsports are apt to deprive him of some of his apparent records on technical grounds. Thus, Drake was not the first Englishman to sail on Pacific waters. He was preceded by John Oxenham, the privateer who coasted the Isthmus of Panama in a pinnace before being captured, in 1575. But a trader named John Chilton had preceded even Oxenham, having sailed from Panama to Peru in 1572 as a passenger on a Spanish vessel. (He later claimed he had lost goods to the value of a thousand ducats when Drake looted Guatulco in 1579.) Was Drake the first Englishman to cross the Pacific? Well, no. Magellan's master gunner was Andrew of Bristol, who died in 1521 just after departing from Guam. But Andrew was a naturalized Spanish citizen, married to a Spanish woman, so all this may be mere quibbling.

On the more positive side, I believe Drake was the real discoverer of the Palau Islands. He was the first Englishman in Mindanao. He was the first Englishman in Indonesia, where he introduced the first English music and heard in turn the thrilling sounds of the gamelan. His truly great accomplishment was to have sailed from California to the Indian Ocean with an incredible mastery of men, navigation, and a tiny but charmed ship.

NOTES

1. Limited space does not allow me to explain the thinking behind many of my decisions, which were arrived at after much research, mostly anthropological but sometimes geographical, demographic, and botanical.

2. "The famous voyage of Sir Francis Drake into the South Sea and there hence about the whole Globe of the Earth, begun in the yeere of our Lord, 1577," in Richard Hakluyt's *The principall navigations, voiages and discoveries of the English nation* (London, 1589).

3. *The World Encompassed, by Sir Francis Drake, being his next voyage to that to Nobre de Dios formerly imprinted: Carefully collected out of the notes of Master Francis Fletcher in this employment, and diuers others his followers in the same* (London, 1628).

4. Printed in Lady Eliott-Drake, *The Family and Heirs of Sir Francis Drake*, 2 vols. (London, 1911), apps. I, II.

5. One Spanish source is a report to his king by Francisco de Dueñas, who had been sent to the Moluccas from the Philippines shortly after Drake had departed and was able to gather some stories about the English captain (MS in the Archivo General de Indias in Seville, *legajo* 1–2–1/13, no. 14). Another is an account by Leonardo de Argensola, *Conqvista de las Islas Malvcas* (Madrid, 1609)—apparently taken from Antonio de Herrera's work *Historia general* (Madrid, 1601), as well as from John Drake's narratives (n. 4 above) and an unknown report by Dueñas. The English "Anonymous Narrative" appears as app. III in the Vaux (1854) edition of *The World Encompassed,* where it is given the title "Short Abstract of the Present Voyage, in Hand-Writing of the Time." The original is British Library Harleian MSS no. 280, fol. 23.

6. Aker expands on all these points, basing his reasoning not only on the records but also on his experience as a navigator in these waters. His reconstruction makes sense if one stresses, as he does, the word "before" in John Drake's statement that "they altered their course towards China before reaching one and a half degrees latitude." In a recent conversation Aker indicated that he stands by this reconstruction and intends to publish it.

7. The identity of this American cultigen remains problematical. Even if we accept the presence of the sweet potato in pre-Hispanic times, the extent of its distribution is unknown. The islanders may have been proffering some sort of aroid or yam.

8. This name is, of course, similar to that given by Magellan to the Marianas, which he called Islas de los Ladrones. Thus some say mistakenly that Drake's islands were the Marianas, but this claim has no support. William A. Lessa, "Drake in the Marianas?" *Micronesica* 10 (1974) 7–11, and idem, *Drake's Island of Thieves* (Honolulu, 1975), pp. 116–131.

9. Andrew Sharp, *The Discovery of the Pacific Islands* (Oxford, 1960), pp. 48–50.

10. Robert Silverberg, *The Longest Voyage: Circumnavigators in the Age of Discovery* (Indianapolis, 1972), p. 321.

11. Most of the books and maps published after Drake's return to England give the 48° latitude, as does John Drake in his first but not his second deposition. Mention of the cold and snow is added in some sources, especially *The World Encompassed*, p. 62. The probable source for the 48° degree latitude is the "Anonymous Narrative" (see n. 5 above). It is important to note that Hakluyt's "Famous Voyage" gives a latitude of only 42° but similarly stresses the cold and snow.

12. These are the Drake-Mellon map (ca. 1587), the Silver map (1589), and the Molyneux terrestrial globe (ca. 1595).

13. Eliott-Drake, *Family and Heirs*, II, 357, 393.

14. There is a dilemma here. If we accept John Drake's veracity with regard to the Island of Thieves, as we have done, we might by the same token accept his latitude of 48° for the northernmost point attained by the *Golden Hind*. If young John was not in on a plot to falsify some of the record, and could not possibly have been influenced by the publications mentioned in n. 11 above or have seen the manuscript of the "Anonymous Narrative," some credence should be given to his parallel of 48°. But he was inconsistent about this, changing the latitude to 44° in his second deposition. In contrast, he was steadfast about the Island of Thieves.

15. Helen Wallis, ed., *Philip Carteret's Voyage round the World, 1764–1766*, Hakluyt Society, 2nd series, 24, 2 vols. (Cambridge, 1965), II, 348–350, 361.

16. See Lessa, *Drake's Island of Thieves*, pp. 182–187, for details and maps.

17. Ibid., pp. 187–188.

18. *Colección de documentos ineditos, relativos al descubrimiento, conquista y organizacion de las antiguas posesiones españolas de ultramar*, 2nd ser., 25 vols. (Madrid, 1864–1884), III, 27–36, 45–49.

19. The source for this episode is Dueñas (see n. 5 above). A translation of this part of his report appears in Henry R. Wagner, *Sir Francis Drake's Voyage round the World* (San Francisco, 1926), p. 173. Dueñas is a good source for much else concerning Drake's Moluccan visit, but he will not be specifically cited in much else that follows. Wagner has published the other relevant parts of Dueñas' report on pp. 176–177, 180, 181–182, 183. The Moluccan adventure is of course described by English sources, too.

20. The Spanish vessel was not the *Nuestra Señora*, as erroneously reported in Lessa, *Drake's Island of Thieves* (p. 212), but a ship captured shortly thereafter. Neither "The Famous Voyage" nor *The World Encompassed* mentions Maria, but the "Anonymous Narrative" and John Drake's two depositions do. Gaspar de Vargas, whose port was sacked by Drake, mentions Maria in a letter to the Viceroy of Mexico written in 1579. William Camden, the leading historian of Elizabethan times, created a furor by mentioning her in his *Annales* (London, 1625), p. 426.

21. The identity of the reef is uncertain, but in a personal communication Raymond Aker gives sound reasons for believing it to be Vesuvius Reef or (less likely) the one adjacent to it.

22. The excommunication episode is described only in the "Anonymous Narrative" and is reprinted by Wagner, *Sir Francis Drake's Voyage*, p. 282, and earlier by Vaux (see n. 5 above). Some say the document may have been dictated by an uneducated seaman named William Legge; others attribute it to John Doughty, brother of the beheaded Thomas. In any event, it seems to be an eyewitness account.

23. Drake took this difficult route to the Indian Ocean for a simple reason: the conventional route through the Strait of Malacca was controlled by the Portuguese, who had a powerful fortress there. Drake's little vessel would have stood no chance of avoiding the guns of the fortress.

Drake and Plymouth

CRISPIN GILL

In considering the theme 'Drake and Plymouth', I want to develop two points: first, explaining why Plymouth (fig. 6:1) was the English port from which not only this voyage but other great Elizabethan voyages were mounted, and second, showing what part Drake played in the life and improvement of Plymouth after the Famous Voyage had established him as a national hero.

Sir Francis Drake was not a native of Plymouth. What we know about his early years comes not from Plymouth records but from family traditions and the interrogations of his nephew and other captured English seamen in the Spanish Inquisition.[1]

There were Drakes in and around Tavistock, fourteen miles north of Plymouth, certainly from 1350 onward. They were small yeomen, farmers, related to many of the best landowning families of the area, but not themselves important. Drake's father was Edmund Drake, who had been a seaman in his youth and had been converted to Protestantism. Francis was born at his grandfather's small farm, Crowndale, just west of Tavistock, between 1540 and 1545—the family accepts 1543 as the probable date. This was a few years after Henry VIII had suppressed the monasteries as part of his break with Rome. The great Abbey of Tavistock had been acquired by the Russell family, and it is said that young Drake was sponsored at his christening by Francis Russell, later the first Earl of Bedford. Hence, the family believes, his Christian name, and they claim that though Francis Russell could only have been twelve when young Drake was born, such a youthful patron was not unknown.

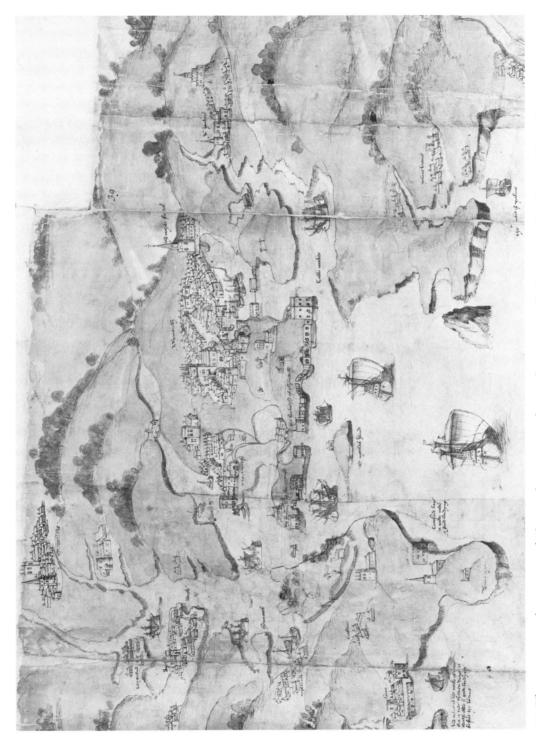

6.1 The estuary and environs of Plymouth, ca. 1536, from what is generally known as the Henry VIII defense map, B. L. Cotton MS, Augustin I. i, 38. Courtesy of the British Library.

The break with Rome and the consequent abandonment of the old Church practices did not please all the population, and there were various uprisings in the more remote parts of England. The Cornish rebelled in 1549 and marched on London. Old Sir Richard Grenville (grandfather of Richard Grenville of Tennyson's *Revenge,* the battle of the one and the fifty-three) shut himself up in Trematon Castle, southwest of Tavistock, but was captured by the rebels and flung into Launceston jail. The Drake family, by tradition, took refuge on St. Nicholas's Island in Plymouth Sound (fig. 6:2). The mayor and aldermen of Plymouth, who commanded the town's defenses, shut themselves up in the medieval castle guarding their harbor. Neither island nor castle was taken by the rebels, who did occupy Plymouth and burn the guildhall. This demonstration of Catholic militancy must have been an alarming experience for a boy about five years old.

Edmund Drake decided that such proximity to the unruly and reactionary Cornish—it was their third rebellion in half a century—was unhealthy, especially given his Protestant views. He obtained a job as Reader in Prayers, a kind of chaplain, to the English Navy and found a place to live on a hulk in the Medway, at the mouth of the Thames, then the principal base of the royal ships.

So, at a tender age, Francis Drake was living in a ship. In due course, because of his father's poverty, young Francis was apprenticed, or "put to the master of a bark" coasting in the Thames estuary, sometimes crossing to the Low Countries and France.[2] It has been suggested that this happened when Edmund Drake lost his naval appointment in 1553, when Queen Mary, the Catholic "Bloody Mary," came to the throne. Francis Drake would have been only ten years old. This is not unlikely. In later years Drake took his own nephew to sea when the boy was ten (Nelson was only twelve when he first went to sea two centuries later).

So, in the sandbanks and swirling tides of the Thames estuary, young Drake learned his seamanship. These are difficult waters, with sandbanks extending ten miles out to sea, barely covered at high tide, and the swatchways and tortuous channels through the banks are learned only with experience. But Drake had lived on the Medway, where boats must have been his toys, from the age of five or six, and the Medway is as difficult a river to navigate as can be found.

Clearly, he was a natural seaman. The legend is that the man to whom he was apprenticed thought so highly of him that on his death he left his ship to young Francis. How long Drake kept the ship, if he owned it at all, is not known, but he is said to have sold it by the time he was twenty in 1563. His father was now comfortably settled as Vicar of Upchurch, beside the Medway (he received the appointment two years after Queen Elizabeth came to the throne), and young Drake was sailing out of Plymouth as third officer in a ship owned by the Hawkins family, who were cousins. Edmund's mother, Francis' grandmother, was a Hawkins. The Hawkinses were the leading family in the port of Plymouth, and Plymouth was a major port.

Plymouth was born out of Sutton, a fishing village at the mouth of the River

6.2 Plymouth harbor and the country inland to Tavistock, showing the conduit or leat built to supply Plymouth with water largely through the efforts of Sir Francis Drake (whose name is close to Buckland Abbey), ca. 1590, Cotton MS Augustus I. i, 41. Courtesy of the British Library.

Plym, in southwest Devon. In the twelfth century the major town in the area was Plympton, at the head of the estuary, the little town clustering around the Earl of Devon's castle and its rich abbey. It had a small trade: we know of a cargo of slate leaving Plympton for Southampton in 1178. But as tin mining developed on Dartmoor (first recorded in 1156[3]), where the river rose, the estuary silted up; ships spent more and more time at the mouth of the Plym, or Plym Mouth. We first hear of a cargo from Plymouth in 1211, bacon for Portsmouth and wine for Nottingham.[4]

The mention of wine is significant. Plymouth is close to rich fishing grounds, and from an early time catches would have exceeded local demand. Fish could be kept only by smoking or salting. Although salt is hard to make by evaporation on the Devon shores, it is easily produced on the shores of the Bay of Biscay, south of Brittany. There has always been a market for fish there, too, so Plymouth's first overseas trade, fish out and salt back, went around Ushant into the Bay of Biscay. From Brittany southward to Bordeaux, the heart of the richest and most extensive vineyards in Europe, is a short haul. Thus, from early days Plymouth had small vessels accustomed to the open waters of the west Channel and to the hazards of rounding Ushant.

When most English trade went to the Low Countries, the Thames was the natural port. As long as Normandy was English, the vessels of the Cinque Ports could cross the Channel to Dieppe, Honfleur, and Harfleur. But these up-Channel ships were less suitable when it came to the open waters of the Atlantic.

The world, too, was getting bigger, and the Crusades were calling men to the Levant. In the First Crusade the armies tried to march across Europe. The second, in 1147, was to go by sea, through the Mediterranean, and a fleet was assembled in Dartmouth, just thirty miles east of Plymouth. There were three comparable ports in the west Channel: Dartmouth and Plymouth in Devon and Fowey in Cornwall. Both Dartmouth and Fowey have narrow cliff-guarded entrances, difficult to enter under sail in bad weather and even worse to leave in headwinds. Plymouth is situated at the head of a wide bay, which eases these problems. It also has better land approaches—in our own times the railway never reached Dartmouth, and it only reached Fowey through a long tunnel. The strong priory at Plympton provided a guest house for great travelers and a safe lodging for any war chest being moved; and in those days war chests were filled with gold. Buckland Abbey, just north of Plymouth, was the center of a vast Cistercian agricultural estate, a natural victualing depot.

So when King John lost Normandy to the French in 1204 and the King of England's possessions were centered in Bordeaux, it was the western ports which could provide ships and seamen for the passage around Ushant, and Plymouth became the chosen base. Edward I mounted expeditions from Plymouth from 1294 to 1296. In 1346 the Black Prince took out from the port an army which won the Battle of Poitiers, and he brought home captive to Plymouth the King of France.[5]

Apart from the armies, there was the constant movement of princes and great nobles, of men and supplies, through Plymouth. Of course, trade went on. Plymouth ships appear in the earliest surviving port records for Bordeaux, from 1303.[6]

The Second Crusade cleared the Moors from northern Portugal. Oporto and Lisbon were open. By 1248 the Muslims had been driven from Seville in Spain. Plymouth seamen, like those of the other ports, were reaching further south, and when the English finally lost Bordeaux to the French in 1451 it was these Portuguese and Spanish ports with which they traded. (Before half a century had elapsed, the Portuguese had reached India by way of the Cape of Good Hope and the Spanish had discovered America.)

Plymouth had a further advantage. The prevailing southwest wind blows straight up the English Channel. Captain John Smith in a later century said it was harder to sail from the Thames to Plymouth than from Plymouth to New England. It is rare, whatever the wind, that a ship cannot clear the chops of the Channel after leaving Plymouth.

William Hawkins moved from Tavistock to Plymouth and by the 1520s was an important man in the port, dealing in cargoes from La Rochelle to Seville. The trade with Spain was a century old; Englishmen had their agents living in Seville and its outport, San Lucar, where they were so numerous as to have their own English church. There were Plymouth men living there too; William Hawkins almost certainly had visited them and heard the stories of the wealth that was coming from Africa, India, and the New World. In 1530 he made the first English trading voyage across the Atlantic, south to the Guinea coast for ivory and probably Guinea grains and African pepper, then southwest to Brazil for brazilwood (much needed in Europe as a dyestuff for the woolen industry), and then home. It was a natural and profitable voyage, with fair winds all the way. Hawkins made three voyages himself in successive years and sent a ship the fourth year. We have the trading figures for a 1540 Hawkins ship which showed a profit of 1,000 percent.[7] This became a regular voyage, and then Bristol, a larger port with greater capital resources, came into the trade; there had always been close Plymouth-Bristol links.

William Hawkins died in 1554, and his sons took over the business. William the younger managed affairs in Plymouth, and John was the seaman who led the voyages. In 1560 John made his first Atlantic round trip, picking up slaves on the African coast for the first time and sailing into the Spanish Main to sell them at the Spanish settlements lining the shores. The move into the Caribbean was sensible. There were fair winds and currents southward along the Spanish and African coasts, across to Brazil and then northeastward to the North Atlantic; but it was easier to take the northeast tradewinds directly to the Caribbean and then out again by the northerly channels to the westerly winds than it would have been to struggle northward along the African coast, as the traders might have done had they confined their trade to that area or to South America. In any case, Spain resented foreigners in her colonies.

Drake joined the business of his cousins the Hawkinses, who by now were a power both in Plymouth and in London, pioneers in this new age. Although it was their enterprise which made Plymouth so great, it was the natural geographical advantages of Plymouth that made their success possible.

Drake's first three voyages to the Spanish Main were not particularly successful. His first venture was in command of a small ship, the *Judith,* in a fleet commanded by John Hawkins. After a difficult cruise with many problems the fleet anchored in San Juan de Ulúa, the outport of Mexico City, to prepare for the voyage home. They were caught and attacked by a superior Spanish fleet, and only Hawkins in his flagship and Drake in the *Judith* escaped, leaving behind men, ships, and treasure. That was in 1569; the next year Drake began to make voyages on his own account, in 1570–71 a reconnaissance and in 1572–73 a voyage during which he captured a mule train bearing Spanish treasure. From a peak in Darien, Drake was the first Englishman to gaze upon the Pacific. He came home to Plymouth with enough money to buy a prominent townhouse at the top of Looe Street, just across the road from the guildhall. It was a newly built street, and the houses had gardens behind. Here Doughty was alleged to have plotted the treason which led to his execution in South America on the circumnavigation. Drake also acquired more property, a house at Thorn Park just outside town and other property in the High Street.

Drake, just thirty years old, already cut a figure in Plymouth. He had been given the freedom of the city of Plymouth in 1570, which gave him the right to trade in the town. On Sunday 9 August 1573, when word spread that he was back from the mule train voyage, the congregation of St. Andrew's Church is said to have rushed out of church in mid-sermon and swarmed down the hill to greet him.[8]

A decade later, when Drake came back from his circumnavigation in 1580, he hailed a fisherman off Rame Head, the western headland of Plymouth Sound, with the call, "Is the Queen alive?" He was told she was, but even so he would not risk himself ashore until messengers had been to London and back to make sure he was still welcome. He anchored under St. Nicholas's Island, where as a small boy he and his family had taken refuge from the Cornish rebellion. His wife, Mary Newman, whom he had married in 1569, sailed out in a small boat with the Mayor of Plymouth to see him.

The town annalist recorded in the Black Book, so called from the black leather which covered the oak boards of the binding:

> 1580. John Blitheman (Mayor). At Mighelmasse this yeare came Mr. Fraunces Drake home to Plymouthe from the Southe Seay and mollocus and wasse round the world and was lacke towe yeares and thre quarters and brought hom great stoore of golde and sylver in blockes. And was afterwards in the same yeare for his good servuice in thatt behalf done kneighted.[9]

The following November Drake was elected Mayor of the Town. The Black Book goes on:

1581. Sr Fraunces Drake, knyghte. (mayor)
The newe Compasse made vpon the Hawe.

1582. Thomas Edmonds, gent (Mayor)
The ale stakes put down & signs set up.
The order for wearing scarlet gowns put into execution.[10]

The wearing of scarlet gowns by the councillors, as well as the aldermen, is said to have been ordered in Drake's mayoralty; perhaps it took a year to have the gowns made. The compass on the Hoe is more of a puzzle. The Hoe is the high open ground between the town and the sea; on the site of the compass now stands the tower of Smeaton's Eddystone lighthouse (rebuilt there when it was removed from the rocks fourteen miles out to sea). An early drawing of the town shows what looks like a round table, and there is a later reference in the town accounts to replacing the "spylle" of the compass. There is no need for an ordinary fixed compass on a land mass; perhaps it was a pelorus, a fixed compass card with a pointer mounted on a spindle, which could be used to take the bearing of ships in Plymouth Sound.

Soon after his election as Mayor, Drake, now thirty-seven, bought his great country house, Buckland Abbey, which remained in the family until 1946. Mary Drake could not long enjoy either this great new house or her new position as Lady Drake and Mayoress of Plymouth. The town had spent £10 on a dinner for Sir Francis "when his lady first came," but she died in January 1582, in Drake's first year of office.

The mayoralty was a position of importance and responsibility. Though Drake had not served on the town council before, he was now chief magistrate, and because the town had few of these justices of the peace, he would be expected to sit in court. He continued in that office, and a few years later the records say that he ordered the arrest of various men for manslaughter. He received £10 for his expenses in office, though the Queen had allowed him to keep £10,000 out of the treasure he brought home from the world voyage, and he gave £1 to the bridewell, the town prison. His name crops up in the town accounts from this time onward: 8d for a messenger to carry a letter to him at Buckland, for example, and later more messengers to him at the abbey and in London, a journey costing 24s. A number of dinners are mentioned at which he was entertained, sometimes with other important guests.

In 1584 Drake, as Member of Parliament for the Cornish borough of Bossiney, was able to help Plymouth. The town had been seeking a new water supply for over twenty years and had surveyed one way to bring water by a leat (an artificial water channel) from the river Meavy on Dartmoor. Once or twice the plan had been taken out and reconsidered, but nothing had happened. Now there was a new bill—for the better preservation of Plymouth haven, the title reads. Bringing the leat into Plymouth would scour out the harbor and keep it clear for shipping; it would enable the fleet to be watered, and it would incidentally provide a better water supply for the town. Drake sat on the parliamentary committee which considered the bill; the committee revised it, inserting the power for half a dozen corn mills to be driven by its water power. But nothing happened for a while, and Drake was busy with other matters.

In February 1585 he married again, this time a lady of rank, Elizabeth Sydenham, daughter of a Somerset knight and landowner. It is said that she was a maid of honor to the Queen and that Drake met her at court, but there is no evidence of this. The Sydenham family had connections by marriage with a family near Tavistock who were Drake's friends, and this may have been the link.

In September 1585 he was off again, westward bound, for the renowned "Descent on the Indies" with a fleet of twenty ships and three thousand men. Though this was part of the war being waged against Spain in the Indies, and not in Europe, it was nevertheless run on a joint stock basis. The town appears to have invested £26 in the voyage; but in the 1586–87 accounts one reads the laconic entry "Item rec of Sr Fra Drake knight for the Townes advent^r xviii^{li} xv^s [£18.15^s]."[11] So it was not a profitable investment.

Drake in fact was still too busy at sea to have much time for the town. He leased his Looe Street house to a neighbor in 1586. In 1587 he raided Cadiz, which delayed the Armada; "singeing the King of Spain's beard" someone called it, but the town records said that Sir Francis "did greatly annoy the king of Spaines flete."[12] The town spent £4 on gunpowder to fire salutes on his return.

In 1588, the Armada came. Lord Howard of Effingham was Admiral of the English fleet; Drake, forty-five years old, was his Vice-Admiral; and John Hawkins was Rear-Admiral. The celebrated legend is that Drake was playing bowls when the message came, and that he merely turned to bowl again, saying "There's time to finish the game, and beat the Spaniards too."[13] There is a 1584 town record of "playing at booles"; and as early as 1625, thirty-seven years after the Armada, a Spanish jibe goes, "We caught you playing at bowls." It is known that the message came at 3:00 P.M. on a Friday afternoon. There had been messages to London on the previous two days saying that the English fleet at Plymouth was in good shape and ready. The light wind bringing the Spanish up-Channel was blowing straight into Plymouth Sound.

The English ships would have to be towed to sea by their boats, and that could only be done on an ebb tide. There was just an hour of ebb left, the weakest hour, to be followed by six hours of flood, when the ships could not move. To finish the game would not only have been in the Drake character, it would also have been far better than to throw everyone into a panic.

The ships were warped out; when Lord Howard could set sail he led his ships due south, across the bows of the Armada, then turned west to get behind the Spanish. Drake was in home waters, and he was a master of tides. He knew that after low tide at Plymouth the current in the Channel flowed eastward for six hours. But there is also a back draft that goes west close under Rame Head and into Whitsand Bay. So he took his ships on that course, a spectacular piece of seamanship. At dawn next morning the Armada found that Drake's squadrons, which they might have trapped in Plymouth, were behind them and that they had the weather gauge, meaning that they were in deep water and could maneuver (fig. 6:3). All day Sunday 21 July the Battle of Plymouth, the first encounter with the Armada, was fought, watched from the Hoe by Mayor William Hawkins and, no doubt, most of the town. A great many men of Plymouth were engaged in the battle. For centuries after, the bells of St. Andrew's Church, Plymouth, rang peals to celebrate the anniversary of this three hours of heavy pounding.

The Armada was driven up the English Channel and up the North Sea to limp home finally to Spain. But the Spanish king was to try again and again. Just a year later, in 1589, Drake led another raid on the Spanish coast to prevent a further attack on England. The men engaged in this expedition thought they had done well, but the Queen was not pleased. Drake was out of favor and thus free to go about his interrupted Plymouth business. The projected leat was built; it was started in December 1590 and finished by April 1591. Drake had been a member of the parliamentary committee which passed it, and he was also chairman of another committee which rejected a petition against the leat lodged by neighboring millers. Now Plymouth gave him the job of building it, allowing him £200 to get the seventeen miles dug and another £100 to compensate the landowners affected. Drake leased the six corn mills driven by the leat—which, instead of emptying into Sutton Harbor, the town's haven, which was supposed to be scoured, emptied into Mill Bay and provided the power for the old tidal mill there. Drake had taken over the lease of this mill from the Hawkins family not long before. In the past century there have been furious arguments and papers published, some to prove that Drake made a small fortune out of the leat, others acclaiming him as a benefactor. It can be said on the positive side that the leat kept Plymouth supplied with water until just before 1900. The switch of the old tidal mill to leat power meant that a large tidal lake behind the mill was no longer needed; it was filled in and by 1850 was covered with houses.

In 1590 Sir Francis Drake was also busying himself about the defenses of Plymouth. News of a new Spanish shipbuilding program that winter had led some people to take their goods out of the town, and "others no doubt, would have followed if they had not been stopped by the coming of Sir Francis Drake who, the more to assure them, brought his wife and family thither." Now he and the Mayor were petitioning the Queen for money to build a new fort on Plymouth Hoe. The old one commanded the harbor; with bigger ships, a new fort was needed to command the Cattewater anchorage.

Traditionally, the Mayor had always been captain of the fort and island. Drake's successor as mayor had petitioned the Crown for Drake to remain captain. There is no record of any confirmation, but Drake always acted as if he had this authority. The lieutenants of both Devon and Cornwall regularly sent him returns of the number of men available to defend Plymouth.

In May 1590 Drake wrote to the Queen about the fort; he also ordered that

6.3 Contemporary map showing the crescent formation of the Spanish Armada and positions of the English in relation to the coast of Plymouth and environs. The zig-zag line shows the course of Drake's advance, the straight line that of Lord Howard of Effingham. Armada Maps, no. 6, from Expeditions Hispanorum. Courtesy of the Trustees of the National Maritime Museum, Greenwich.

a regular guard should be mounted each night on St. Nicholas's Island, the key to the town's defenses. Sir Francis himself took command of the first guard, and it is said that from this time forward the island was known as Drake's Island. It certainly is today, but some writers claim that the heirs of Drake, in the eighteenth century the Whig political managers in Plymouth, built up this legend—just as they had published *The World Encompassed*—to exalt their own authority by borrowing from the first Sir Francis.

The Queen gave authority for the new fort in May 1592, but to pay for it she taxed all pilchards landed in Devon and Cornwall and made a grant of £100 a year out of the customs duties raised in those counties. That of course led to problems. The fort was started but the work went slowly; there were endless arguments with West County ports about their contributions; and every dodge was tried by the pilchard merchants.

When Drake, just turned fifty-two, sailed with John Hawkins on that last 1595 voyage to the West Indies from which neither returned, the fort had not yet been completed. It was eventually finished, and it had protected Plymouth for over sixty years when Charles II ordered a new and bigger Citadel on Plymouth Hoe. The builder started with a conventional five-point star fortress of the period alongside Drake's fort but eventually incorporated Drake's fort into his. Pepys, observing this new construction on a visit to the town, commented that "de Gomme [the engineer] has built . . . very sillily,"[14] but the Citadel is still there, incorporating Drake's fort. No enemy fleet has entered Plymouth Sound since. The leat is still there; when it was repaired at the outbreak of World War II for a reserve means of bringing in water, the cost was only £200. What Drake did, he did well.

Drake never returned home to Plymouth from that last voyage. He lies, not "slung atween the roundshot in Nombre de Dios Bay," but in a lead coffin off Portobelo, just a few miles from the eastern end of the Panama Canal. It is fitting that he should have been buried at sea, in the Atlantic but as close to the Pacific as could be, for in his time he dominated both oceans.

NOTES

1. Lady Eliott-Drake, *Family and Heirs of Sir Francis Drake,* 2 vols. (London, 1911); Crispin Gill, *Plymouth: A New History,* vol. I (Plymouth, 1966).

2. William Camden, *Annales rerum anglicarum et hibericarum regnante Elizabeth,* ed. Hearne (1717).

3. *Dartmoor: A New Study,* ed. Crispin Gill (Newton Abbot, Eng., 1970), p. 100.

4. Gill, *Plymouth,* vol. I, p. 57, from the Pipe Rolls, Public Record Office (Plymouth, 1966).

5. R. N. Worth, *History of Plymouth,* rev. ed. (Plymouth, 1890), p. 30.

6. Gill, *Plymouth,* vol. I, p. 68, from the Pipe Rolls, Public Record Office (Plymouth, 1966).

7. J. A. Williamson, *Hawkins of Plymouth* (London, 1949), p. 33.

8. L. Jewitt, *A History of Plymouth* (London, 1873), p. 108.

9. R. N. Worth, *Plymouth Municipal Records* (Plymouth, 1893).

10. Ibid., p. 18.

11. Ibid., pp. 18, 19.

12. Ibid., p. 127.

13. Richard Boulind, Crispin Gill, Martin Wright, and G. Chowdary-Best, "That Game of Bowls," *Mariner's Mirror* (London), 57 (November 1971) 447–450. A series of letters on the subject.

14. *The Tangier Papers of Samuel Pepys,* ed. Edwin Chappell, Publications of the Navy Records Society, vol. 73 (London, 1935), p. 114.. The reference is to Sir Bernard de Gomme, a Dutch-born military engineer (1620–1685), who was employed in Plymouth in 1667.

6.4 Southwest view of Buckland Abbey, Sir Francis Drake's home in Devon from 1581 to 1596. Built by the Cistercian Order in 1278, the Abbey remained with the Order until the dissolution of its monasteries (1539). The Grenvilles bought it and later converted the Abbey church to use as a residence. Drake acquired the property after his circumnavigation; it remained in the family until 1946 and was given to the National Trust in 1948. It is now a maritime and folk museum of Devon administered by the City of Plymouth. Courtesy of Trans Globe from their collection of Historic Houses.

6.5 Contemporary portrait of Sir Francis Drake by Marc Gheeraerts, in the Great Hall, Buckland Abbey. Courtesy of Trans Globe from their collection of Historic Houses.

6.6 Portrait of Elizabeth Sydenham by John Gower. In 1585 Drake married Elizabeth (his second wife), the daughter of a wealthy West Country landowner. Drake's first wife, Mary Newman, whom he had married in 1569, died in 1582. There were no children from either marriage. Courtesy of Trans Globe from their collection of Historic Houses.

6.7 The Great Hall, part of the Grenville conversion of Buckland Abbey, has an elaborately designed plaster ceiling; on the west side of the hall, above the portrait of Elizabeth Sydenham, there is an exceptionally fine plaster frieze commissioned by the Grenvilles. Over the fireplace is another plaster frieze bearing the date A.D. 1576, the year Sir Richard Grenville completed his restoration of the property. The paneling is of oak, with finely carved pilasters and a pediment inlaid with holly and boxwood. Furnishings include a large oak drawer-leaf table from the sixteenth century and an oak chair which is a replica of the one in the Bodleian Library made from the timbers of the *Golden Hind*. Courtesy of Trans Globe from their collection of Historic Houses.

6.8 Drake's drum, kept in the Great Hall. The drum has Drake's coat of arms and crest painted on one side and a decorative pattern of metal studs around the vent hole on the other. Drake's coat of arms was granted to him by letters patent in 1581. After his death, the drum was brought back to Buckland Abbey. The legend which grew up around the drum provided the inspiration for this poem by Sir Henry Newbolt:

> Take my drum to England, hang et by the shore,
> Strike et when your powder's runnin' low;
> If the Dons sight Devon, I'll quit the port o' Heaven,
> An drum them up the Channel as we drummed them long ago. . . .

Courtesy of Trans Globe from their collection of Historic Houses.

6.9 Portrait of Queen Elizabeth I, attributed to Federigo Zuccaro, in Drake's Drawing Room, Buckland Abbey. This painting of the Queen, formerly preserved in Mothecombe House, is in a rich frame surmounted by symbols of royalty, a crown and a scepter, for example. Courtesy of Trans Globe from their collection of Historic Houses.

6.10 Drake's Drawing Room. This fine oak-paneled room is Sir Francis Drake's major structural contribution to Buckland Abbey. The room contains contemporary portraits, including one of Drake's kinsman and fellow voyager Sir John Hawkins, by Hieronymous Custodis (over the fireplace), and the Zuccaro portrait of the Queen. The room is handsomely furnished with contemporary pieces. Courtesy of Trans Globe from their collection of Historic Houses.

6.11 The Tithe Barn at Buckland Abbey, built in the fifteenth century, one of the finest in England. It is 150 feet long, 32 feet wide, and 60 feet high at the highest point. This cathedral-like structure is supported by buttresses; woodwork pegs, rather than nails or screws, are used throughout for fastening the magnificent roof timbers. The barn is now part of the museum, and it houses the larger agricultural and transport exhibits. Courtesy of Trans Globe from their collection of Historic Houses.

Charles Fitzgeffrey's Commendatory Lamentation on the Death of Drake

MICHAEL J. B. ALLEN

Joy is the best healer
Of labours decided, and Songs,
The Muses' wise daughters,
Charm her forth by their touch,
Nor does warm water so drench and soften the limbs
As praise joined to the harp.
Longer than actions lives the word.

Pindar's *Nemean* IV is a choral ode dedicated to Timasarchos of Aigina, a winner in the boys' wrestling. As in other odes to winners of foot races, wrestling and boxing bouts, chariot, horse, and mule-car races, sprints and trials of strength, Pindar's guiding theme is, in the words of Sir Maurice Bowra, "the part of experience in which human beings are exalted or illumined by a divine force"; for at such times man's consciousness is enhanced and his "whole being has a new spaciousness and confidence."[1] The poet's task is to capture this joy as it transcends the fleeting moment of athletic victory and to render homage to sandaled Hermes or to golden-haired Apollo for their gift of jubilation in physical triumph.

From the Greek beginning, western poets have been fascinated by men of action, and by the deities presiding over them. While songs ostensibly praise deeds, the more mysterious if paradoxical dependency is that of deeds on songs—Pindar's "longer than actions lives the word." We recall the memorable lines from the Old English poem *Widsith*, "The poets always meet someone, in the northern or southern lands, who understands their art, an open-handed man who does not wish his fame to disappear."

Sir Francis Drake has not been totally neglected by the poets. Seen as Miltonically Satanic by the Spaniards, Juan de Castellanos and Lope de Vega,[2] he was eulogized in Latin verses by various contemporaries, the Hungarian Parmenius, the Englishman William Gager, and others,[3] and similarly in English by Nicholas Breton.[4] D'Avenant, who claimed to be Shakespeare's illegitimate son, made him the protagonist of a patriotic opera in 1658; Alfred Noyes of an unreadable twelve-book epic; Walter Henderson of a heroic poem in eight cantos; and Newbolt of a celebrated war song.[5] In addition, Drake has been the hero of novels by George Henty, Rupert Holland, and Leonard Wibberley;[6] and of two musicals, one as recently as 1977,[7] as well as of fugitive and occasional poems by such sea and song birds as Tryphena Archer, Thomas Evans, and John Masefield.[8] Of Renaissance panegyrists, by far the most impressive is Charles Fitzgeffrey.

Fitzgeffrey—he spelled his name in different ways—was born in Fowey, Cornwall, in 1575, 1576, or 1578, a clergyman's son. He entered Broadgates Hall (now Pembroke College) in Oxford in 1590 or 1593 and received his degree in January 1596 or 1597. While an undergraduate he won a name for himself as a Latin poet, particularly of epigrams, and was later to publish a genial collection entitled *Affanioe* (1601).[9] In 1596, the probable year of his graduation, when he was between eighteen and twenty-one, Joseph Barnes of Oxford published his long poem *Sir Francis Drake, His Honorable Lifes commendation, and his Tragicall Deathes lamentation.* It ran to a second edition only a few months later when it was accompanied by a prose "epistle to the reader" and a series of poetical tributes. Having received his M.A. in 1600, Fitzgeffrey was presented with the living of St. Dominic (which included Fowey), where he acquired a considerable reputation as an exemplary and witty divine. He lived there until his death in 1636, 1637, or 1638. In 1634 he published a collection of religious verse, *The Blessed Birth-day*, and we also possess a number of his sermons to vouch—according to Grosart, his nineteenth-century editor and only critical champion to date—that he was "a man, every inch of him—brave, high-hearted, out-spoken, patriotic, and in the finest sense, 'evangelical'."[10] Though the religious poems and the Latin epigrams are not without interest, and though the sermons display an Elizabethan exuberance and conceitedness of language in discussing even the darkest mysteries, the long biographical-historical poem on Drake is Fitzgeffrey's chief call to literary notice, if not distinction.

Published in octavo with the motto "Conamur tenues grandia," the poem was prefaced by a sonnet to "the beauteous and vertuous Lady Elizabeth, late wife unto the highlie renowmed Sir Francis Drake deceased," and by various commendatory verses to the author by three poetastric friends. Written in rhyme royal—the stanza form of Chaucer's *Troilus and Criseyde,* of Lydgate's *Fall of Princes,* of *A Mirror for Magistrates,* and of Daniel's *The Complaint of Rosamond,* the form the Elizabethan critical treatises recommended for testaments, complaints, and tragic matters generally—it ran to all but three hundred stanzas. Beginning with the descent of Night to mourn Drake's passing, it went on to invoke the panoply of sources needed for sixteenth-century poetic inspiration:

> O who will leade me to that two top't mountaine,
> The *Heliconian* Muses laureat hill?
> Who will conduct me to that sacred fountaine,
> Whence soule-infusing *Nectar* doth distill,
> That Poets sp'rites with winged furies fill:
> Where naked *Graces* use to bathe and swim,
> While *Nymphs* and *Fairies* daunce about the brim? (B3v.3)[11]
>
> . . . .
>
> Phoebus faire wel-springs, fountaines cristall bright,
> Oile of invention, Poets paradise,
> Impressures of conceite, sap of delight,
> Soules sweete Emplastrum, unguent of the eies,
> Drops, making men with Gods to sympathize,
> Baths of the Muses, *Hebes* sugred wine,
> Pure *Helicon,* the very name divine.
>
> Mount me, faire offspring of *Mnemosyne,*
> Vpon *Bellerophon's* winde-winged steede;
> Lift up my leaden sp'rite, *Euphrosyne,*
> Above the pitch of pastors rurall reede:
> For he that sings of matchlesse DRAKE, had neede
> To have all *Helicon* within his braine,
> Who in his hart did all heavens worth containe. (B4r.2,3)

While other European poets of the period utilize the same array of invocations, Fitzgeffrey does so with a vigor and gusto and a learned enthusiasm for mythological detail that bespeak a personal commitment to his subject and his role. He assumes that only the most serious and lofty kind of verse can serve as the proper medium for lauding and lamenting Drake, and that his poem will surely dwarf the ancient masterpieces if only his powers can rise to their matter. There is no self-deprecating hint, no Chaucerian flicker of irony here, despite the continual play of trope, of argumentative wit and wordplay. Indeed, the coexistence of high seriousness of intention, even at times of polemical zeal, with the surface decoration and the full deployment of all the rhetorical devices and figures available to him as a trained Latinist make for a typically Renaissance portrayal of the poet's task. Clearly, Drake inspired in Fitzgeffrey a surge of patriotic pride in his achievements and a determination to preserve his memory:

in part perhaps because Drake championed the radical Protestant cause which he espoused himself, in part because they were both West Countrymen, but mainly because he genuinely believed him worthy of an epic, one that would outshine Homer's and Virgil's alike (B6r.1).

In the course of justifying the poetical merits of Drake's story, Fitzgeffrey describes the state of poetry in late Elizabethan England and passes some notable judgments on poets now enshrined in the literary canon:

SPENSER, whose hart inharbours *Homers* soule,
If *Samian* Axioms be autenticall:
DANIEL, who well mayst *Maro's* text controule
With proud *Plus ultra* true note marginall:
And golden-mouthed DRAYTON musicall,
Into whose soule sweete SIDNEY did infuse
The essence of his Phoenix-feather'd Muse. (B5r.3)

Drake would make a fitter subject for *The Faerie Queene* than Red Crosse or Guyon, and a fitter subject—and historians feel this is a reference to Marlowe's *Edward II* and to Shakespeare's *Henry VI* plays—than the Mortimers, Lancasters and Yorks who bestride the stage (B5v.3).

Fitzgeffrey then pens one of his best formal similes:

Even as the Larke, when winters wast drawes neere,
Mounteth her basinetted head on high,
And through the aire doth tune her trebles cleere
Quav'ring full quaintlie forth her Tireli,
Beyond the ken of any piercing eie;
While as the Red-brest on an humble thorne,
With weeping notes the summers lost doth mourne. (B6v.3).

Having bewailed the predominance of love poetry, he apostrophizes the tragedians to "straine [their] tragicke Muses to rehearse / The high exploites of *Iove* borne Martialists" (B8r.1), martialists in the campaigns against Spain, and Drake above all. This in turn leads him to decry the envy of the times and the malice of Drake's detractors:

False in election, false in amitie,
And only true in infidelitie . . . . (C1r.3)

Some such there are, (o shame! too great a summe!)
Who would impeach the worth of worthy DRAKE,
With wrongfull obloquies sinister doome,
And eagerly their serpent-tongues they shake, . . . (C2r.2)

Monsters of nature, *Nile*-bred Crocodiles,
Sight-slaying Basilisks, poyson-swolne toades, (C2r.3)

and so on for a number of sonorously contemptuous stanzas. He prays that Posterity personified will catalog Drake among her saints and banish Neptune to make Drake the next god of the sea "Either to loose, or binde the windes restraints" (C3v.3). It might be more fitting even for him to become Jupiter himself, "For who more fit than DRAKE to rule the thunder?" (C4v.3). Single-handedly, Drake could have quelled the primordial rebellion of the Giants against Olympus and put Hercules to shame (C5r.2; cf. D1r.1–D3r.1). When he sails the seas, the nereids and oceanides dance about his ship, longing to kiss and embrace it (C5v.2). And Spain's cities have learned to dread his approach as they would Doomsday itself; even St. James of Compostela (who one might have thought would have welcomed Doomsday) is too terrified to show his head (C6r.2). Drake leads the gods themselves to battle (C6v.2), and Fitzgeffrey embraces the obvious pun on *draco* to glory in his nostrils "burning flakes of fire" (C7r.2,3). Depicted again as the giant-queller, Drake is then compared to the mathematical geniuses of antiquity, Archimedes and Archytas (D3r.2,3), and—rather curiously and inappropriately—to the eagle that enraptured Gan-ymede, Jove in his gayest moment (D3v.3–4r.1).

Having sung of his hero's exploits against Spain in this grandiloquent vein, the poet turns to Drake's civic triumphs as mayor of Plymouth (see Gill, ch. 6, above), and particularly to his installation of a new flushing and drainage system, a feat Fitzgeffrey compares to Hercules' diversion of the Alpheus to cleanse the Augean stables:

> Her now-bright face, once loathsomly defilde,
> He purg'd and clensed with a wholesome river:
> Her, whom her sister-citties late revilde,
> Vp-brayding her with her unsavory savor,
> DRAKE of this opproby doth now deliver. (D7r.3)

Immediately, and with no attempt to bridge the incongruity, he next speaks of the great circumnavigation:

> Bound on an high adventure shee intends
> To tell the world that all the world can tell,
> How all the triple earth's unbounded ends,
> And landes where no inhabitants do dwell,
> Where darke obscuritie still keepes his cell,
> Whereas the sunne dares scarce appearance make,
> Have heard, and seene the fame of famous DRAKE (D7v.3)

> . . . .
> A GOLDEN-HYNDE, led by his art and might,
> Bare him about the earth's sea-walled round,
> With un-resisted Roe out-running flight. (D8r.2)

Once again, Homer is called upon to cease singing of the perfidious Odysseus while Fitzgeffrey sings instead of the marital fidelity of his Devon hero, so conspicuously lacking in the Ithacan forebear (E3r.2). Little of the actual events or even the itinerary of the Elizabethan *Odyssey* appear at this point, and the poet digresses for a while to praise other English heroes and adventurers, starting with Edward III and including Richard the Lionheart, Madoc (who, the poet claims, discovered America long before Columbus or Vespucci had [E5r.1]), Mandevil, the Cabots, Wyndham, Chancelour, Grenville, Cavendish, Gilbert, Frobisher, the Hawkins brothers, and others immortalized by Hakluyt.

Eventually Fitzgeffrey returns to the circumnavigation, though he gives the impression that one has to pass through the Strait of Magellan to get to Moroccan Mogadore (Bojador), and takes Drake from the Cape Verdes to California to home in one stanza:

> He that at *Brava* sawe perpetuall spring,
> Gracing the trees with never-fading greene,
> Like Laurell branches ever flourishing:
> He that at *Taurapaza's* port had beene:
> He that the rich *Molucces* Iles had seene:
> He that a new-founde *Albion* describe,
> And safelie home again his barke did guide. (F6r.1)

Finally, having praised the monetary success of his privateering escapades in the Caribbean, Fitzgeffrey mourns England's loss of Drake on the voyage with Hawkins, the morality of which he adroitly turns to patriotic advantage:

> Whether to win from *Spaine* that was not *Spaines,*
> Or to acquite us of sustained wronge,
> Or intercept their *Indian* hoped gaines,
> Thereby to weaken them, and make us stronge;
> Heere to discusse, to me doth not belong. (G1r.1)

"Scudo" and "Portbella," where Drake sickened and died respectively, are formally execrated (G2r.2–3), and England is told to seek for consolation in the fact that, though it has lost its dragon, it still harbors the rampant lions, Essex, Cumberland, and Howard, who will continue to guard it from "Proud *Spaine*" (G7r.3). At the elegiac climax, Drake is translated into his eponymous constellation (Draco) and then into sainthood (G8r.1). The poem concludes on a cosmological key:

> Phoebus himselfe shall chronicle thy fame,
> And of a radiant sunne-beame make the pen;
> The inke, the milke whence Via Lactea came;
> Th' empyrean heaven, the volume shalbe then;
> To register this miracle of men;
> The sunne and moone, the letters capitall;
> The stars, the commas and the periods all. (G8r.3)

The story of Drake will become the bedside reading of the pagan gods and Christian saints alike (G8v.1), the wished-for consummation of all Elizabeth's naval commanders. Fitzgeffrey ends with a suitable quotation from Horace (*Carmina* I.vi.13–14).

This combination of conceited, hyperbolic, irritated wit, ablaze with literary enthusiasms and mythological allusions, decorative analogies and patriotic ardor, extraordinary distortion of historical perspective and elegiac excess, high-mindedness, a sensible admiration for civic as well as martial achievements, love of epigrammatic pointing as well as extended figures, a pride in the literary and political past and present of the nation, and above all a youthful, pedantic, grandiose, lyrical conception of the poet's duty—all these serve to render Fitzgeffrey's poem an attractive curiosity, redolent of its age. They do not succeed however in turning Drake into a literary hero. This failure is not due to Fitzgeffrey's wanting poetic gifts, which are in many ways quite considerable, but rather to his ignoring two dimensions of the problem that faced him in his commitment to aggrandizing his countryman: one modal, the other thematic.

Even from this distant point of vantage, we can imagine a Marlovian Drake in his narrow cabin, the charts of the half-discovered globe in front of him, the master of a navigational expertise beyond the scope of ordinary mortal mathematicians, contemplating the straits and headlands of both the outer and the inner world, a Drake metamorphosed from a Protestant adventurer into a Scythian sea tyrant. Or, more appositely perhaps, we can imagine a Donnean Drake swiveling a compass and running down the line of his own hard palm, the circumnavigation an intellectual exercise in hyperbole and paradox, in the contorted logic that sails us westward to an eastern truth at the intersection of a rhyme. We might even imagine Sir Francis as the dreamer in a lost Spenserian canto of the fourth book, waking in a copse beside the Meavy to find the plate of brass the delusion of an Archimago, the *Golden Hind* a false Florimel.

In short, the circumnavigation could well have provided the subject matter of drama, metaphysical lyric, or sustained allegory. A poet-persona, Drake might have dropped anchor in Plymouth Sound, having won the knowledge of his own and all men's limitations from the hemispheres of memory and expectation, a man who had cast the world's circle about himself. Ironically, Fitzgeffrey himself glimpsed some of these possibilities, not in his long lamentation, but in a commendatory sonnet he contributed for John Davies of Hereford's interesting poem *Microcosmus,* which appeared in 1603. Fitzgeffrey's sonnet is addressed to Drake and Columbus, and it reads:

Goe *Drake* of England, *Doue* of Italie,
Vnfolde what ever Neptune's armes infolde,
Trauell the Earth (as Phoebus doth the skie)
Till you begette newe Worlds vpon this olde.
Would any wonders see, yet liue at rest,
Nor hazard life vpon a dangerous shelfe?
Behold, thou bear'st a World within thy brest,
Take ship at home, and sayle about thy selfe.
This Paper-Bark may be thy Golden-Hinde,
Davies the *Drake* and true discou'rer is,
The end, that thou thy-selfe thy-selfe maist finde;
The prize and pleasure thine, the trauell his:
See here display'd as plaine as knowledge can,
This little World, this wondrous Ile of Man.

In its modest way this is probably the best English celebration of the circumnavigation: witty, eloquent, pointed, a genuinely successful sonnet, fusing conceit with concept.

In his 1596 poem Fitzgeffrey obviously wanted in part to compose an elegy, as the adoption of rhyme royal attests. But Drake's death presented some of the same pitfalls Tennyson encountered with the death of the Iron Duke: how to portray the outpourings of public grief authentically. Fitzgeffrey could have turned to several elegiac models: to the medieval de casibus and dream elegies or, particularly since it had been rediscovered and revitalized by a number of continental Renaissance poets such as Garcilaso and Ronsard, to the ancient pastoral elegy as developed by Theocritus, Bion, and Moschus. Such a choice would have allowed him both to dovetail his intensely personal admiration for Drake into the national sorrowing to which the poem itself is a self-conscious witness and to use the conceited, allusive language and the mythological underpinning that he dearly loved as an artist and could effectively deploy. To begin with, there would have been a firmer structure for what is now a loose narrative listing of exploits: traditional sections, such as the invocation of the gods or the procession of mourners, to subject it to more complex ends. In the event, Fitzgeffrey's lamentation is not keyed to any triumphal, processional, seasonal, or ritual patterns. His assertion of Drake's immortality and apotheosis springs from personal conviction alone; it is not the climax generated by a form with traditional associations and conventions for which the poet is not responsible individually but which he is free to exploit as a poetic inheritance, as Milton did in *Lycidas* or Shelley in *Adonais*.

Fitzgeffrey chose, however, to write something without any elegiac precedent: a biographical eulogy-elegy-epic which surveyed the glories of Drake's life in the light of the triumph of Protestantism and of England. Yet, in eschewing elegiac models, he was also unable to draw upon the themes, motifs, and dimensions that endow the great epics with their own enduring life. In particular, he gives little indication of being aware of the web of mysterious forces of which Drake was just one gossamer and which stretched across not only England but all the western seapowers, as the world opened up to their discoverers and traders in its Renaissance beauty, variety, and cruelty. Not that we can criticize him for failing to attain the tragic sweep of a new *Iliad:* had there been one, it would probably have belonged to Philip and his Armada, and centered upon the inexplicable and implacable ire of the very God whom the Spaniard strove so devoutly to worship and to glorify. But, with the Muses' help, Fitzgeffrey could have created perhaps a new *Odyssey,* as he himself was obviously aware and hoped, one centered upon the circumnavigation, with Drake as the resourceful, perdurable prince of an archetypal voyage, a man divinely favored by the reformed gods of Canterbury if not Geneva, whose bark was to escape both Atlantic Polyphemuses and Pacific Circes. Drake could even have been Neoplatonized, as Odysseus was in late antiquity, his voyage becoming more than a *nostos,* a return to a Tudor Penelope, but rather a Plotinian circle of emanation, conversion, and return to the Uranian Aphrodite, second daughter of Henry VIII—the episodes in his active life gradually transformed by some

English Tasso into a series of contemplative dilemmas, his landfalls into initiatory mysteries. Drake was not per se intractable material for such a transformation. Consider the case of Vasco da Gama, the hero of *The Lusiads*.

In celebrating da Gama, his distant relative, Luis de Camoëns created an epic of knowledge. Into it he poured his humanistic delight in cosmography and geography, classical and modern; his Renaissance obsession with the marvels of the natural world and its alien cultures; his nationalistic pride in Portugal's history as he had absorbed it from learned chronicles and travelers' tales alike; his Neoplatonic idealism and Counter-Reformation fervor; and his poetic love of language, allusion, rhetoric, and mythology. The result was a unique combination of lyrical intensity, sensuality, intellectuality, and learning, having little to do with da Gama himself.

The climax of Camoëns' vision occurs in the last book of the poem, where the sailors, on Venus' Isle of Love, are given a vision of their nation's future destiny. Tethys, the sea goddess and da Gama's companion, shows them the Ptolemaic universe of ten spheres, beginning with the empyrean and the primum mobile and ending with the earth, the whole fashioned in God's image: "Infinite, perfect, uniform, self-poiz'd, / Brief, like the Architect that made the same" (X.79).[12] She next indicates the three continents: Christian Europe "higher by the head / In *Arms* and *civill Arts* than all the rest"; "untill'd AFFRICK, covetous, ill-bred," terminating in its mighty cape, the giant Adamastor (X.92); and Asia, which commences with the Arabias and the Persian Gulf, then stretches eastward to India, Singapore, Cambodia and Vietnam, China, Japan, the east Indies and the oriental seas ("Sown infinite of *Isles* that have no name" (X.132), and legendary for their birds of paradise, camphor and nutmegs, their bituminous springs and fiery volcanoes)—and which returns at last to Ceylon and Madagascar. Finally she sings of the newly discovered continent, "another World, which from the *North* / Extends it self to the opposed *Pole*" (X.139). Though this is in the hands of Spain, Lusitanian exploits shall not be wanting:

> Alongst this *Coast* (to find out, and to view
> The end thereof) shall wander Magellan,
> Who in reality of *Fact* shall be
> A Portingall, but not in *loyaltie*. (X.140)

Camoëns briefly describes the Patagonian giants, the great Strait, the new Pacific sea, and the icy Terra Incognita. At this messianic point, Tethys concludes her prophecy:

> Thus farr, O Portingals, ye are allow'd
> Your *Nation*'s future Actions to survay,
> Which through the *Sea* by *you* left ope her prowd
> And never wearied *Ensigns* shall display . . . . (X.142)

She promises the sailors favorable winds and tranquil seas for their voyage home, secure in the perpetual love of amorous nymphs. In one stanza da Gama's men depart for and arrive at "Sweet Tagus's Mouth" (X.144), and Camoëns breaks into a memorable outburst at Sebastian's and the court's neglect not just of himself but of the whole nation's cheerful dedication and tireless commitment to its imperial task:

> Behold how cheerfully, a thousand ways,
> Like *fearlesse Lions* and *wilde Bulls* they run,
> Expos'd to *watch* whole *Nights,* to *fast* whole *days,*
> To *fire* and *sword,* the *Arrow* and the *Gun,*
> To *torrid Regions,* and to *frozen Bays,*
> To Moors, and People that adore the *Sun,*
> To unknown perils, a *new* World to find,
> To *Whales,* to *shipwracks,* to *tempestuous Wind!*
>
> To *doe* and *suffer* All for *You* prepar'd,
> And to obey in the remotest *Land*
> (Though ne'er so *bitter,* and though ne'er so *hard,*
> Without *Reply,* or *stop*) what *You* command . . . . (X.147–148)

Suffusing Camoëns' vision is a sense of coming failure, of the ebbing of direction, energy, and faith, as Portugal loses hold on its manifest destiny as a nation in the vanguard of Christian expansion. The achievements of da Gama and Magellan, of Dias, Cabral, and Albuquerque, had brought a small Atlantic seaboard kingdom into contact with Roman greatness, only to betray it to an inner darkness. Even at the beginning, the magnitude of the discoveries and conquests was in most ways lost upon the participants themselves. For the sea, as Melville was to contend so powerfully centuries later, often makes monomaniacs of men, deluding them with dreams of wealth and power, not leading them to a Stoic clarity. The mythology of the deep—white behemoths, St. Elmo's fire and waterspouts, the wings of the albatross and the storm petrel, phantom sails and flying fish and phosphorescent weed—these constitute the images and setting of the sixteenth-century sea, but a setting in which men more often degenerated than acquired a Hytholodayan wisdom. Though *The Lusiads* concludes with a sea vision and a sea prophecy of the nation's destiny by water, expressing the fervent hope that her kings will rise to their subjects' crusading struggle, the reality—as Camoëns knew only too well, and as he voiced through the lips of the old man on the waterfront the day da Gama embarked from Lisbon—was the unbridled savagery of the occupation of Goa and other Indian towns, the exploitation of vulnerable cultures and communities, and eventually the moral blindness inflicted inevitably on the mother country.

While Fitzgeffrey had a forthright—Grosart would say manly[13]—picture of Drake as a national leader, as the embodiment even of Protestant virtue, he lacked precisely these Camoënic insights into the complex of personal and public involvements in an imperial enterprise that brought, along with enormous prosperity, a cancerous corruption to the individuals and the institutions committed to it. True, while Portugal and England in the sixteenth century had something in common as maritime powers, the two were not in phase in terms of their maritime destinies. As well as being passionately Catholic, Portugal was already deeply tainted by the wealth and power, the crazed dreams, the brutality, the spiritual torpor, the over-extendedness that had come with her discoveries; England by contrast still stood upon the threshold of imperial expansion. Consequently, though ironically perhaps, the true poet of the sea voyages, not just of da Gama's rounding of the Cape and crossing to India but also of Drake's and Magellan's circumnavigations, is the one-eyed Camoëns; for he saw so clearly the delusions and tragedies which the youthful Fitzgeffrey gives no inkling of perceiving.

Camoëns also anticipated joys and triumphs that Fitzgeffrey would have misinterpreted as pagan sensuality. Seven years before Drake's landfall in present-day Marin County, Camoëns' readers were presented with a California in the Venusian Isle of Love, a sensual and intellectual paradise where man's body and soul were for an Edenic moment aspects of a unitary being:

> A thousand gallant *Trees* to *Heav'n* up-shoot
> With *Apples* odoriferous and faire:
> The *Orange-tree* hath in her sightly *fruit*
> The colour Daphne boasted in her *Haire*:
> The *Citron-tree* bends almost to her Root
> Under the yellow burthen which she bare:
>> The goodly *Lemmons,* with their *button-Caps,*
>> Hang imitating *Virgins* fragrant *Paps.* (IX. 56)

In Tethys and the nymphs, who enamor and make love to the Portuguese sailors, Camoëns portrayed the forces which man must always call upon to regain his humanity after the dehumanizing effects of voyaging and foreign toil; the forces which enable him to return to his native hearth as a welcome husband, son, and father, rather than as a dreaded mariner disrupting the wedding feasts of kinsmen or, worse, as an Ahab made lunatic by the perpetual flood. For Venus, the Lusitanians' goddess, was more than the patroness of love and beauty; ultimately, for the Renaissance humanists, she watched over humanity itself. On Camoëns' Isle, da Gama and his triumphant, homesick crew are drawn into the embraces not of Circe or Acrasia, sirens or lotus eaters, but of generous and ennobling impulses, passion and tenderness, the contentment and gladness of body and of mind. These, when united, become the *humanitas* we strive for as both a psychological and a cultural goal. Without the experience of Venus, the voyage would have been simply a tale of endurance, debility, disease, treachery, and war; with it, it also became the witness to an entire country's potentiality for joy and self-fulfillment.

Drake returned to England in 1580 with a fortune but no vision, no Nova Albion as an enchanted isle, nothing which served to stir the contemporary poets directly. Only gradually, obliquely, inconspicuously almost, in the imagery of *The Tempest,* in Donne's hymn in his sickness with its fatal straits of Anian and Magellan and Gibraltar, in Marvell's ode to the pilgrims keeping time with their falling oars to where the remote Bermudas ride, did the deeper significance of Drake's—of all the Elizabethan voyagers'—romance with the western seas enter into the literary consciousness. The subsequent efforts of Newbolt, Noyes, and Masefield amount to little more than nautical jingoism or sentimentalism. Arguably, given the absence of a Camoëns, Drake's finest interpreter might have been Conrad: unerringly he could have penetrated both to the heart of the Doughty affair and to the doom that Drake's landing ultimately signaled for the Miwok Indian tribes. But Conrad remained committed to the eastern seas he had known personally, and left Drake unillumined by his intricate, musical prose.

Drake remains a history book, at most a Hakluyt hero—not someone the great poets have chosen in their unfathomable ways to measure face to face. His circumnavigation was only one instance after all, however courageous and magnificent, of the attempt by Renaissance man to come to terms with the paradoxes of his flat map's relationship to a round world. Still, more than Timasarchos the wrestler, Drake deserved a Pindar; and Fitzgeffrey would have been the first to agree, in a flurry of oxymora and antitheses.

NOTES

1. C. M. Bowra, *The Odes of Pindar* (Harmondsworth, Eng., 1969), p. xvi.

2. Juan de Castellanos, *Discurso de el Capitan Francisco Draque* (written in 1586–1587 but not published until 1921 in Madrid); Lope Félix de Vega Carpio, *La Dragontea* (Valencia, 1598; repr. Burgos, 1935).

3. Parmenius, *De Navigatione* (1582), lines 294–298 (ed. and trans. David B. Quinn and Neil M. Cheshire in *The New Found Land of Stephen Parmenius* [Toronto, 1972], pp. 102–103): "Ni frustra, quod mortali tot secla negarant, / Hac tuus immensum nuper Dracus ambiit orbem / Qua patri Oceano clausas circumdare terras / Concessit natura viam, mediaque meare / Tellure et duplici secludere littore mundos." Gager, "Verses to Francis Drake," British Library Additional MS 22583 (n.d.), fol. 84. Compare similar references by Laurence Humfrey (see Quinn and Cheshire, *New Found Land*, pp. 10–11) and by Thomas Watson (in Quinn and Cheshire, pp. 23, 67–69, 135).

4. Nicholas Breton, prefatory poem to *A Discourse in Commendation of the Valiant as Vertuous Minded Gentleman Maister Frauncis Drake, with a Reioysing of His Happy Adventures* (London, 1581). The earliest poetic reference to the circumnavigation, anticipating Parmenius' by a few months, this consists of three six-line stanzas.

5. Sir William D'Avenant, *The History of Sr Francis Drake: Exprest by Instrumentall and Vocall Musick, and by Art of Perspective in Scenes, &c.* (London, 1659; first performed in 1658 in the Phoenix Theatre, London); Alfred Noyes, *Drake: An English Epic* (New York, 1906); Walter Henderson, *The New Argonautica* (London, 1928)—Drake is one of several other "immortal spirits," including Raleigh and Ponce de Leon; Sir Henry Newbolt, "Drake's Drum," *Poems: New and Old* (London, repr. 1933), pp. 16–17.

6. George Alfred Henty, *Under Drake's Flag* (New York, 1894); Rupert Sargent Holland, *Drake's Lad* (New York and London, 1929); Leonard Patrick O'Connor Wibberley, *The King's Beard* (New York, 1952).

7. James C. Cross, *Sir Francis Drake, and Iron Arm* (with music by Sanderson; first performed at the New Royal Circus, London, 1800); Lynne Riley, Richard Riley, and Simon Brett, *Drake's Dream* (first performed at the Shaftesbury Theatre, London, 1977).

8. Tryphena Matilda Archer, "Drake's Bay, 1579," in *Drake's Bay and Other Poems* (Milwaukee, 1913), pp. 1–3; Thomas J. Evans, *Sir Francis Drake, and Other Fugitive Poems* (Richmond, Va., 1895); John Masefield, "A Word with Sir Francis Drake during His Last Night in London," in *The Atlantic*, 208 (July 1961) 50–54. All the items in this and the previous notes are merely a selection from scores of other literary and semiliterary Drakeana. For several of these references I am indebted to the late Benjamin Draper.

9. Leicester Bradner, *Musae Anglicanae: A History of Anglo-Latin Poetry, 1500–1925* (New York, 1940; repr. 1966), pp. 83–85.

10. Alexander B. Grosart, *The Poems of the Rev. Charles Fitz-Geoffrey, 1593–1636* (Manchester, 1881), p. xxxiv. Grosart has a number of corrections for the entry on Fitzgeffrey in the *Dictionary of National Biography* but was himself "corrected" on several biographical points by G. C. Moore Smith, "Charles Fitzgeffrey, Poet and Divine," *Modern Language Review* 14 (1919) 254–270.

11. Henceforth all references will be to the signatures of the Huntington Library's copy of the first edition (the poem itself runs from B1r to G8v), the last figure indicating whether the stanza is the first, second, or third on the page. I have kept to the spelling and punctuation of the original but have used the modern *s* throughout.

12. I shall quote throughout from the brilliant, if overly free, verse translation by Richard Fanshawe, ambassador to both Portugal and Spain in the 1660s. The uncorrected first edition was published in London in 1655 and reedited for Harvard University Press by Jeremiah D. M. Ford (Cambridge, 1940). My references are to this second edition, and they consist of canto and stanza.

13. Grosart, *Poems of Fitz-Geoffrey*, p. li.

Sir Francis Drake Revived: From Letters to Legend

W. T. JEWKES

Some think it *true whilst* other some do doubt
Whether Captaine Drake compast the worlde about;
Some say he did it in the Devil's name
And none *ever* since could doe the like againe.
But these are all *deceived,* why should they doubt it;
They know each yeare theres some that goe about it.
ANONYMOUS, published by "J. H. Gent.," 1619

It is curious that Drake's voyages and exploits have made such a small impact on major English literature, particularly in his own age. The first published account of a Drake voyage appeared in 1587, seven years after the circumnavigation. *Newes out of the Coast of Spaine,* by Henry Haslop, told of Drake's Cadiz raid of that year, certainly his most brilliant exploit as far as immediate political impact was concerned, but nonetheless his sixth voyage since he had begun to command his own ships. It is particularly surprising that although Hakluyt published *Divers voyages to America* in 1582, he makes no mention therein of the circumnavigation completed two years earlier.[1] Not until 1589 did reports of two previous voyages (an account of the 1572 Nombre de Dios trip and "The Famous Voyage" narrative of the circumnavigation) appear in Hakluyt's *The principall navigations*. One other publication appeared that year: Walter Bigges's *A Summary and True Discourse*, telling of Drake's 1585–86 West Indies voyage. In Drake's lifetime, then, there appeared only one long account of a late voyage, one medium-length summary of the circumnavigation, a brief reference to the Cadiz raid, and a short narrative of Drake's third voyage almost twenty years before.

This lack of publicity did not go unnoticed even in Drake's day, and it gave rise to several complaints. The first appeared in a ballad by Henry Robarts (or Roberts) published in 1585 and entitled "A most Friendly Farewell, Given by a welwiller to the right worshipful Sir Frauncis Drake Knight . . . ." Issued on the occasion of Drake's departure for the Caribbean, this is a piece, according to the title page, "wherein is briefely touched his perils passed in his last daungerous voiage." Here at last we encounter the circumnavigation in what might be called literature. Although the ballad recalls the "stirring up of hero-icall spirits" motif of many such accounts published in this and the next century, Robarts' motives, to judge from the dedicatory "Epistle," seem self-serving.

Despite its rather fulsome adulation, this poem is revealing. Robarts complains in the "Epistle" that his countrymen

> have not given you that honor worthie your desartes, have sought to rob you of your worthines, a base thing in schollers and the learned who seeth other countreymen that hath not undertaken the one halfe of your troubles to be registred in the mindes of all men forever, by their meanes which hath by wrything given them their desarts: as the conquest of the west Indyes can witnesse, wherein many of theyr names is explained in other wryters also.

Robarts warms to his theme with even more fervor:

> Then Englishmen what dishonour doe you our famous Drake, that you have left his name so long unwritten of, whome fame hath bruited in all the whole worlde for his most famous enterprises, and hath made him to be admired among his mortall foes for his valour, O noble English heart never yet daunted. . . . Unthankfull Englishmen that can suffer your worthy countreymen to rest in oblivion, and his renowmed deeds with unthankfulnesse, so soon to be forgotten.

Yet, after noting the failure of English Parnassians to record the great circumnavigation in suitable strophes, Robarts himself dwells mainly on the excitement of the forthcoming Caribbean voyage. The perils of Drake's round-the-world exploit are indeed, as the title page asserts, but "briefly touched" upon, taking up only the first four lines of the poem and never really mentioning the fact that the voyage was a circumnavigation. Sounding like Shakespeare's Bottom reciting the lines of Pyramus, they begin:

When true report was blazed abroad the III yeares taken toile,
Of that rare Knight Syr Frauncis Drake through many a foreign soil,
Who by his travile on the Seas unto his endless fame
Did purchase for his countrey wealth, and credit to his name.
I did expect some Ovids pen to paint his worthy praise,
But none hath writ that earst I sawe which makes me saye,
The brunt was spread of traviles his the poets did dismay,
My minde was forward with ye first, but yet my heart did faile
That gainst my will I forced was to strike my simple sayle.

The rest of the tedious poem devotes itself to repairing this delinquency in himself (and other English poets) by striking a rather heavy-handed note about the forthcoming expedition. Little of it is interesting, except perhaps for some scattered classical allusions. Although it never quite elevates Drake to the status of a sea god, as the Reverend Charles Fitzgeffrey does some years later, Robarts in his "Epistle" compares Drake to Alexander conquering Darius, to David killing Goliath, and to Mucius Scaevola, who put his right hand into the fire to prove his hardiness in defense of Rome. In the ballad he continues in the same vein, likening Drake to Ulysses for his policy and Achilles for his valor. He closes by dubbing Drake "the Phoenix of our age," calling upon Neptune to protect Drake as he did Achilles.

The next self-consciously literary treatment of Drake was printed two years later, in 1587. An even more tedious doggerel ballad by one Thomas Greepe, it deals again not with the circumnavigation, but with Drake's exploits in the 1585–86 West Indies venture. It is titled "The true and perfect Newes of the worthy and valiant exploytes atchieved and doone by that valiaunt Knight, Syr Frauncis Drake."

In his patronizing dedication to the Earl of Cumberland, Greepe, in spite of being a self-confessed farmer rather than a poet, nevertheless follows pretentious models. Robarts may have tried to take the place of an English Ovid, but Greepe had higher ambitions:

The worke is a true breefe discourse of the most rare and worthy exploytes, performed by the right worshipful Sir Frauncis Drake Knight, and his consortes in the fortunate Isles, which, although the trueth thereof be not unknowne to your Honor, yet the vulgar sort of people in the Realme having hearde, and yet wanting the verite of the same, may by this pamphlet be the better advertised.

Though "not pend in lofty verse, not curously handled," Greepe continues in his "Epistle to the Reader,"

there is nothing can more profit thy posteritie heereafter, than the leaving in memory so worthy a thing, for how shoulde we know the woorthy deedes of our Elders, if those learned Poets and Historiographers had not sett them downe in wryting, as Josephus for the state of the Jewes: Homer and Euripides for the Grecians: Titus Livius for the Romaines: Quintus Curtius for the life of Alexander the great, and so of all others.

Though not so outspoken as Robarts in his reproof of his fellow would-be poets for failure to mention Drake, Greepe clearly feels that Drake has not been sufficiently appreciated for his contribution to England's maritime glories. Besides comparing him to Gideon among the Midianites, Daniel in the lion's den, and Shadrach, Meshach, and Abednego in the fiery furnace, Greepe reminds his readers that "none the like hath ever woone," and he sums up his feelings about Drake's accomplishments with these robust though heavy-handed words:

When Siedge is layd to towne or fort
And when the same bee yeelded straight:
The valour's then of small report,
And the exploites of no great weight.
   But where with force they bide the brunt:
   Theyr conquests are of great account.
Ulisses with his Navie great,
In ten yeeres space great valour woone:
Yet all his time did no such feat,
As *Drake* within one yeere hath doone
   Both Turke and Pope and all our foes:
   Doe dread this Drake where ere he goes.

Heroic analogues to the exploits of famous voyagers were by no means uncommon in the narratives of the time.[2] But the plaintive note struck by Robarts and Greepe is more unusual, and it implies that they feel their task of giving proper recognition to Drake is both a more onerous and a more important one than that usually faced by the aspiring laureate.

This plaintive note is sounded once again in 1596, in Richard Rous's commendatory verses appended to the long epic poem by Charles Fitzgeffrey, *Sir Francis Drake: His Honorable Lifes commendation, and his Tragicall Deathes lamentation* (see Allen, ch. 7, above). Rous begins by claiming that "thrise worthie Drake," though "once dead," is now "twise alive," presumably because of Fitzgeffrey's attempt to immortalize his hero. Then he proceeds with this sonnet:

When to the banks of sweet *Elysium*
Came worthy DRAKE, to get his passage there.
The ferriman denied his ghost to come,
Before his exequies solemniz'd were:
But none t'adorne his funerall hearse did prove:
And long he sate upon the haplesse shoare,
Untill thy Muse (whom pittie still did move)
Helpt thee to rise, and him to rest no more:
And sent her mournefull teares unto his ghost,
And sweete (though sad) complaintes, as exequies,
Passing him to those fields which long he lost,
And won his soule the joy, thy pen the prise;
So still thy funeralles shall adorne his name,
And still his funeralles shall enlarge thy fame.

The attempt at reviving Drake was now well under way.

After Drake's death, with the exception of *The World Encompassed* (1628) and additional materials in Hakluyt's second, expanded edition of *The principal Navigations* (1598–1600), major literary works dealing with Drake seem to be concerned mainly with resurrecting his spirit rather than with assessing his significance in the political, social, economic, and intellectual cross-currents of his age. Two quite independent books appeared in the seventeenth century with the curious title *Sir Francis Drake revived*.

The first of these two books was written by Phillip Nichols in 1626 (see Quinn, ch. 3, above). It is a highly editorialized account of the 1572–73 Nombre de Dios voyage and is chiefly interesting for its general tenor, well summarized by the title page subscription, "Calling upon this Dull or effeminate age, to follow his noble steps for gold and silver," and for its inclusion of a "Dedicatory Epistle" purportedly by Drake to Queen Elizabeth dated 1 January 1592 (1593). The "Epistle," if authentic, makes it clear that Drake was planning to publish his own account of his "services against the Spaniard," which may mean a narrative of all his previous exploits, not just the 1572–73 voyage. Such a narrative would be, as he declares, "the first fruits of your Servant's pen."

At this time, of course, Drake was in the period of his deepest disgrace, after the disastrous Portugal expedition. A possible political motive for this intended publication is hinted at: "Not as setting sail for maintaining my reputation in men's judgment, but onely as sitting at helme, if occasion shall be, for conducting the like actions hereafter." Drake seems to have in mind his own vindication, however modestly he may phrase it. Elsewhere in the "Epistle," he expresses his hope that "our present age (at least), may be satisfied, in the rightfulnes of these actions, which hitherto have been silenced." Nevertheless, his intended narrative was not published at that time, possibly because no publisher would touch it and perhaps even because the Queen continued to frown upon him. He did not receive his desired next command for two more years.

Drake's curious words, "which hitherto have been silenced," hinting as they do at some sort of official prohibition, may indeed explain why so little about him was published in his lifetime. This speculation is supported elsewhere by the comment of the Seigneur de la Popellinière in his *Les Trois Mondes* (1582) that the Queen withheld the record of Drake's circumnavigation so that it could not be published—probably because she feared that some other nation might profit from it. This may explain why no account of the circumnavigation was published until Hakluyt's *The principall navigations*. It seems reasonable to speculate that similar strictures may have shrouded Drake's other exploits during his lifetime, and even for some considerable time thereafter, so that his nephew's vindication of his famous uncle could not safely appear until thirty-four years later.[3]

The other seventeenth-century work on Drake appeared in 1692 under the title *The English Hero: Or Sir Francis Drake Revived . . . Being a full account of the Dangerous Voyages, Admirable Adventures, Notable Discoveries and*

Magnanimous Atchievements of that Valiant and Renowned Commander . . . Recommended to all Heroick Spirits, to endeavour to benefit their Prince and Country by the like Worthy Undertakings. This is a rambling compilation of material on Drake's voyages which lays thematic though not detailed stress on the circumnavigation, as the author (R. Burton) indicates in his epistle "To the Reader":

> Among these Gallant Adventurers none is more renowned than our
> present Hero Sir Francis Drake, who may be the pattern to stir up Hero-
> ick and active spirits in these days to benefit their Prince and Country,
> and immortalize their names by the like noble attempts, who by first turn-
> ing up a furrow about the whole World, hath exceeded all that went be-
> fore him. Of those worthy Travels and Exploits there having not hitherto
> been published any just or exact Account, I have collected all I could any-
> where meet with upon this Excellent Subject.

The most interesting thing in this whole patchwork of material is perhaps Burton's note that John Davies of Deptford had some planks from the *Golden Hind* made into a chair, which was presented to the University Library at Oxford. Burton quotes a poem by "a Renowned Poet of this kingdome"[4] entitled "Upon the Poet's sitting and drinking in the chair made out of the Relicks of Sir Francis Drake's Ship":

> Chear up my Mates, the wind doth fairly blow,
> Clap on more sail, and never spare,
> Farewell all lands, for now we are
> In the wide sea of drink, and merrily we go.
> Bless me, 'tis hot! another bowl of wine,
> And we shall cut the burning Line.
> Hey Boys! she scuds away, and by my head I know
> We round the world are sailing now.
> What dull men are those that tarry at home
> When abroad they might wantonly roam,
> And gain such experience, and spy too
> Such countries and wonders, as I do!
> But pr'y thee, good pilot, take heed what you do,
> And fail not to touch at *Peru*!
> With gold there the vessel we'll store,
> And never, and never be poor,
> No, never be poor any more.

The poem continues in this exhilarated vein for two more long stanzas, and one can justly question whether it was the spirit of Drake or alcoholic spirit which moved its composition.

Nevertheless, the circumnavigation had at last begun to surface as the essential expression of Drake's genius, and attempts were being made to eternize what it seemed to represent. Interest in Drake was again revived in the mid- to late nineteenth century, this time mainly (apart from the work of the historian Sir Julian Corbett) in the form of such inspiring fiction for young people as Charles Kingsley's *Westward Ho* and G. A. Henty's *Under Drake's Flag.*

Perhaps of greater interest is the surfacing of folklore traditions begun about Drake soon after his death which seem to have continued until recently. John Stow tells us, in his *Annales* of 1615, that after Drake had been knighted, books, pictures, and ballads were published in his praise. If this is true, it is probable that most were in the form of broadsides or chapbooks. They therefore would have belonged to what we call popular literature, which may explain why they have not survived. Folklore, although it too is part of the popular tradition, works the opposite way: it persists for a long time solely in oral form, and often only much later does it surface in literary form.

The popular tradition that Drake would survive as a guardian spirit of England first appeared in print in 1885 in Henry Newbolt's poem *Drake's Drum.* It is impossible to tell how far back this legend goes, or even whether Newbolt's idea of the drum summoning up Drake's spirit was inspired by folklore or whether he made it up. Yet as early as 1799 the public knew of the existence of Drake's drum at Buckland Abbey, together with his Bible and sword (all three items were sent there after his death).[5] Perhaps Newbolt supplied the story that Drake had commanded that the drum be hung on the Plymouth seawall (certainly an unlikely place to preserve such a fragile object). On the other hand, the notion that the drum would sound again if ever England were threatened by an enemy from the sea may not have been his invention. Be that as it may, the legend had achieved wide circulation by World War I, thanks perhaps to Newbolt's poem, which had been set to music and had become part of the common entertainment in drawing rooms, pubs, and music halls. A new literary treatment in Alfred Noyes' poem "The Admiral's Ghost" may also have helped:

> But—ask of the Devonshire men; for they heard in the dead of night
> The roll of the drum and they saw him pass
> On a ship all shining white.

Noyes developed this idea further in a letter to *The Times* of London on 28 August 1916:

> There is a tale in Devonshire that Sir Francis Drake has not merely listened for his drum, during the last three hundred years, but has also heard and answered it on more than one naval occasion. It was heard, as the men of the Brixham trawlers can testify, about a hundred years ago, when a little man, under the pseudonym of Nelson (for all Devonshire knows that Nelson was a reincarnation of Sir Francis) went sailing by to Trafalgar.

Only a little before the naval action of Jutland, word came from the Brixham trawlers again. They had "heard Drake's drum beat" and were assured that the ghost of Drake was inhabiting the body of Sir John Jellicoe.[6]

So strong had this tradition about Drake become by this time that it gave rise to a curious incident at the end of the war. At the time of the surrender of the German fleet at Scapa Flow, the beating of a drum was heard by the captain, commander, and other officers aboard the *Royal Oak,* a West Country ship manned by a crew mostly of Devonshire and Cornish men. The incident was investigated thoroughly, but no drum could be found. Still, its beat continued until orders were given for the German flag to be lowered.

In World War II the tradition surfaced again in a British Broadcasting Corporation broadcast on 16 August 1940 by Isaac Foot, which was later published in *London Calling* under the title "Drake's Drum Beats Again." In this curious piece Foot goes far beyond Newbolt and Noyes, claiming that the drum was heard by the citizens of Plymouth on the visit of Fairfax and Cromwell during the Civil War; by Admiral Blake when, "sick unto death,"[7] he reached Plymouth harbor; by Nelson; by Wellington; and by Napoleon when a prisoner aboard the *Bellerophon;* and by those who watched the troopships arrive in Britain from the Commonwealth countries, as well as those who sailed the little ships to Dunkirk.

Foot's fancies may seem ludicrously romantic to us now, yet the documented incident at Scapa Flow reminds us that they are not entirely idiosyncratic. Another curious incident which occurred on the Hampshire coast in September 1940 is equally well attested. Two army officers on duty on the evacuated seafront claimed to have heard a drum beating, and a widespread security check was ordered because no signals of any kind were allowed in the area. The beat was described by one of the officers as "a distinct call . . . a very incessant beat, pause, two sharp beats in quick succession, one sharp beat." Despite the convincing precision of these details, no drum was turned up by the search.

It is not easy to be certain how far back in time, or in what specific form, the folk tradition of Drake's guardian spirit may have originated. It is consonant with reports in his own time that Drake had supernatural powers.[8] Some of these reports persisted until the nineteenth and twentieth centuries and are recorded by Anna Elizabeth Bray and Robert Southey, and also by Katherine Briggs.[9] These reports tell of Drake's construction of the leat from Dartmoor to Plymouth by means of magical powers (see Gill, ch. 6, above); of his making fire ships to fight the Armada by chipping slips off a wooden block; of his preventing his wife's remarriage when he seemed to have been lost on a voyage (by firing a cannon shot through the globe to emerge just between the couple at the altar); and so on. All of these seem much more trivial than the drum legends, but they do at least evidence an old folk tradition. That people early attributed necromantic powers to Drake in no way precludes the possibility that they may also have attributed benign powers to him.

Whatever may have governed the sensitivity of published material about Drake in his lifetime, the fact remains that neither then nor later have his life and achievements inspired any major work of literature. The writings that do survive about him seem to be inspired by something redolent of a "dying and reviving hero" myth; and here folk tradition appears to have played more than a supporting role. In this respect, Drake takes his place with other legendary figures like King Arthur, Charlemagne, Barbarossa, and many others whose deaths have seemed unacceptable because in life they embodied so much vitality and exercised so much influence on larger affairs. Despite the seeming indifference of the major poets to Drake, the memory that has been preserved somehow attaches him to the spirit of England's greatness and the fortunes of her survival. Perhaps that is why the nation keeps re-reviving him.

NOTES

1. There are only a few references to Drake in Hakluyt's *Divers voyages,* John W. Jones, ed., Hakluyt Society (London, 1850). In the first, Drake's name is listed in a chronology of travellers following the date, 1578 (p. 6). The other references allude to Drake's experiences on "the back side of America" (p. 12) and how Hakluyt tried to get Sir Francis Drake, "seeing God hath blessed him so wonderfully" (p. 16) to provide for a lecture in navigation (see Waters, ch. 2, above).

2. Some years ago I made this point in an analysis of the travel narratives of numerous voyages of the time ("The Literature of Travel and the Mode of Romance in the Renaissance," *Bulletin, New York Public Library* 67, no. 4., pp. 219–236). Later studies of the period suggest that this whole "heroicall" motif may have been part of a larger movement in Elizabeth's reign, on the part of courtiers, artists, and literary men, to revive the glamour of past chivalric ages, and thus distract the minds of Englishmen from more immediate political and social anxieties; see Roy Strong, *The Cult of Elizabeth: Elizabethan Portraiture and Pageantry* (London, 1977).

3. On the title page of *Sir Francis Drake revived* we are told that the ensuing narrative was "reviewed also by Sir Francis Drake himself, before his death; and much holpen and enlarged by divers notes, with his own hand, here and there inserted."

4. That is, Abraham Cowley. See *Works of the English Poets,* Vol. VII (London, 1790) p. 216.

5. See G. Lipscomb, *A Journey into Cornwall through the Counties of Southampton, Wiltshire, Dorset, Somerset and Devon* (London, 1799), p. 315. The sword is now kept at H.M.S. *Drake,* the shore base of the Royal Navy and Royal Marines in Plymouth. The drum remains at Buckland Abbey. A silver replica of the drum was presented to H.M.S. *Devonshire* in 1929, but in 1936 it was given to the Church of St. Nicholas in Devonport after the crew of the ship became convinced that the replica of the drum was responsible for a series of extraordinary misfortunes they experienced; see Edith M. R. Ditmas, *The Legend of Drake's Drum,* West Country Folk Lore Series no. 6, 1973, p. 12.

6. Quoted in Ditmas, *Legend of Drake's Drum,* pp. 11–12. This pamphlet, together with an article by Ditmas, "The Way Legends Grow," *Folklore* 85 (1974) 244–253, provides some useful information about Drake and folklore tradition.

7. The phrase is Foot's.

8. Lope de Vega claimed in 1598 that he had heard of Drake's occult powers from Spanish soldiers taken prisoner from the Armada, who had apparently heard of them from the Devonshire men who had guarded them as prisoners.

9. See Anna Elizabeth Bray, *Traditions, Legends, Superstitions and Sketches of Devonshire* (London, 1838), II, 168–174; Robert Southey, *English Seamen* 2nd. ed. (London, 1887); and Katherine Briggs, *Dictionary of British Folk Tales,* 1968, pt. B, I, 138–139, and II, 38–40.

The Cartography of
Drake's Voyage

HELEN WALLIS

And the 26. of Sept . . . we safely with ioyfull minds and thankfull hearts
to God, arriued at Plimoth, the place of our first setting forth after we
had spent 2. yeares 10. moneths. and some few odde dais beside, in seeing
the wonders of the Lord in the deep, in discouering so many admirable
things, in going through with so many strange aduentures, in escaping out
of so many dangers, and ouercomming so many difficulties in this our en-
compassing of this neather globe, and passing round the world.

The narrator in *The World Encompassed by Sir Francis Drake* (1628) described thus the day of the *Golden Hind's* return from the voyage around the
world, 1577–1580.[1] Within a week Queen Elizabeth had summoned Drake to
court, telling him to bring with him some specimens of his labors and not to fear
anything. Bernardino de Mendoza, the Spanish ambassador in London, reported on this visit to Philip II of Spain in an urgent despatch of 16 October
1580. He said that Drake had spent more than six hours with the Queen and
had presented her with "a diary of everything that had happened during the
three years and a very large map" (un diario de todo lo quele ha succedido en
los tres años y una gran carta).[2] Mendoza's letter, which was intercepted by the

English, provides the earliest record of the two prime documents of the voyage, Drake's journal and chart. The phrase "una gran carta" was mistranslated as "a very long letter" by the editor of the *Calendar of State Papers* in 1896. The significance of the reference was therefore overlooked until the misreading was corrected in 1977.[3] It is in fact the first record of Drake's chart, which was to become famous as one of the showpieces in the Palace of Whitehall.

PRIMARY SOURCES: CHARTS AND JOURNALS

The chronicler Samuel Purchas, introducing the third book of the second part of *Purchas his Pilgrimes* (1625), gives an eyewitness account of Drake's chart.[4] He must have seen it in or after 1618, when the account of the circumnavigation of the Dutchmen Willem Schouten and Jacob Le Maire was published. Commenting peevishly on Dutch claims to priority of discovery in "remotest Navigations," Purchas was prompted to advance (with some exaggeration) Drake's title to "the S. Streights called Maires" and the adjacent seas. Referring to the Dutch, he wrote:

> I adde their New Straights Southwards from those of Magelane were discovered by Drake, as in the Map of Sir Francis Drakes Voyage presented to Queene Elizabeth, still hanging in His Majesties Gallerie at White Hall, neere the Privie Chamber, and by that Map (wherein is Cabotas Picture, the first and great Columbus for the Northerne World) may be seene. In which Map, the South of the Magelane Straits is not a Continent, but many Ilands, and the very same which they have stiled in their Straits, Barnevels Ilands and long before beene named by the most auspicate of Earthly Names, and let themselves be Judges, with which the other is as little worthie to be mentioned, as a kind Mother, and an unkind Traitor. The Name Elizabeth is expressed in golden Letters, with a golden Crowne, Garter and Armes affixed: The words ascribed thereunto are these, Cum omnes ferè hanc partem Australem Continentem esse putent, pro certo sciant Insulas esse Navigantibus pervias, earumque australissimam Elizabetham à D. Francisco Draco Inventore dictam esse. The same height of 57. degrees, and South-easterly situation from the Magelan Westerne Mouth give further evidence. [The Latin inscription may be translated: Whereas almost everyone believes this to be part of the southern continent, they know for certain these islands to be passable by navigators, of which the most southerly island is named Elizabeth by its discoverer, Sir Francis Drake.]

Drake's chart thus had an honored place next to the world map of Sebastian Cabot of 1549. The two maps provided Englishmen of a less valiant age with a record of England's maritime triumphs under the Tudors. Purchas gives more information in a marginal note: "In the said Map is Queene Elizabeths Picture, with Neptune yielding his Trident, and Triton sounding her Fame, with these Verses: 'Te Deus aequor eus donat Regina Tridente, Et Triton Laudes efflat Ubique tuas.'" The fact that Purchas mentions Sebastian Cabot's portrait as being on Cabot's chart, and Elizabeth's portrait as being on Drake's, seems evidence by default that Drake's portrait was not displayed on his own chart; and there is other evidence to support this.

Two other manuscript maps of Drake's voyage were made, presumably as copies of the Queen's chart. Henry of Navarre, later Henry IV of France, wrote from Paris to Sir Francis Walsingham, Secretary of State, in March 1585, requesting the "collection" (presumably of charts) and the "discourse" of Drake's great voyage":

> Je vous prie par mesme moyen [through the agency of Jacques Ségur-Pardaithan, Henry's envoy to England] me maintenir en la bonne grace dune si tres excellente Royne & la prier de commander au cheualier de Drac de m'enouyer le recueil & discours de ce quil a remarqué en son grant voyaige duquel le djs^r de Segur ma parlé & qui m'est fort necessaire pour l'execution d'aucuns de mes desseins.[5]

A chart "diapré et doré" (many coloured and gilded) was sent to Paris in answer to the request.[6] It is also recorded that Drake presented to his friend the Archbishop of Canterbury (probably Edmund Grindel, 1519?–1583, archbishop from 1576 to 1583) a map of his voyage "richly decorated with coloured and gilded designs."[7] No trace of either map can be found.[8]

Drake's journal was a cartographic document. It was illustrated with drawings, including views and presumably maps, as Drake's Portuguese prisoner Nuno da Silva reported: "Francis Drake kept a book in which he entered his navigation and in which he delineated birds, trees and sea-lions. He is an adept in painting and has with him a boy, a relation of his, who is a great painter. When they both shut themselves up in his cabin they were always painting."[9] On Fenton's voyage, in 1582, William Hawkins and Simon Wood, both of whom had sailed on the circumnavigation, stated that Drake "went to his cabin at 8 a clok and wind or rayn never stird."[10] Another of Drake's prisoners, Don Francisco de Zárate, wrote: "He also carries painters who paint for him pictures of the coast in its exact colours. This I was most grieved to see, for each thing is so naturally depicted that no one who guides himself according to these paintings can possibly go astray."[11]

So far as we know, the only members of Drake's company who drew maps and painted pictures were Drake himself and his young cousin John Drake. The journal of Francis Fletcher, the chaplain, also contained maps and drawings, presumably copied from those of Francis and John Drake, although this remains a conjecture. Like the maps of Henry of Navarre and the archbishop, all the primary records of the voyage have disappeared.

Drake's chart probably perished in the fire which destroyed the Palace of Whitehall in January 1698. The journal was presumably still in the Queen's possession in 1585 when Henry of Navarre requested it. Lancelot Voisin, le Seigneur de la Popellinière, stated in *Les Trois Mondes* (1582) that the Queen had custody of Drake's records in order to prevent publication: "Toutesfois qu'elle garde les memoires de sa nauigation affin qu'ils ne soient publiez. Ie ne doute pointe que plusieurs ne luy persuadent de retenir telles instructions, affin quelles ne soient communiquees aux estrangers ny mesmes à ses suiets."[12]

The journal was evidently not available to Richard Hakluyt in 1589 when he prepared his account "The Famous Voyage" for *The Principall Navigations*. It is not known whether the Dutch artist Jodocus Hondius, an émigré in London, had access to it (or to Drake's map) when from 1589 onward he was engraving the terrestrial globe of Emery Molyneux, published in 1592, and at the same time preparing his own map of Drake's voyage, issued in England ca. 1590. It is doubtful that Drake himself was able to consult his journal. In a letter to the Queen dated 1 January 1592 (1593), printed by Philip Nichols in *Sir Francis Drake Revived* (1626), he reported that he was planning to publish the narrative of his voyages in order to correct the misrepresentations already printed. We can assume that his sources for the compilation (which was probably to be made by a writer on his behalf, as D. B. Quinn conjectures) did not include the journal.[13] It was not available to Drake's nephew, Sir Francis Drake, Bart., when he prepared *The World Encompassed* for publication in 1628. Referring to the journal's "irreparable loss," Zelia Nuttall commented:

> The precious journal, if not already lost, was at all events inaccessible in 1628, else Drake's nephew, namesake and heir, would not have "offered now at last to publique view both for the honour of the actor . . . and for the stirring up of heroick spirits" the narrative of the voyage *"carefully collected out of the notes of Master Francis Fletcher* which he published as *The World Encompassed by Sir Francis Drake.*"[14]

There is at least one seventeenth-century reference to "Drake's Journal," but what it meant is not clear. Samuel Pepys wrote in his *Naval Minutes*: "Obtain of Mr. Evelyn his History of the late Sea War . . . and Sir Francis Drake's Journal, which he says he has and promised to look up for me."[15] Whatever this was, it is not to be found today in the Pepys Library at Magdalene College, Cambridge, despite J. R. Tanner's editorial note to the contrary. The loss of the journal with its graphic records explains why many problems concerning Drake's voyage remain unsolved.

Illustrated "rutters" (books of sailing directions, normally illustrated with views) were an accepted type of maritime record dating back to the fifteenth century. The Portuguese were skilled in the technique of making rutters, as illustrated by two manuscripts, the "Book of Francisco Rodriques," MS, ca. 1513, and the *roteiros* of the Red Sea by João de Castro, MS, 1540–41. French hydrographers of the so-called Dieppe School, who were much influenced by the Portuguese, followed the same practice. The name "painter" was given to a man who sailed on maritime expeditions as artist and map maker. Besides making profiles of the coast, a favorite device of these men was to draw "bird's-eye views" of the coast as seen from the ship. This would produce, in style, a map and view combined.

A coincidence should be mentioned here. On the expedition to Nombre de Dios in 1573, Drake had met and joined forces with the pilot Guillaume le Testu of Le Havre, who died on the expedition. Le Testu was one of the most accomplished French "painters" and map makers of the Norman school, and author of an illustrated "Cosmographie Universelle," 1556 (1557). Drake may perhaps have learned something of the marine arts from le Testu during their short association.

However that may be, Drake by 1577 had evidently become convinced of the importance of drawings as a record of navigation. There are various references to a French painter being taken on the voyage around the world, but this may arise from a misunderstanding about the nature of the "Huth Journal," another manuscript associated with Drake. On Drake's West Indian voyage, 1585–86, Baptista Boazio, page to Lieutenant General Christopher Carleill, acted as draftsman and mapmaker and was responsible for the maps illustrating the *Summarie and true discourse of Sir Francis Drakes West Indian Voyage* (1589).[16] On Drake's last voyage, his expedition to the West Indies in 1595–96, he ensured that all the principal landfalls should be recorded in color by a "painter." The illustrated rutter is preserved along with other English manuscripts in the Bibliothèque Nationale in Paris (Manuscript Anglais 51). It may previously have been in the collection of the Flemish diplomat Henri-Florent Laurin de la Haye, whose portrait is pasted to the flyleaf.[17] The drawings of coastal profiles and descriptive texts of this manuscript give precise details of the hydrography of places visited, and in particular they record the approaches to harbors, the setting of currents, the depth of water, and the nature of the seabed.

If Drake's journal included such details for the Pacific coast of America, it is no wonder Zárate considered its future use by Englishmen a serious danger to Spain. In the seventeenth century the Spaniards themselves used as their main navigational aid to the South Sea rutters or waggoners, as the English called them, of the west coast of America, and they treated them as highly secret documents. Spanish rutters were great prizes, and in the 1680s those captured by English buccaneers were copied by English hydrographers (notably William Hack) of the so-called Thames or Drapers' Company School and presented to royal persons and members of the nobility. The views which they display of places along the coasts of Mexico, Peru, and Chile provide the best record of the towns Drake attacked and spoiled—except that, as a result of Drake's raids, the towns were now fortified.

Francis Fletcher's journal must have given a good impression of the drawings in Drake's journal, but this too has disappeared. It is known from the copy made in 1677 by John Conyers, "pharmocopolist" of London.[18] Only the first part of the voyage is transcribed (fig. 9:1). The manuscript, which was acquired by Sir Hans Sloane for his collection (British Library, Sloane MS 61), is inscribed on folio 1: "ex libris Joh. Conyers Pharmocopolyst. Memorandum hacklyts Voyages of Fletcher." The map on folio 2 bears the caption: "This a

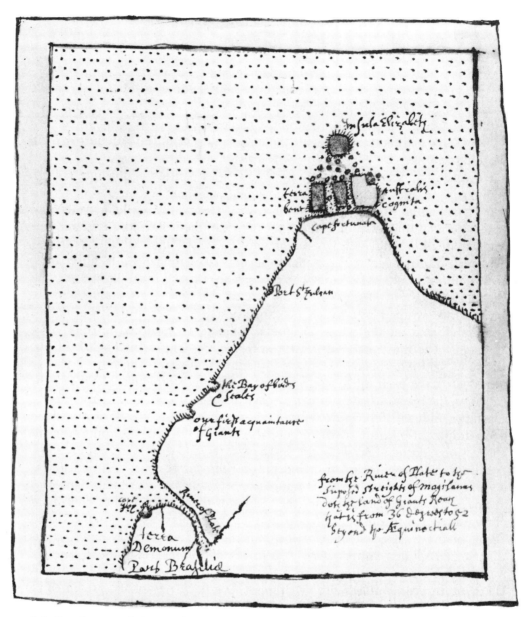

9.1 Sketch map of the southern extremity of South America, by Francis Fletcher, Sloane MS 61, fol. 35r. Courtesy of The British Library.

Mapp of England an Exact Coppy with the Originall to a haire: that don by Francis Fletcher in queen Elizabeths tyme this copyed by Jo: Conyers Cittizen & Apothecary of London together with the rest and by the same hand as Follows." The title of the manuscript (folio 3) reads: "The first part of the second voiage about the world attempted continued and happily accomplished within the tyme of 3 yeares by Mr Francis Drake at her highness commaund &

his company written & faithfully layed down by Francis Fletcher Minister of Christ & Preacher of the Gospell adventurer & traueler in the same voyage."

The text ends on folio 43, taking the voyage to the island of Mocha, which Drake visited in November 1578. Fletcher completed the narrative of this first part with the statement (squeezed by Conyers onto the bottom of folio 41v):

> of this Valdivia you shall heare more in the second part of this navigation about the world wth which I will attempt to finish wth all convenient speed I may & thus I end this first part of this Trauaile wth description & mapp of the Iland of Mucho & the forme & the monuments w^che I made to have ben sett up uppon the Southermost Cape of America att the entering into the Sowth Sea but could not as hath been said.[19]

An illustration of "Mucho Insula" follows (folio 42r), then a short discourse on the "giants" of Patagonia in the same hand, beginning "now as the transcriber may here make inquiry why som (in these dayes vizt 1677) may accoumpt the stoarye of these Giants fabulous" (folio 43r). The wording of the text shows that Fletcher was the author of the main narrative of the voyage, and also of comments made after the voyage, notably on Thomas Cavendish's circumnavigation (1586–1588), which some scholars have thought might be Conyers' interpolations.[20] Conyers, who generally referred to himself in the third person as "the transcriber," added the section on giants (folio 43r). Blank pages follow.

It is not known what happened to Fletcher's original journal after Conyers had copied it, or whether Fletcher went on to complete the second part of his text, which was evidently made as a compilation after the voyage. A complete version must have existed, for it was the source of *The World Encompassed* in 1628. The blank pages in Sloane MS 61 suggest that Conyers did not complete his transcript with the second part of the journal, perhaps because he did not possess it. It is possible that more clues may be found through investigating the life and activities of Conyers himself. He was well known in Royal Society circles and was a friend of the society's Secretary, Robert Hooke, who records visits to Conyers in his diary, 1674 to 1676. On 27 May 1674, Hooke writes "At Mr. Coniers, Apothecarys in Fleet Street. Saw some stones of his Collection . . . ." Other visits occurred on 28 May 1674 and 28 March 1676.[21]

The disappearance of Fletcher's original manuscript makes Conyers' copy, Sloane MS 61, one of the most important sources for the voyage. The drawings copied by Conyers from Fletcher are (at third hand) a record of the sketches and maps drawn by Drake and his cousin John. Conyers made careful notes on his maps to show how they differed in size from the originals. Some were enlarged, presumably in order to fill the page. A caption beneath the map of the island of Mayo (folio 6v) reads: "This Coppy here much larger than the Originalle viz. deeper." The map of the island of Santiago in the Cape Verde Islands (folio 8) is certified: "Vera Copia J. Conyers." None of the maps has a scale or indication of latitude and longitude. Fletcher had included a sketch map of England as a guide to the relative size of the southern part of South America from 36°S to 52°S, as the caption notes. Conyers therefore made two copies of the map of

South America, one exact (folio 19r), and the other enlarged (folio 34r), as he explains:

> this scheame below & that of England at the beginning of the booke being both I suppose made by one scale may serve for a Paterne to the bignes I suppose of other Ilands here described by the transcriber but not with that exactness as this here & that of England at the beginning is by which the rest may be adjusted wch is only a Caution & the original being exactly to a haire with this & that of England therfore this is twise inserted the other of these in the Place of being larger than the originall must be considered accordingly.

The words "John Conyers Apothecary" follow but have been crossed out.

A second document which has been regarded, mistakenly, as Drake's journal is the Huth manuscript.[22] This work contains some material relating to the circumnavigation. A title added in the eighteenth century reads: "Histoire Naturelle des Indes: contenant Les Arbres, Plantes, Fruits, Animaux, Coquillages, Reptiles, Insectes, Oyseaux, &c, qui se trouvent dans les Indes; représentés par les Figures peintes en couleur naturelle; comme aussi les différentes manières de vivre des Indiens; savoir: La Chasse, La Pêche, &c. avec des explications historiques." On 15 November 1911 the manuscript was put on sale by Messrs. Sotheby, Williamson, and Hodge as lot 144 in "the famous library of Printed Books, Illuminated Manuscripts [and so on] collected by Henry Huth."[23] It is described as comprising two hundred watercolor drawings on 121 leaves of the natural history, manners, and customs of the inhabitants of Peru and other parts of South America.

A fuller account was given in 1928 by the owner then, C. F. G. R. Schwerdt, who had acquired the manuscript as part of his collection of books, manuscripts, prints, and drawings on the subject of hunting, hawking, and shooting. The "illustrated manuscript (c. 1586) describing one of Sir Francis Drake's Voyages," as Schwerdt records it, was one of two items outside the limits assigned to his theme but was included because of its paramount interest.[24]

Bernard Quaritch, writing in 1867, had supposed the manuscript to have been written by a Frenchman who had accompanied Drake on his voyages to the South Seas and Florida. This is explained by a comment of the French translator in his preface of dedication to a Baron de Courtomer. He mentions that he had made his account at the insistence of the baron, who had informed him that one of his tenants had been with Drake during the voyage.[25] Two illustrations refer to Drake, one derived from the circumnavigation (folio 43).[26] It illustrates a "Canau de la Mer du Sus" and has the following caption:

Ce Canau est de la Mer du Sus
Dune Ille nommee gilolo en laquelle
Franscique Drac englois fit nettoier
Son navire pour parfaire son navire
Et voyage de la mer du Sus.

The drawing shows a chief of "Gilolo" under an awning in the canoe, which is manned by two ranks of eleven rowers (one is obscured by the chief). The word "cacique" is written on the canoe, indicating the ruler of Ternate, Sultan Babu, who sailed in ceremonial state to greet the *Golden Hind*. Gilolo was evidently a mistake for Ternate.

The other drawing associated with Drake is "Hinde de Loranbec" (folio 92r), showing an Indian hunting. The text mentions Drake being in 36.5°N on the coast between Florida and Newfoundland in 1586, which suggests that this is a reference to the Roanoke colony, whence Drake brought home 103 settlers in June 1586. It is not certain that the drawings in the manuscript were by the Frenchman who wrote the text, as the titles under the pictures are reported to be in a different ink and hand from the text.[27] A full investigation of the manuscript, now in private hands in the United States, has not yet been made.

DRAKE'S DISCOVERIES

Drake achieved the second circumnavigation of the globe. He was the first commander and the first Englishman to make the circuit. He brought back remarkable graphic records of the voyage, a fact which became widely known. He made two major geographical discoveries, the first in the far south of the American continent, the second in its remote northwest. By showing Tierra del Fuego to be an archipelago and not part of the southern continent Terra Australis, he pushed the continent to the south, revealing open sea beyond and a new passage to the Pacific. Thitherto the only known way around the world had been through the Strait of Magellan. Two maps of the southern part of South America in Fletcher's journal (Sloane MS 61, folios 19r, 35r) illustrate the discovery. Fletcher gives the islands on the south side of the Strait of Magellan the ironic epithet "Terra australis bene cognita" (see fig. 9:1). The southernmost island of the group is "Insula Elizabethae." Here Drake with typical panache made an act of possession on behalf of Queen Elizabeth, prostrating himself at its southernmost point, as Sir Richard Hawkins recounted:

> going ashore, [he] carried a Compasse with him, and seeking out the Southermost part of the Iland, cast himselfe downe upon the uttermost poynt groveling, and so reached out his bodie over it. Presently he im-barked, and then recounted unto his people, that he had beene upon the Southermost knowne land in the world, and more further to the South-wards upon it, then any of them, yea, or any man as yet knowne.[28]

Fletcher reported that Drake set up a monument recording the event (figure 9:2).[29]

At the opposite end of the continent, on the northwest coast of America, Drake discovered beyond California the land which he named Nova Albion, with its fine harbor in 38°N, Portus Novae Albionis, where he stayed for five weeks from 17 June to 23 July 1579. Here too he made a formal act of

The Description of Elizabeth Iland

This Iland Broader, deeper then the Originall: vizt: |......|

9.2 Francis Fletcher's map of Elizabeth Island (probably Henderson Island, 55°36′S), Sloane MS 61, fol. 39. Courtesy of The British Library.

possession for Queen Elizabeth, after a ceremony in which the Indians of the region crowned him, apparently yielding their sovereignty. How far north Drake sailed in his search for the western entrance to the Northwest Passage around North America remains a matter of debate. The anonymous account gives 48°N, but the map evidence varies between 43°N and 48°N. The numbers 3 and 8 may have been confused in the reading of one of the manuscripts, or perhaps there was an attempt to suppress the fact that Drake had sailed to 48°N. One of the most authoritative pieces of cartographic evidence, Molyneux's terrestrial globe of 1592, supports the more northerly limit (see fig. 9:11 below).

Although these were the two outstanding discoveries of Drake's voyage, others he made in the Pacific were considered worthy of record. One was a correction to the shape of South America. Drake found that the coast of Chile extended northeast not northwest, and thus he disproved the existence of the bulge shown on Spanish and Dutch maps of South America. Fletcher accused the Spaniards of a deliberate falsehood: "Wee following the directions of the comon Mapps of the Spanyards were utterly deceaued for of a Malitious Purpose they had set forth the mapp false that they might deceave strangers if anny gave the attempt to trauail that way that they might perish by Running ofe to the sea rather than Touch with anny part of the land of America."[30] These suspicions were unfounded. The error arose from the navigators' difficulty in establishing longitude and the chartmakers' problem in compiling maps from charts with coastlines shown in widely different positions.[31]

The voyage across the Pacific from Nova Albion to Guam revealed the great width of the ocean. Ortelius' world map "Typus Orbis Terrarum," 1570 (fig. 9:3), has 110 degrees of longitude between the Cape of California and Malacca, whereas the Molyneux globe of 1592 and Edward Wright's map of 1599 show 120 degrees. In the East Indies Drake was the first to discover and navigate the south coast of Java, with its port, identified as Tjilatjap (see Lessa, ch. 5, above).

The errors which Drake uncovered on the maps and charts he had with him illustrate the paucity of good charts at the time and the difficulties of these remote navigations. He probably carried a copy of Ortelius' world map published at Antwerp in 1564 since this was known in London in the 1560s. Sir Humphrey Gilbert copied it in reduced form to illustrate his *Discourse of a Discoverie for a New Pasage to Cataia* (written in 1566, published in 1576), and it is notable as the earliest English printed world map now extant (figure 9:4). A world chart is said to have been made for Drake in Lisbon for use on his voyage, and this is conjectured to have been done by Fernão Vaz Dourado, whose maritime atlases survive in a number of examples.[32] Lacking adequate charts for his voyage, Drake took every opportunity to commandeer the services of pilots and to make use of their charts. Mendoza's account of Drake's interview with the Queen includes this statement: "Drake asserts that had it not been for two Portuguese pilots whom he took from one of the ships he plundered and sunk on the coast of Brazil on his way out, he could never have made the voyage." Nuno da Silva in his sworn deposition said of Drake: "On capturing vessels, the first things that he seized were the navigation charts, the astrolabes, compasses and needles, which he cast into the sea without making any use of them" (the final comment must refer only to the compasses and needles).[33] After he had taken Nuno da Silva's chart of the Rio de la Plata and the Cape of Good Hope, he had it translated into English.

From the *não del plata*, the silver ship, Drake seized "two pilots of the China seas" with all their sea charts and papers. One of them, Alonso Sánchez Colchero, was ordered to conduct Drake on the China route, but he managed to secure a release.[34] Referring to the route of the Lima ships, Nuno da Silva reported: "This Francis Drake is well acquainted with this route, having learnt everything about it from all the pilots whom he captured, there not being a single thing about which he did not inform himself."[35]

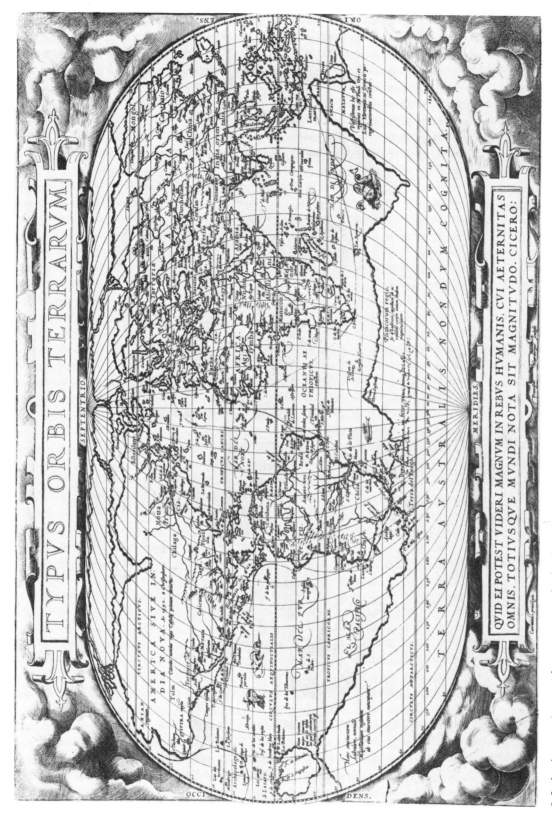

9.3 An impression, without text on the back, of the world map in the *Theatrum Orbis Terrarum* of Abraham Ortelius, Antwerp, 1579. The track of Drake's voyage and a note on the discovery and naming of Insulae Elizabethae, to the south of Tierra del Fuego, are added in the manuscript. Courtesy of The British Library.

9.4 World map showing the Northwest Passage to China as advocated by Sir Humphrey Gilbert in *A Discourse of a Discouerie for a New Passage to Cataia,* London, 1576. Courtesy of The British Library.

A POLICY OF SECRECY

Drake returned to England with many charts, sketches, and pictures from which a new and greatly improved map of the world could be made. The paradox of the voyage was that his feat of navigation and his discoveries were kept concealed. Only the inner circle of backers and the Queen's ministers were allowed to share the secrets revealed to the Queen. Even the fact that he had sailed round the world was not disclosed, as we learn from Mendoza's secret despatches. Mendoza had informants at court who kept him apprised of every report and rumor. His dispatch of 16 October 1580 included further gleanings: the Queen's councillors, Lord Burghley and his colleagues, together with Robert Dudley, Earl of Leicester, Sir Christopher Hatton, and Sir Francis Walsingham—the principal promoters of the venture—"are very particular not to divulge the route by which Drake returned, and although, as I wrote to your Majesty, Hatton's trumpeter had said that the road home had been by the Portuguese Indies, Drake himself signifies to the contrary." Mendoza added that Drake's men "are not to disclose the route they took, on pain of death. Drake affirms, that he will be able to make the round voyage in a year, as he has found a very short way." This led to the mistaken conclusion that Drake must have returned by the Strait of Magellan.

The reason for the policy of secrecy was political: the Queen was anxious to conceal the nature of Drake's privateering activities, which had secured for the

Crown and the adventurers a booty amounting to more than ten tons of silver bullion, as well as 101 pounds of gold and other treasures.

The fact that as early as October 1580 a new expedition was being planned to exploit Drake's discoveries was a further reason for secrecy. "He is arranging to return with six ships," Mendoza reported of Drake; "at present there is hardly an Englishman who is not talking of undertaking the voyage, so encouraged are they by Drake's return." Projects for usurping the Portuguese trade with the Moluccas and for more raids to plunder Spanish colonies in the Pacific were variously considered as the entrepreneurs vied with one another in their heady plans for overseas adventure. The union of the Spanish and Portuguese crowns in 1581 provided an added incentive for the prosecution of any project which would diminish the power of Philip II, now astride two empires.

First Drake was to lead an expedition to the Azores and thence to the Caribbean in December 1580. Then, as Mendoza reported on 6 April 1581, "it is decided that Drake himself shall not go, although, no doubt, he has arranged the matter through other hands in order that he may not be too conspicuous."[36] A second enterprise was proposed, this time for trade in spices on the Malabar coast of India. When this in turn fell through, a third enterprise, organized by the Earl of Leicester, with Drake as adviser, did finally materialize. Three ships set off in May 1582 under the command of Edward Fenton. John Drake, the young cousin who served as Drake's page on the circumnavigation, sailed as captain of the bark Drake sponsored, the *Francis*. Ostensibly this was a trading voyage to the Moluccas by way of the Strait of Magellan. In fact, it was alleged, probably correctly, that the voyage had been bought and sold by Fenton to the Spaniards before the ships sailed.[37] Fenton turned back from Brazil before he had reached the Strait of Magellan. John Drake defected from the expedition, hoping to continue the voyage alone. The *Francis* was wrecked as she tried to leave the River Plate. John Drake, captured by Spaniards, reached Lima in 1587, facing a lifetime in enforced exile. Despite the failure of Fenton's expedition, Drake in company with Hawkins and Leicester was still planning a voyage to the Moluccas in 1584. Again nothing came of it, and his interests turned to the West Indies. The successful voyage which followed Drake's expedition was that of Thomas Cavendish, who sailed through the Strait of Magellan and around the world in 1586–88.

With such ventures in prospect or in progress, and hopes of plunder never far below the surface, Drake's geographical discoveries not only remained secret but seemed somewhat irrelevant. Mendoza himself did not learn until April 1582 the secret of Drake's major geographical discovery, the fact that Tierra del Fuego was not part of the southern continent but an archipelago with open sea beyond. Referring also to John Winter, captain of the *Elizabeth*, who had separated from Drake and sailed home in 1578–79, Mendoza reported this new intelligence in a letter of 20 April 1582.

That the straits are really formed by islands is proved by what happened to Winter . . . which made cosmographers here think that Winter had not entered the straits at all. Although he affirmed that the straits were formed by islands, he was not believed until Drake himself returned, who has not explained the secret to any one but some of the councillors and the chiefs of this expedition who placed before him the danger which would be run by sending these ships whilst your Majesty had so large a fleet in the Straits of Magellan. Drake replied "So much the better; as they were thus assured that your Majesty's vessels would stay there and keep guard to prevent anyone entering the South Sea," but, after all, they would find themselves deceived, as it was not continent but only very large islands, and there was the open sea beyond Tierra del Fuego. The person who has given me this statement, although he saw Drake's chart and has discussed it with him, does not understand navigation and cosmography sufficiently to tell me exactly the degrees of latitude, but only asserts the point that the land consists of islands and not continent.[38]

Despite Drake's hint that the expedition could use the new route around Tierra del Fuego, there was no plan for Fenton in 1582 to take advantage of it and thus to avoid any Spanish ships waiting in the Strait. The chart shown to Mendoza's informant was probably Drake's sketch of the Strait of Magellan which Fenton's men took with them. Richard Madox, who kept the records of Fenton's voyage, wrote in his secret diary:

The charts and plans are taken out, even the drafts so that examining all arguments we might more easily ascertain in what place we are. We examined, as it happened, the sketch of the Straits of Magellan which that golden knight of ours who had once passed through had made. Then the question arises by what art or industry he could express so vividly all the islands he had drawn there or decide for certain that they were so situated when he had gone through the Straits within the space of only seventeen days and for eight days had been sedulously struggling with much circuitousness and many windings to round one single cape. His companions confess to having seen certain gaps in the land and long recesses of the sea, and thence they surmise that it had been some such thing. But I am convinced that that Drake of ours either found some kind of draft among the Portuguese or Spaniards and thus put forth their little commentaries as his own or I believe him to be a man who cast off all shame and dared boldly to determine things unknown and to present them to her majesty as explored and already claimed. Either of these things should be reproved.[39]

Marginal notes in cipher read: "Sir Francis Drak cards fals," and "his theft of the portingale [charts]."

The sketch of the Strait of Magellan was probably similar to one of the two maps of the southern part of South America in Fletcher's journal. It is significant that there was already doubt about Drake's claimed discoveries even though he was a promoter of and consultant for this voyage. Another of Madox's anecdotes adds a further gloss to the confused picture of Drake's doings. On 15 March 1582 Madox, before he sailed, was introduced by his friend Cyprian Lucar, the mathematician, to a certain John Ashley, who was preparing beads and other devices for trade to be used on Sir Humphrey Gilbert's voyage to Newfoundland in 1582. "He told me that he thowght to se when a letter dated at London the first of May shold be delyvered at China before midsomer folowing *et econtra* for he avowched upon report as he sayd of the Yndians that ther was a saylable passage over America between 43 and 46 degrees throe which he sayd Sir Frances Drak cam home from the Moluccas."[40]

Although rumors of Drake's discoveries were circulating, a strict control of the graphic and written records was successfully enforced. As J. G. Kohl surmised, it appears that

> the instructions given to Francis Drake were the same as those given later by the Lords of Council to M. Fenton, one being: "18.Item: you shall give straight order to restraine that none shall make any charts or descriptions of the said voyage but such as shall be deputed by you the Generall; which said charts and descriptions we think meete that you, the Generall, shall take into your hands at your return to this our coast of England, leaving with them no copie, and to present them unto us at your return; the like to be done, if they find any charts or maps in those countries.[41]

A further prohibition of any publication giving details of the route and reports of the discoveries appears to have been in force until at least 1588, the "Annus Mirabilis" when the Armada was defeated. "Bookes, pictures and ballads" were published in Drake's praise, as Edmund Howes recorded,[42] but none gave any geographical information. The earliest printed "celebration" of the voyage now known ("account" would imply a more factual record) was *A Discourse in commendation of the valiant as vertuous minded Gentleman, Maister Frauncis Drake . . .*, by Nicholas Breton, a poet and writer, and it was written and published before Drake's knighting on 14 April 1581. Breton refers in cryptic terms to Drake's achievement: "Our Countrey man hath gone rounde about the whole world." He also wrote that Drake had found "the Land where Treasure lyes, the way to come by it and honor by the getting of it." Breton omitted the name of the land in question.[43]

The navigator William Borough, who sailed as Drake's vice admiral on the expedition to Cadiz in 1587, praised Drake's circumnavigation in the preface (dated 26 September 1581) to *A Discours of the Variation of the Cumpas*, published in 1581: "till now at length our Countrieman Sir Francis Drake for valorous attempt, prudent proceadying, of fortunate performyng his voiage about the worlde, is not onely become equall to anie of them, but in fame farre surmounteth them all."[44]

The secrecy, the rumors, and the false reports perplexed serious geographers and made them suspicious. In a letter of 12 December 1580 Gerard Mercator wrote to Ortelius, thanking him for the despatch about the new English voyage on which you have previously sent me a report through Rumold [Mercator's son]. . . . I am persuaded that there can be no reason for so carefully concealing the course followed during this voyage, nor for putting out differing accounts of the route taken and the areas visited, other than that they may have found very wealthy regions never yet discovered by Europeans, not even by those who have sailed the Ocean on the Indies voyages.[45]

Drake thus entered the ranks of the great explorers and navigators in a very different way from that of his predecessors. Columbus had hastened to report his discoveries of 1492. A Latin edition of his letter to the Treasurer of Aragon "concerning the islands lately discovered in the Sea of India," *De insulis nuper inuentis,* was published in 1493, and an edition illustrated with woodcuts (the earliest representations of the New World) appeared in 1494. The account of Magellan's voyage (completed after his death by Juan Sebastián de Elcano), 1519–22, was publicized in the printed version of a letter from Maximilian of Transylvania, Secretary to the Emperor, to his father the Cardinal-Archbishop of Salzburg. The letter, dated from Valladolid 22 October 1522, was printed at Rome in November 1523 and at Cologne in January 1524 under the title *De Moluccis Insulis.* The much fuller account of the voyage written by Antonio Pigafetta was produced in four manuscript copies, one in Italian and three in French, presumably for four different patrons. A French version was printed in Paris and appeared sometime between 1526 and 1536. Richard Eden's edition of 1555, or the later Willes edition of Eden, was one of the books Drake took with him on the voyage.

Drake was, in comparison, a hero without a true history. Le Seigneur de la Popellinière commented shrewdly on the disadvantages of the policy of secrecy:

> Mais ie ne sçay, s'ils ont grande raison de ce faire: car la communication, ne peut estre qu'à l'honneur de sa nation, si elles sont telles que les autres peuples en puissent tirer profit ou quelque commodité. Et au rebouts un desdain et mal contentement que tous et mesmement ceux qui desirent voyager en recevront contre tels qui leur envient ce bien.[46]

National pride was ill served by such a policy. Claims of priority of discovery have to be made in good time to gain general recognition.

HAKLUYT'S PUBLICATIONS

Despite the policy of secrecy, Richard Hakluyt, as editor, saw to it that Drake's discoveries were recorded on two printed maps of the period. Hakluyt was promoting the publication of works on English and foreign ventures overseas, and he arranged that Drake's discoveries be added to two maps illustrating these works, but without attribution. One was Michael Lok's map of North America, published in Hakluyt's *Divers Voyages touching the discouerie of*

9.5 The Drake-Mellon world map (manuscript), drawn after 1586. Courtesy of Yale Center for British Art, Paul Mellon Collection. (See text on page 141.)

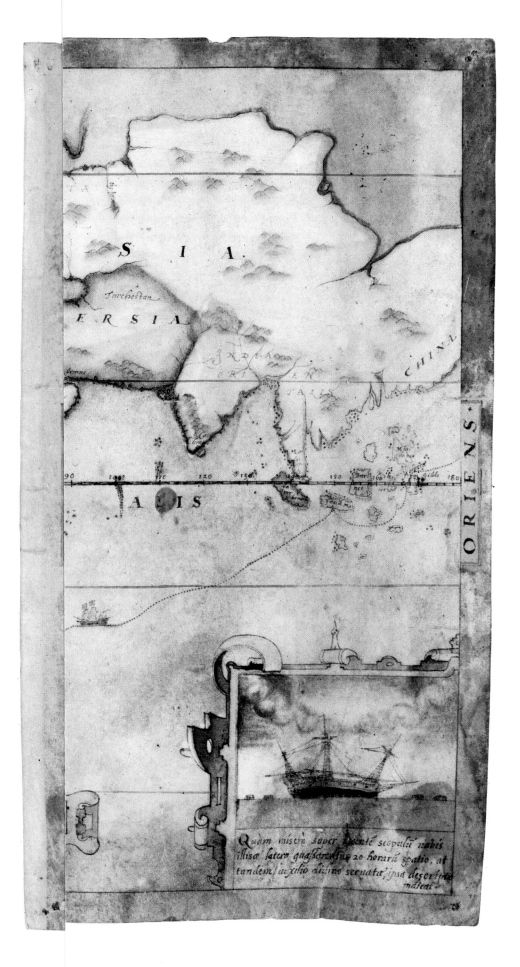

TATA

SIA

Turchestan

ERSIA

INDIA
ORIEN

CHINA

Ormus

90   100   110   120   130   140   150   180

ORIENS

A IS

Quam miseri super vicente scopulu nabis
illisa latere quassereusti 20 horaru spatio, at
tandem auxilio diuino seruata, ipsa descriptio
indicat

America (London, 1582). Lok was a leading advocate for the discovery of a northwest passage to Asia and a promoter of Frobisher's three expeditions, 1576–78, in search of it.

Lok also possessed an "olde excellent mappe" which Verrazzano had given to Henry VIII. This showed "a little necke of land" in 40°N, the characteristic feature of Verrazzanian cartography. Lok depicted this on his own map as a narrow isthmus between the Atlantic Ocean and "Mare de Verrazana, 1524," a gulf of the Pacific. The south coast of this sea trends west to "Sierra Neuada," off which a ship ("nauis") is drawn. The legend against the coast listing the voyages to the region ends "Anglorum [navigationes] 1580." This is the first record of Drake's voyage on a printed map.

The text of the book, unlike the map, names Drake in reference to the voyage. "Francis Drake Englishman" appears under 1578 in the list of "names of certaine late trauaylers," and his discoveries "on the back side of America" are noted as encouraging to the hope of finding a northwest passage to Asia. Hakluyt also reveals that he had discussed with Drake his project of establishing in London a lecture on the art of navigation. He should therefore have been able to obtain information about the voyage from Drake. If so, Drake was vague in his report, or the report became garbled, for both of Hakluyt's maps give the wrong dates for the discovery of the islands of Tierra del Fuego and of Nova Albion: that is, 1579 and 1580 instead of 1578 and 1579.

Hakluyt's other map was of America, entitled "Novus orbis," and he used it to illustrate his 1587 edition of Peter Martyr's celebrated work *Decades of the New World* (fig. 9.6). The map was engraved by "P.G.," probably Philipp (or Filips) Galle; the initials "P.G." appear in the border and the Latin inscription reads "F. G. S." (Filips Galle Sculptor?) It is dedicated to Hakluyt and was printed in Paris.[47] This map ranks as one of the best depictions of America for its day, as a comparison with Lok's map shows; and the choice of a prime meridian through Toledo may suggest a Spanish source, among other possibilities. Hakluyt presumably provided information on Drake's voyage to the engraver. The islands of Tierra del Fuego are depicted in detail, somewhat as on the Drake-Mellon and the Van Sype maps, with the attached legend "Ins. Reginae Elizabethae 1579 ab Anglis," beyond which there is open sea. The bold outline of the northwest coast of North America ends in 50°N and carries the legend "Nova Albion inventa an. 1580 ab Anglis."

That Hakluyt's discretion about Drake's discoveries reflected government policy is confirmed by intelligence sent from Paris, where Hakluyt worked from 1583 to 1588 as chaplain and secretary to Sir Edward Stafford, resident English ambassador to France. Stafford wrote to Walsingham on 16 October 1584: "I find from 'Mr. Haklitt' that Drake's journey is kept very secret in England, but here is in everyone's mouth. When questioned about it, I have answered as an ignorant body, as indeed I am, except for what I find by their speeches here. It may [be] they hit not all right, but they guess at great part."[48]

When the defeat of Spain in 1588 brought to an end the need for discretion in the publication of Drake's discoveries, Hakluyt provided the first narrative

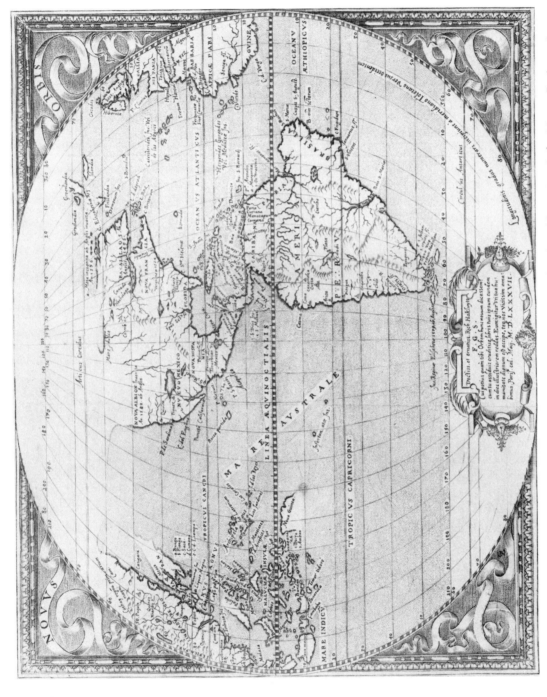

9.6 Map of the Americas engraved by "P. G." (Philipp Galle), in Richard Hakluyt, *De Orbe Novo*, Paris, 1587. Courtesy of The British Library.

account of the voyage. "The famous voyage of Sir Francis Drake into the South Sea, and there hence about the whole Globe of the Earth" appeared in six unnumbered leaves between pages 643 and 644 in Hakluyt's one-volume collection *The Principall Navigations, Voiages and Discoveries of the English Nation, made by Sea or over Land* (London, 1589). Hakluyt decided to include this account at the last minute when the *Principall Navigations* was almost ready for publication. He explained in the preface that he had first intended to insert an account of the voyage but then had been, "contrary to my expectations, seriously delt withall, not to anticipate or prevent another mans paines and charge in drawing all the services of that worthy knight into one volume." The projected volume was not published, and it can be conjectured that the would-be author was John Stow, in whose collections are preserved two of Hakluyt's main manuscript sources: John Cooke's narrative (Harley MS 540, folios 93–110) and the "Anonymous Narrative" (Harley MS 280, folios 83–90). Presumably Hakluyt had access also to Fletcher's manuscript. It might be expected that Hakluyt would have illustrated the *Principall Navigations* with a map of Drake's discoveries because he had indicated them on the two maps of America in his earlier publications. Instead, he contented himself (to use his own words) "with inserting into the worke, one of the best generall mapes of the world onely, until the comming out of a . . . terrestriall Globe . . . composed by M. Emmerie Mollineux." The general map was a copy of a world map engraved for Abraham Ortelius in 1587, and it included none of Drake's discoveries. As D. B. Quinn has remarked, the *Principall Navigations* of 1589 "had to float on its sea of words alone."

MAPS DERIVED FROM THE QUEEN'S MAP

It is probable that Drake's map was not put on public view in 1589. Only Purchas records it, and much later. From his account it is possible to identify three maps as derived versions made in the 1580s, or not later than 1590, probably as unauthorized copies.

A manuscript map (24 × 25 cm) now known as the Drake-Mellon map appears to be the closest copy of the Queen's map because its legend about Drake's discovery of islands south of America, the most southerly of them Elizabeth Island, follows almost word for word that text as recorded by Purchas (fig. 9.5). The title of the map runs: "Vera descriptio expeditionis nauticae, Francisco Draci Angli, cognitis aurati, qui quinque decimo Decembris An M.D.LXXVII, terraru[m] orbis ambitum circumnavigans, unica tantu[m] naui reliqua (alijs fluctibus, alijs flamina correptis) redux factus, sexto supra Vegesimo Sep. 1580."[49] The fact that the map not only displays the track of the *Golden Hind* around the world, but also illustrates Drake's route and activities on his West Indian voyage of 1585–86, shows that it was drawn not earlier than 1586–87. Its insets illustrate two incidents of the voyage in the Eastern Archipelago: Drake's arrival at the island of Ternate in the Moluccas and the *Golden*

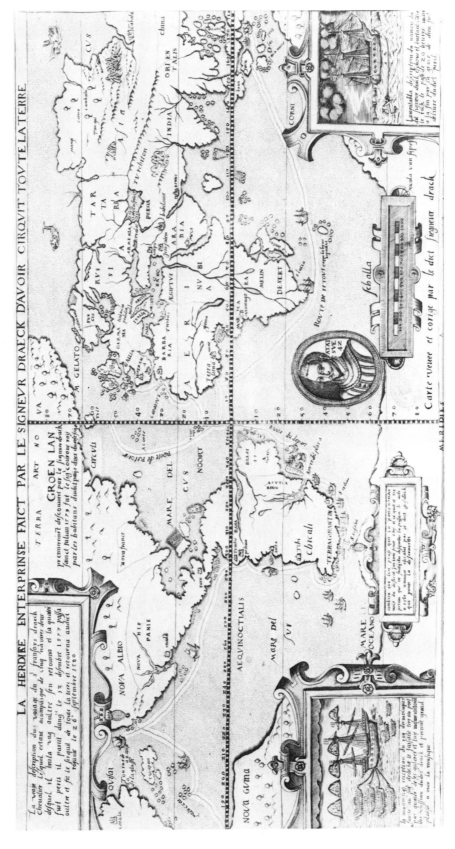

9.7 World map, by Nicola van Sype, engraved and probably published at Antwerp, ca. 1583 or later. Courtesy of The British Library.

Hind stuck on a reef at Celebes.[50] It can be deduced from this that the Queen's map displayed the same vignettes and perhaps others. Drake's acts of possession in America, at Insula Elizabethae in the south and at Nova Albion in the north, are indicated on the Drake-Mellon map by flags of St. George. The northern boundary of New Spain is drawn across the continent, giving the impression that the northern parts of North America lie open to England's imperial designs. On the eastern seaboard a third flag flies over Raleigh's Virginia colony (established in 1585), and a fourth in the northeast celebrates the act of possession at Meta Incognita (Baffin Island) on Frobisher's first voyage in 1576.

Of the two engraved maps derived from the Queen's map, the earlier can be identified as the world map (24 × 44 cm), entitled "La Herdike [Heroike] Enterprinse faict par le signeur Draeck" and bearing the engraver's inscription, "Nicola van Sype f." (fig. 9:7). The map shows Drake's route with some accuracy. The islands comprising Tierra del Fuego are carefully delineated, and Insula Elizabethae has the Royal Arms of England set below it. The adjoining legend gives a French version of the legend on the Drake-Mellon map as rendered in Purchas. A legend in the top left-hand corner beginning "La vraije description du voiage du s^r francoys draeck" is similar to the descriptive title-legend of the Drake-Mellon map. Its decorative cartouche extends well into North America. This explains why the legend attached to Drake's discovery of Nova Albion (corresponding to that on the Drake-Mellon map) is awkwardly and misleadingly placed under the name "Groenlan" (Greenland, which as on the Drake-Mellon map, seems to be part of northeast America). The Royal Arms are fitted below the corner cartouche so as to appear attached (appropriately) to Nova Albio (*sic*). Both the van Sype map and the Drake-Mellon map depict Java as an island, with the *Golden Hind's* track passing to the south and calling in at a port, presumably Tjilatjap.

The van Sype map has the same insets as the Drake-Mellon map but differs from it (and from the third derivative map) in two notable respects. It includes an oval portrait of Drake, aged forty-two. Assuming that Drake was born in 1540 or 1541, the completion of this map and its engraving can be dated at 1582–83 or later. The portrait was evidently derived from the miniature painted by Nicholas Hilliard in 1581 that gave Drake's age as forty-two. Further, a statement asserts that the map was seen and corrected by Drake ("veuee at corige par le dict siegneur drack"). This legend was presumably displayed on the original and copied by van Sype. These two features suggest that van Sype's original was not the Queen's map, but a copy of it, probably made for Henry of Navarre. For we can assume that Drake would not have signed his own chart as seen and corrected by himself, and Purchas' omission of any reference to Drake's portrait on the Whitehall chart implies that it did not display the portrait. With Hilliard's miniature as a model, a copyist would naturally add the portrait as an embellishment for an important presentation copy.

No other work by the engraver "Nicola van Sype" has been found, but a family of engravers of this name flourished in Germany during the first two decades of the seventeenth century. A Dutch version of the map is also known

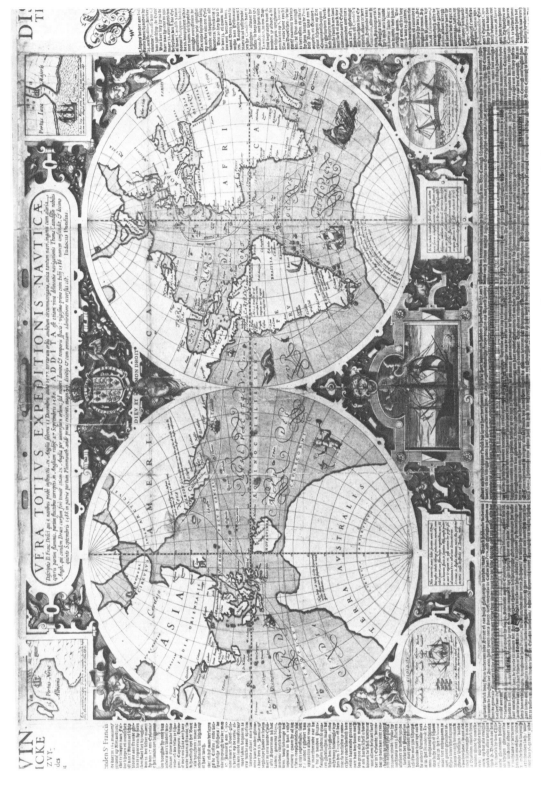

9.8 The Drake Broadside map, by Jodocus Hondius, probably issued in Amsterdam, 1595. Courtesy of The British Library.

and is generally considered to be a copy from the French edition. Both versions may have been unauthorized copies made from a drawing smuggled out of the country. Whether the Drake-Mellon map was also unauthorized or, on the contrary, was a reduced version of the Queen's map made for the benefit of some official or other person remains another of the unanswered questions concerning the Drake maps.

The later printed map derived from the Queen's map is the double-hemispheric map by Jodocus Hondius. It is commonly called the Drake Broadside map because the example first known (that in the British Library) is mounted with accompanying Dutch text comprising a version of "The Famous Voyage" and of Cavendish's circumnavigation taken from Hakluyt's *Principall Navigations* (fig. 9:8). Portraits of Drake and Cavendish are included in the text, displaying inset hemispheric world maps. The portrait of Drake, which erroneously displays Cavendish's track, is now best known in Crispin van de Passe's engraving after Hondius, published in 1598 (see frontispiece).

The publication of the Dutch text of the Broadside map in 1596 as a separate pamphlet with similar accompanying portraits seems to suggest that the map was issued in Amsterdam in 1595. But other evidence indicates that the map was printed in London, perhaps as early as 1590. The "life" of Hondius presented in the preliminary text to the Mercator-Hondius atlas of 1636 states that Hondius, while in London, "drew many fine draughts, and master peeces, as Sʳ *Francis Drakes* voyage about the World." This shows that the map was designed and engraved in England. Further, an early version of Hondius' portrait of Drake bears the inscription "Iudocus Hondius Flander fecit Londini." It correctly displays Drake's route on the hemispheric map, and the delineation is similar to that on the Drake-Hondius map.

The provenance of the six surviving copies of the map also seems to indicate two places of issue. Three were found inserted in or bound into English works, and three seem to have a Dutch provenance. This may mean that the map was issued in England around 1590 and later, in the Netherlands, around 1595. It seems reasonable to assume that the preparation of Hondius' map in England was unauthorized, and this would explain the difficulty in establishing its place and date of issue.

Although Hondius' map has many similar features to the Drake-Mellon and van Sype maps, there are some striking points of difference. In showing the world as a double hemisphere instead of as a plane chart Hondius was exploiting the facilities of the stereographic projection made popular by Rumold Mercator in his world map of 1587, published in the first volume of Gerard Mercator's *Atlas* (1589). This arrangement gave Hondius scope to use the margins for decorative devices and legends. His map is the only one of the three derivatives to be adorned with a portrait of the Queen, placed in the center beneath the Royal Arms. It may have been directly copied from the Whitehall map, which displayed Elizabeth's portrait. Of special interest are five vignettes, of which the two at the bottom are the same as those in the Drake-Mellon and van Sype maps. In the bottom center the *Golden Hind* is depicted. At the top of the map Hondius has two inset plans, one of "Portus Novae Albionis," the other of "Portus Javae Majoris." These are the only details of local topography to survive in the printed contemporary records of Drake's voyage. The plan of the port of Java is clearly recognizable as Tjilatjap with its narrow inlet or canal. That of Portus Novae Albionis is likewise important as the harbor where Drake spent five weeks on the coast of Nova Albion. Whether this is a true depiction of that historic site has been endlessly debated, all the more so because there is no harbor on the California coast which exactly fits its topography. The fact that Drake was making such a careful record of his landfalls gives us every reason to accept it as authentic; and Hondius as the engraver would surely have made a faithful copy of the manuscript plan, which he may have taken from Drake's journal, or Fletcher's, rather than from Drake's chart. (This would explain why the other two maps, derived from Drake's chart, did not include these two additional insets.)

Hondius' map also differs from the other two in its expression of doubt about the nature of Drake's discoveries in the southernmost and northernmost limits of America. In a legend referring to Tierra del Fuego, Hondius explains that whereas Drake placed islands there, Cavendish and all the Spaniards deny the truth of this, affirming that there was nothing but a strait. Hondius reports that in Nova Albion, latitude 42° on 5 June, Drake turned back because of the cold ("Hic prae ingenti frigore in Austrum reuerti coactus est lat.42 die 5 Iunij"). An asterisk against the legend attaches it to the northern limit of Drake's track in 42°N, which is also asterisked. There are indications that the track was first marked as continuing to about 48°N and was then partially deleted from the plate. As the information in the legend is derived from "The Famous Voyage" of Hakluyt, this suggests that Hondius corrected the plate after reading Hakluyt's account.

Hondius' map thus incorporates a later interpretation of Drake's discoveries than that of the Drake-Mellon and the van Sype maps. By 1589 the results of Cavendish's circumnavigation were available for comparison with Drake's discoveries. Hondius had already given some record of Drake's discoveries on two maps dated 1589 (Hondius' earliest surviving maps). One is a small circular map, 3.25 inches in diameter, showing a heart-shaped world and inscribed "Typus Orbis Terrarum. Iudocus Hondius fecit 1589." South of America are the islands of Tierra del Fuego in a form similar to that appearing on Fletcher's two maps, and with the attached legend in 48°N: "In reginae Elizab."[51] The other is a map of America and the Pacific Ocean entitled "1589. Americae Novissima descriptio." An inscription on the southern continent, reading "I Hondius inuen. I. le Clerc excu. 1602," shows that although Hondius drew the map of 1589, Isaac le Clerc engraved it some years later, in 1602. The map appears to have been copied from Abraham Ortelius' map "Maris Pacifici . . . descriptio," dated 1589, published in the *Additamentum IV Theatri Orbis Terrarum* (1590). The major difference between the maps of Hondius and Ortelius is in the delineation of Tierra del Fuego. It is shown by Hondius as an archipelago closely matching Fletcher's. An attached legend reads: "Insule Reginae Elisabetae ab Anglis detectae anno 1579" (the incorrect date, as also given on P.G.'s map of 1587). On the north shore of the Strait of Magellan, Hondius records the establishment of the fortress in 1582 by order of Philip II.

The nature of Hondius' contract with le Clerc is not clear. A copy of the map is to be found in Jean le Clerc's *Theatre géographique du Royaume de France* (Paris, 1621), together with five other maps of the world and the continents drawn by Hondius and engraved by I. le Clerc. Of two world maps, the one entitled "Orbis Terrae Novissima Descriptio" is double-hemispheric after Rumold Mercator's, and the other, "Nova Vniversi Orbis Descriptio," is oval after Ortelius. Both show the discoveries of Drake south of America, and the oval map carries on the southern continent the legend "Cum omnes hanc partem australem esse continentem putent, pro certe sciant insules esse." This expresses Hondius' earlier idea of Drake's discoveries, before conflicting opinons became current. There is no sign of Drake's discoveries in Nova Albion on this map, nor on the map of America of 1589 and the circular map of 1589. The double-hemispheric map engraved by le Clerc, on the contrary, has the legend "Nova Albion ab Anglis nominata anno 1580." This map must also predate Hondius' Drake map of ca. 1590.

The map of America and the circular map, both of 1589, are probably the earliest maps made by Hondius, and his designs for the other le Clerc maps were presumably drawn not much later. The circular maps show some similarity to the silver map of 1589 (the earliest map of Drake's voyage of known date), and Hondius' Drake map (ca. 1590) is also similar. This may suggest that Hondius was involved in the production of the silver map.

As an engraver and map maker, Hondius from 1589 onward played a prominent role in mapping Drake's discoveries. His engraving of Molyneux's terrestrial globe in 1592 must have made him one of the best authorities on the subject of the voyage. Yet he became increasingly dubious about Drake's discoveries to the south of America. On his world map "Typus totius Orbis Terrarum, in quo & Christiani militis certamen super terram . . . graphice designatur, a Iud. Hondio caelatore," commonly known as the Christian Knight map, probably published in Amsterdam about 1597, there is no record of Drake's voyage in North or South America, despite the map's dedication to R. Brewer, Henry Briggs, and Edward Wright. "Tierra del fogo" appears as part of the southern continent, on which the Christian Knight is fighting the forces of darkness. This equivocal handling of the evidence probably resulted from Hondius' being too attentive to Spanish influences while engraving the Molyneux globes.

On his return to the Netherlands, Hondius reverted for the most part to the traditional idea of Tierra del Fuego. His maps and globes must have helped to confirm the Dutch belief that their countrymen Le Maire and Schouten in 1617 were the first to discover the existence of a passage around South America. Yet relics of Drake's discoveries remained on some of Hondius' maps. There is no sign of the Tierra del Fuegan archipelago on Hondius' large world map on Mercator's projection, published in 1608 and now preserved at the Royal Geographical Society.[52] Even its miniature inset map of Drake's circum-

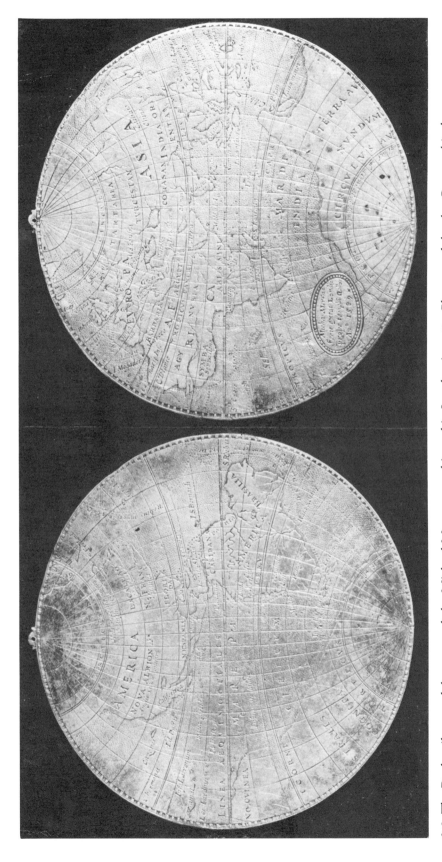

9.9 The Drake silver medal map, made by Michael Mercator and issued in London in 1589. Photograph by the *Geographical Magazine*, London, of the original in the Hans P. Kraus Collection at The Library of Congress.

navigation is of the traditional style. The large double-hemispheric world map of 1611,[53] on the other hand, shows islands off South America labeled "I. F. Drack." Adjacent to these is a record of "Lameyrs passage," showing that the map was completed or altered in about 1618, after the return of Le Maire and Schouten. This was presumably done by Hondius' eldest son, Jodocus Hondius, Jr., who in that year published a description of the map.

THE SILVER MAP

The year 1589 was notable not only for Hakluyt's publication of "The Famous Voyage," but also for the first publication in England of a map commemorating Drake's voyage, the famous silver map or medal (fig. 9:9). Purchas referred to it after describing the Whitehall map: "And my learned friend Master Brigges told me, that he had seene this plot of Drakes Voyage cut in Silver by a Dutchman (Michael Mercator, Nephew to Gerardus) many yeeres before Scouten or Maire intended that Voyage." Master Brigges was Henry Briggs the mathematician. The medal itself became known in the later years of the nineteenth century as an anonymous and undated record of Drake's voyage. The similarity of the silver map to the map of America by P.G. in Hakluyt's *Decades* led such historians as Miller Christy to suggest that the 1587 map was based on the medal and that the two works were by the same engraver.[54] In April 1967, however, a unique and hitherto unknown exemplar of the medal appeared in Christie's salesrooms as the property of the Earl of Caledon. Unlike the eight medals thitherto known, this one was found to bear an author's inscription and date, "Micha Merca: fecit extat Londi: prope templum Gallo: An° 1589," translated as "Michael Mercator made [this]. It is available in London near the French Church, 1589."

An inscription with such specific details has the ring of truth. Yet this would not rule out the possibility that a forger knowing Purchas' reference had made the medal. Asked to investigate the authenticity of the medal when it was brought to the Map Room of the British Museum immediately after Christie's sale, we followed up the clue of "templum Gallo." The term indicated a French Protestant church, identified as the Huguenot Church in Threadneedle Street. In the Public Record Office, London, we found under St. Benet Fink the following record for the collection of the first payment of two subsidies granted by Parliament in the thirtieth and thirty-first years of Elizabeth I: " Michael Mercator servaunte to Baptista . . . iiijd," with the date 18 June of the thirty-second year (1590). Michael Mercator can be identified as the son (born April 1567, died 1614) of Arnold Mercator, the grandson (not nephew) of Gerard Mercator the elder, and brother of Gerard Mercator the younger. The record proves that he was in London from 1589 to 1590 as the guest of one Baptista. The word following "Baptista" is rubbed and cannot be deciphered, but it definitely was not "Boazio," disproving the natural conjecture that Mercator's host might have been Baptista Boazio (fl. 1588–1606), the Italian artist living in London who sailed with Drake on his West Indian voyage and made the five maps illustrating the voyage. This documentary evidence of Mercator's visit to London authenticated the medal, which therefore ranks as the earliest dated map depicting Drake's track and voyage and the first map of the voyage published in England.

The Mercator medal (now in the Drake collection of H. P. Kraus which was presented to the United States Library of Congress in 1980)[55] was presumably the prototype. The omission of the author's legend on the later medals was probably done for commercial and patriotic reasons, for the medal so inscribed gave prominence to Mercator and only passing reference to Drake in the legends recording his departure: "Draci Exitus" and "D. F. Dra. Exitus anno 1577 id. Dec." By following the 1587 map engraved by P.G., Mercator repeated the incorrect dates of 1579 and 1580 in the inscriptions attached to Drake's American discoveries. The two maps differ in that Mercator, using as his source Rumold Mercator's hemispheric world map of 1587, depicts the southern continent but moves the coastline southward to show a passage south of Tierra del Fuego. Similarities to Hondius' circular map of 1589 and the Drake map of ca. 1590 may suggest that Hondius was consulted in making the medal. If so, this probably took place before Hondius made his own Drake map because the erroneous dates for Drake's discoveries in the American hemisphere (1579 and 1580) found on various maps of the 1580s (and on the medal) are not perpetuated by Hondius on that map.

Another version of the silver map has recently come to light. In the collection of the shoemaker, book collector, and antiquary John Bagford (1650–1716), which passed to the British Museum Library (now the British Library), there is preserved a unique paper impression of the silver medal.[56] It shows the eastern hemisphere only, and it has been identified as a counter-impression of the silver medal in the Department of Coins and Medals of the British Museum (registration 1882, 5.7.1.). The paper impression shows not only the intaglio lines of the medal map, but also the various accidental imperfections on the surface of this copy of the medal. The process for making such an impression was as follows: a reversed impression of the medal was pulled from the inked surfaces of the silver, as from a copper plate, and before the ink could dry this reversed image on paper was passed through a press with a second piece of paper so that an impression the same way around as the engraved medal could be printed. This paper impression was on exhibition for the first time in 1977, side by side with the silver medal from which it was taken, in the British Library's 1977 exhibition "The Famous Voyage of Sir Francis Drake."[57]

One other curious fact deserves to be recorded. Michael Mercator the map maker was not the first of that name to come to England. A medalist also named Michael Mercator (1490/1–1544), member of one of the leading families in the town of Venlo, the Netherlands, was active from 1527 to 1541 as an instrument maker and diplomat in the service of Henry VIII. Early in 1539 Henry granted him an augmentation to his arms and a knighthood. Michael Mercator commemorated the event by making a medal of himself dated 1539.[58] It is inscribed in Latin, "Portrait of the first knight from Venloo created by the king of the English." Investigations suggest, however, that there is no connection between the two Michael Mercators. We have the authority of Purchas and Briggs for believing that the Michael Mercator (fl. 1589) of the silver map was one of the well-known geographical family, although no other example is known of a medal by the cartographer Michael Mercator. The circumstances of his making the medal, and whether he was commanded by Drake to make it, are questions still unresolved. It would seem appropriate that in the year after the Armada, Drake would commission a medal as a commemorative piece for himself, his family and friends. Whatever the answer, the silver map now has a place of added importance among the cartographic relics of Drake's voyage.

THE MOLYNEUX GLOBE

By 1590, ten years after Drake's return, there was still no detailed map of his voyage available in England. This lack was remedied when Emery Molyneux, the mathematician and instrument maker of Lambeth, issued in 1592 the pair of globes whose publication had been heralded by Hakluyt three years earlier (fig. 9:10). [59] Sixty-two centimeters in diameter, these were the largest printed globes yet made and the first globes published in England. The terrestrial provided an impressive record of England's achievements in navigation, exploration, and discovery, the most spectacular of which were the recent circumnavigations of Drake and Cavendish. The globe is the earliest printed work of known date to show the tracks of both voyages, and to record notable incidents in explanatory legends. It is therefore one of the most authoritative documents as evidence of Drake's track. The fact that the northwest coast of America, inscribed Nova Albion, extends beyond 50°N, with "F. Dracus" named against what seems to be an indication of a harbor in about 48°N, is noteworthy. This would explain why Hondius first marked Drake's track to about 48°N on his Drake map ca. 1590.

There is one outstanding omission, nevertheless: Tierra del Fuego is not shown as a group of islands ending at Insula Elizabethae, but retains the traditional outline indicating a possible connection with the southern continent. Yet Molyneux was assisted by the mathematician Edward Wright, who depicted Drake's discovery of the islands of Tierra del Fuego clearly enough on his world map published in Hakluyt's *Principal Navigations* (1599–1600). It is significant also that Hakluyt ignored or suppressed the fact of Drake's discovery in "The Famous Voyage" (1589). Whatever the reasons for Hakluyt's omission, it can be conjectured that Molyneux was influenced by Jodocus Hondius, who developed growing doubts about the discovery because Cavendish's voyage and the Spaniards seemed to provide contrary evidence.

One Spaniard in particular who may have used his influence to persuade Hondius and Molyneux that Drake's claims were false was Drake's old adversary Pedro Sarmiento de Gamboa. In 1579–80 Sarmiento had led the Spanish

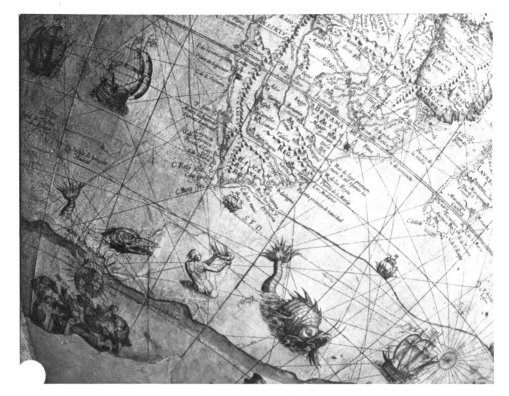

9.10 Detail from the terrestrial globe of Emery Molyneux, London, 1592, showing Drake's track from the Indian Ocean to the Atlantic. From Petworth House, collection of Baron Egremont. Courtesy of the National Trust.

expedition to survey the Strait of Magellan, and he established his ill-fated colony there in 1584. After his capture at the Azores, Sarmiento was brought to London in 1586 as the prisoner and honored guest of Sir Walter Raleigh. While in London he evidently provided information which was incorporated on the Molyneux globe, for various features in the delineation of the Strait of Magellan and the portrayal of the Solomon Islands as Sarmiento's own discovery (recorded on the globe) must have come directly from him. In contrast, the detailed representation of the Solomon Islands by Hondius on his map of America dated 1589 (engraved in 1602) was copied from Ortelius' map of the Pacific, published in 1590.

Of Sarmiento's visit, Raleigh relates an anecdote which later became famous:

I remember a pretie jeast of Don Pedro de Sarmiento, a worthie Spanish Gentlemean, who had beene emploied by his King in planting a Colonie upon the Streights of Magellan: for when I asked him being then my Prisoner, some questions about an Iland in those streights, which me thought, might have done either benefit or displeasure to his enterprise, he told me merrily, that it was to bee called the *Painters wiues Iland*; saying, That whilest the fellow drew that Mappe, his wife sitting by, desired him to put in one Countrie for her; that shee, in imagination, might hauue an Iland of her owne.[60]

Peter Heylyn, geographer and divine, commented in 1652 on Sarmiento's jest: "I fear that Painters wife hath many Ilands and some Countries too."[61]

It is possible to make more sense of the story if we interpret it in light of Drake's discoveries. There was only one island within the Strait which was of interest to Raleigh and which could do "benefit" or "displeasure" to Sarmiento's enterprises in 1579–80 and 1584: Elizabeth Island, of which Drake had taken possession in the Queen's name. If, alternatively, Raleigh was referring to the islands south of the Strait, these included Drake's other (and more southerly) Insula Elizabethae, where he made his most dramatic act of possession. Raleigh would naturally point to the fact that Elizabeth Island constituted an English possession standing in the way of Spanish enterprise. He might also raise the question of the insular character of Tierra del Fuego. Sarmiento's allusion to the painter in his answer recalls the alarmed comments of the Spaniard's about the activities of Drake and his cousin John as painters recording the coasts. His jest can be interpreted as an attempt to ridicule and so discredit Drake's cartographic exploits. The jest, I suggest, accuses Drake of inventing the island—for who else, apart from John, was a painter in those parts? It makes play perhaps of the fact that Drake's second wife (whom he married in 1583), like his sovereign, was named Elizabeth. Sarmiento had every reason to discourage, by jest or otherwise, the idea that England had nominal possession of any islands in the region. He would work, above all, to discredit the report that Drake had discovered Tierra del Fuego to be an archipelago with open sea beyond. Thus "the painter's wife's island" became a popular phrase, divorced from its exact historical context, and at the same time Drake lost credit for one of his two major discoveries.

The Molyneux globes became famous. Their publication in 1592 was a major event in London. Shakespeare's comparison of a kitchen maid to a terrestrial globe in *The Comedy of Errors* (III.ii) was a topical allusion. The globes were financed by the merchant adventurer William Sanderson, who spent more than £1,000 on the pair. At his house in Newington Buttes, two special entertainments were held at which first the terrestrial and then the celestial were presented to the Queen. When she received the terrestrial, she commented: "The whole earth, a present for a Prince, but with the Spanish King's leave"—an ironic reference to King Philip's claim to the whole world and to his motto, "Non sufficit orbis."[62]

While Elizabeth was casting an imperial eye on the territorial delimitations of the globe, mathematicians were making a close geographical study of it. In *M. Blundevile His Exercises* (1594), Thomas Blundeville included "a briefe description of the two great Globes lately set foorth by M. Molinaxe: and of Sir Francis Drake his first voyage into the Indies." He measured Drake's route and worked out that he had sailed 12010 leagues, "which is almost twice so much as the Compasse of the whole world, which if you measure upon the Globe by

9.11 Detail from the Molyneux terrestrial globe, revised in 1603, showing North America, including Drake's Nova Albion. Photograph by the *Geographical Magazine*. Courtesy of the Master and Benchers of the Middle Temple.

the Equinoctiall line . . . you shall finde . . . to amount to 21600 miles . . . which by allowing three miles to a league doe make no more but 7200 leagues."[63]

Hondius returned to the Netherlands in 1593, followed by Molyneux in 1596 or 1597, and one of them took with him the copper plates of the globes. Hondius then revised the terrestrial, altering the original date to 1603 and adding new discoveries.[64] The pair issued by him in 1603 was acquired (and had perhaps been ordered) by William Crashaw, preacher at the Middle Temple (the Inn of Court) from 1605 to 1613, who had the globes in his private library and described them as "one of the fairest paire of globes in Englande."[65] The Middle Temple was well known for the geographical interests of its members (of whom Drake was one), so it is appropriate that this has remained the home of these magnificent globes—the terrestrial one displaying across the North American continent with prophetic fervor the finely embellished arms of Queen Elizabeth (fig. 9:11).

Only one example of the terrestrial globe now survives in its original state. This belonged to the Ninth Earl of Northumberland, the "wizard earl," and by family tradition was given to him by Sir Walter Raleigh while they were fellow prisoners in the Tower of London.[66] On his release in 1622 the Earl carried it with him to Petworth House, where it has remained. When Hondius or Molyneux removed the copper plates to the Netherlands, England lost the opportunity of keeping the Molyneux globes up to date. From 1622 onward, Englishmen had to make use of the large Dutch globes of Willem Jansz Blaeu and his successor Joan Blaeu. Knowledge of the exploits of Drake, Cavendish, and the other navigators and explorers of Elizabethan times faded as the Molyneux globes wore out and were discarded.

LATER PRINTED MAPS

Two other works printed in England in the 1590s are important as records of Drake's voyage. John Blagrave, a Reading mathematician, designed a pair of terrestrial and celestial planispheres based on the Molyneux globes and engraved by Benjamin Wright, the London artist, in 1596. The terrestrial marks the tracks of Drake and Cavendish. Nova Albion is clearly displayed, extending beyond 50°N, and Drake's track reaches about 48°N, as on the globe, before it turns back south. There is of course a continental Tierra del Fuego to match the globes.

The second map is Edward Wright's "true hydrographical description of so much of the world as hath beene hetherto discouered, and is come to our knowledge" of 1599. With this map, published in the 1599–1600 edition of the *Principal Navigations*, Hakluyt made amends for his omissions in the *Principall Navigations* of 1589. The map is drawn on Mercator's projection, which Wright adapted using a mathematical formula. Like the Molyneux globe, the map gained Shakespeare's attention. He refers to it in *Twelfth Night* (III.ii), where Maria says of Malvolio: "He does smile his face into more lines than are in the new map, with the augmentation of the Indies." The lines were the compass lines radiating across the chart; the "augmentation of the Indies" presumably referred to the Solomon Islands, which stretched eastward from New Guinea. Drake's Tierra del Fuego and Insula Elizabethae are properly depicted. In the second state of the map, Wright includes an additional legend in the southeast Pacific. In this he records Drake's discovery that Tierra del Fuego was an archipelago and that the coast of Chile trended not north-westward but east of north.

THE CARTOGRAPHIC RECORD

Adorned in gilt paint or cut in silver, the special commemorative maps of Drake's voyage can be seen as fitting records of an expedition which had brought home a fortune in silver and gold. The Queen played up to the theme. When Drake gave her a coconut, she returned it to him set in gold.[67] The sailors spoke, ironically, of the "golden knight."[68] But the fame of the hour does not leave a lasting record. Decorative pieces made in special materials for presentation do not necessarily have a long life or wide circulation. Wall maps in particular are vulnerable to decay and destruction. Drake's map had an honored place next to Sebastian Cabot's in the gallery at Whitehall but, like Cabot's map, it did not survive to come to the British Museum with the Old Royal Library in 1757. Silver medals are locked away in cabinets and can remain unknown for many years, as happened to the Mercator medal.

A printed map from a copper plate engraving or a wood block, on the other hand, has more enduring qualities and normally enjoys a wider currency. Frobisher's voyages in search of the Northwest Passage (1576–1578) were in print by 1578, illustrated by woodcut maps. But for political reasons Drake, the first commander to complete a circumnavigation of the world (as English chroniclers were quick to point out), did not enjoy the advantage of instant publication.

Even when publication was no longer prohibited, few good printed maps of Drake's voyage were produced. England had not yet developed a flourishing map trade and still depended on foreign engravers for such ambitious projects as publication of the Molyneux globes. This helps to explain Hakluyt's perfunctory attitude to maps in his *Principall Navigations* (1589). "O good Hakluyt, how short, how unsatisfactory, how tyranically spoken!" exclaimed Kohl in protest to Hakluyt's lame excuse that he was waiting for publication of the Molyneux globes. Drake was one of those who suffered from "this singular and much to be lamented omission" (as Kohl described it), for Hakluyt "made no attempt of delivering by print some of those treasures by which he was surrounded."[69] The removal of the Molyneux globe plates to the Netherlands soon after their publication likewise contributed to the lack of an authoritative record of Drake's voyage in the seventeenth century.

Drake was also unfortunate in not having secured an appropriate contemporary biographer. The would-be author of the biography spoken of by Hakluyt (John Stow?) never fulfilled his intention. The paintings in the journal made by Drake and his cousin would have provided posterity with the information which Blundeville in 1594 sought for Drake's voyage: "But if it might please Sir Francis to write a perfect Diarie of his whole voyage, shewing howe much he sayled in a day, and what watring places he found, and where hee touched, and how long he rested in any place, and what good Ports and Hauens he found . . ." (the passage continues with a prospectus for systematically reporting navigation and discovery, including every form of human society and physical feature). "In thus doing the saide Sir Francis I say should greatly profite his countrie men, and therby deserue immortall fame, of all which things, I doubt not but that he hath alreadie written, and will publish the same when he shall thinke most meete."[70] But Blundeville's hopes were disappointed. Drake did not live to publish the narrative of his voyages as planned in 1593.

Drake's discoveries appeared on later maps in strange places. The idea that Drake had actually discovered the coast of the southern continent southwest of the Strait of Magellan was perpetuated on a series of maps from 1602 until as late as the 1760s. The mistake arose from the observation of an eclipse of the moon on 15 September 1578, from which the *Golden Hind's* position was calculated to be 90°W of London, as Edward Cliffe recorded, whereas her true position must have been 75–80°W. Drake's landfall on Tierra del Fuego was therefore displaced westward on the maps of Levinus Hulsius (1602) and of Sir Robert Dudley in his *Dell' Arcano del Mare* (Florence, 1646–47, second edition 1661).[71] The marking of "Portus Francisci Draci" or "P. Francisci Draci" may have encouraged the later naming of Drake Passage between South America and Antarctica. Paradoxically, this mistaken record of Drake's discoveries may have served to keep his name on the map in these regions, though for the opposite reason to the truth. Drake Passage is a final and appropriate commemoration of his discovery of what was then the "southernmost knowne land in the world," with open sea beyond.

The cartographic record of Drake's explorations in Nova Albion also became confused. When California after 1602 came to be portrayed as an island, Drake's Nova Albion with its Portus Novae Albionis was usually located on the coast of the island. Henry Briggs's map "The North Part of America," published in the third volume of *Purchas His Pilgrimes* (1625) became a prototype for the insular California in the eighteenth century. One of the most popular maps of this kind was Herman Moll's map of North America, published after 1712, which gave Jonathan Swift the geographical setting for Gulliver's visit to Brobdingnag in the second book of *Gulliver's Travels* (1726). Its bulbous peninsula protrudes from the coast of North America to the north of New Albion, beyond the narrow "Streights of Annian." A portrayal of Nova Albion which was as

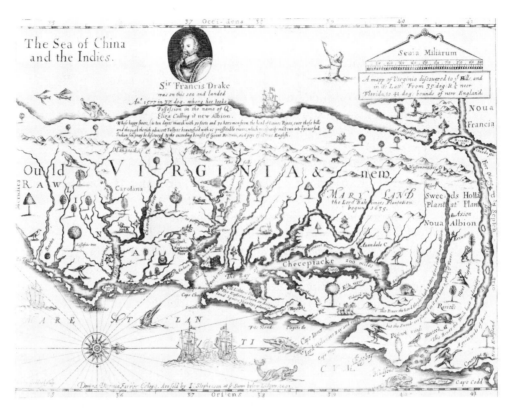

9.12 Map of Virginia, by John Farrer, showing Nova Albion at ten days' march to the west. Published in Edward Bland, *The Discovery of New Brittaine,* 1651. Courtesy of The British Library.

bizarre as the imaginary Brobdingnag appeared on John Farrer's map of Virginia (1651), published in John Bland's *The Discovery of New Brittaine* of 1651 (fig. 9:12). Nova Albion, complete with Drake's portrait, is represented as ten days' march from the head of the James River. This mistake arose from the belief that the Pacific Ocean lay not far beyond the hills of tidewater Virginia, a relic of Verrazzanian cartography of the sixteenth century.

However confused was the cartographic record of Nova Albion, Drake's visit there and his act of possession were quickly taken into the literature of colonial enterprise, although they were not followed up by further voyages, at least not for some two hundred years. In contrast to the history of Drake's discoveries in the southern part of South America, there was no question of these northern events being forgotten. One of the earliest references came from the pen of the young Hungarian Stephen Parmenius, a friend of Hakluyt and of Sir Humphrey Gilbert, who sailed with Gilbert on the fateful voyage to Newfoundland in 1582. To his poem of embarkation on the voyage, "De Navigatione," Hakluyt adds a marginal note "Nova Albion," showing that the verses were referring to Drake's annexation of California in 1579. He personified America as reaching out her hand and, with downcast crown, begging to be liberated by England.

If map makers did not forget Drake's voyage, the same was true of English mariners. Drake won great acclaim for his achievement as the first Englishman to navigate the Strait of Magellan and enter the Pacific Ocean.

> Such a mighty and valuable thing also was the passing this Straight, that Sir Francis Drake's going thro' it gave birth to that famous old Wives Saying, viz, that Sir Francis Drake shot the Gulph; a Saying that was current in England for many years, I believe near a Hundred after Sir Francis Drake was gone his long [est] journey of all; as if there had been but one Gulph in the world, and that passing it had been a Wonder next to that of Hercules cleansing the Egean Stable.

Thus Daniel Defoe's imaginary circumnavigator comments in *A New Voyage round the World, by a Course never sailed before* (1725). The phrase that Drake "shot the gulf" appears in various documents of the sixteenth and seventeenth centuries and became a subject of one of the many Drake legends.[72]

Such was the fate of the maps and drawings of Drake's voyage. If more documents had survived, Portus Novae Albionis might have been revealed with the precision of the landing places on Drake's last voyage. It is in keeping with Drake's devious and equivocal temperament that he provided posterity with a legacy of mysteries and legends. The four-hundredth anniversary of Drake's visit to Nova Albion is an appropriate time to commemorate the event with an account of Drake's maps, some lost, others preserved and treasured as records, however imperfect, of that remarkable voyage. In trying to decipher their secrets we should remember Raleigh's words: "Therefore the fictions (or let them be called conjectures) painted in Maps, doe serue only to mislead such discouerers as rashly believe them, drawing upon the publishers, either some angrie curses, or well deserued scorne, but to keep their owne credit they cannot serue alwaies." Telling the story of Sarmiento's jest, he continues: "But in filling up the blankes of old Histories, we neede not be so scrupulous. For it is not to be feared, that time should runne backward, and by restoring the things themselves to knowledge, make our conjectures appeare ridiculous."

This is a warning from Drake's own time not to place too much credence on map evidence alone. Filling in the blanks of old histories also has its perils. Time may be reserving some surprises which would reduce our speculations to the level of Sarmiento's painter's wife's island.

One strange cartographic coincidence is noteworthy. Gerard Mercator included stars on his terrestrial globe of 1541 (fig. 9:13), an innovation which few cartographers thought fit to follow. In the far northwest of America, north of Hispania Nova, the star Caput Draconis, head of the dragon, is inscribed in the otherwise empty territory where Drake ventured nearly thirty years later. Among Spaniards, Drake was known, of course, as the Dragon, and even today South American children are admonished, "The Dragon will get you." Perhaps Drake with his claims to occult powers would have seen it as more than a coincidence. It seems an appropriate tailpiece to this cartographic study of the Famous Voyage of this "most famous Capitaine in the world."[73]

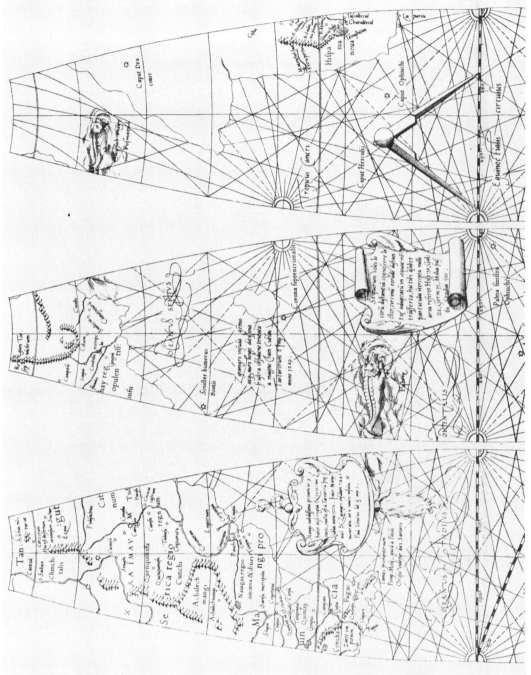

9.13 Detail of the North Pacific from the gores of Gerard Mercator's terrestrial globe, 1541 (facsimile), showing the star Caput Draconis in northwest America. Courtesy of The British Library.

NOTES

1. *The World Encompassed By Sir Francis Drake . . . Carefully collected out of the notes of Master Francis Fletcher . . .* (London, 1628), p. 108. The text opens with a dedicatory letter to Robert Earl of Warwick by "Francis Drake" (Sir Francis Drake, Bart.), whose name does not appear elsewhere.

2. British Library (B.L.) Additional MS 28420, fol. 30.

3. The interception explains why no copy is to be found at Simancas. *Calendar of Letters and State Papers relating to English Affairs, preserved principally in the Archives of Simancas*, vol. III: *Elizabeth, 1580–1586* (London, 1896), item 44, p. 55. Patricia M. Higgins of the Department of Manuscripts, British Library, clarified the reference. See the catalogue of the British Library exhibition *Sir Francis Drake: An Exhibition to Commemorate Francis Drake's Voyage around the World, 1577–1580* (London, 1977), item 99, p. 98.

4. Samuel Purchas, *Purchas His Pilgrimes* (1625), III, iii, p. 461; in the MacLehose ed. (Glasgow, 1906), XIII, 3–4.

5. B.L. Harleian MS 376. fol. 5. Zelia Nuttall surmised that this request may have led to the loss of Drake's journal. See Nuttall, ed., *New Light on Drake . . .* , Hakluyt Society (London, 1914), p. xlv. But the Queen's response, it appears, was to send not the journal but a copy of Drake's map. It is interesting to note that a request for Drake's journal was also received from William, Landgrave of Hesse, a supporter of the King of Navarre's cause. A memorandum of the Privy Council on "Considerations to be weighed concerning the negotiations of Germany and Denmark," dated at the beginning of November 1585, includes the note: "And the Landgrave of Hesse having asked for a discourse touching Sir Francis Drake's first voyage, his request should be satisfied." *Calendar of State Papers, Foreign, September 1585–May 1596*, vol. XX (London, 1921), p. 136. Hereafter cited as *C.S.P.*

6. Bibliothèque Nationale, Paris, MS Français 15454, fol. 133.

7. Nuttall, *New Light on Drake,* p. xxvii.

8. In answer to enquiries made in Paris in 1977 about Henry's map, the Bibliothèque Nationale replied that no trace could be found. Investigations into the Archbishop's map have so far proved fruitless.

9. Nuttall, *New Light on Drake,* p. 303.

10. E. S. Donno, *An Elizabethan in 1582: The Diary of Richard Madox, Fellow of All Souls,* Hakluyt Society (London, 1976), p. 23.

11. Nuttall, *New Light on Drake,* pp. 207–208. Nuttall suggests (p. xxvii) that the colored representations of the coast seen by Zárate may have been drawn by Drake, probably the sole competent cartographer on board, and colored by his assistant.

12. Lancelot Voisin, Seigneur de la Popellinière, *Les Trois Mondes* (1582), bk. 3, fol. 38v.

13. See Quinn, ch. 3, above.

14. Nuttall, *New Light on Drake,* p. xxviii. The wording of the title *The World Encompassed,* as given, is incorrect in some small details.

15. J. R. Tanner, ed., *Samuel Pepys's Naval Minutes,* Navy Records Society (London, 1926), p. 95.

16. Mary Frear Keeler, *Sir Francis Drake's West Indian Voyage, 1585–86* (London, 1981), pp. 317–319.

17. The manuscript was reproduced by Charles de la Roncière, *Un atlas inconnu de la dernière expédition de Drake* (Paris, 1909). It was loaned to the B.L. exhibition in 1977; *Sir Francis Drake: An Exhibition,* item 147, p. 126.

18. Henry R. Wagner mistakenly gave the name as Joseph Conyers; *Sir Francis Drake's Voyage round the World* (San Francisco, 1926), p. 290.

19. Fletcher's journal, B.L. Sloane MS 61, fol. 41v.

20. For example, Wagner, *Sir Francis Drake's Voyage,* p. 292.

21. Guildhall Library, London, MS 1758.

22. See, e.g., A. Anthiaume, *Cartes marines, Constructions navales, Voyages de découverte chez les Normands, 1500–1650* (Paris, 1916), I, 179.

23. *Catalogue of the famous library of Printed Books, Illuminated Manuscripts . . . collected by Henry Huth . . . which will be sold by auction, by Messrs Sotheby, Williamson & Hodge . . . on Wednesday 15th November, 1911* (London, 1911), no. 144, p. 39.

24. C. F. G. R. Schwerdt, *Hunting, hawking, shooting, illustrated in a catalogue of books, manuscripts, prints and drawings* (London, 1928), I, xvi; II, 321–326; frontispiece and pls. 155, 156. The drawings are listed according to their inscriptions. See also P. H. Hulton and D. B. Quinn, *The American Drawings of John White, 1577–1590* (London, 1964), I, 34.

25. Schwerdt, *Hunting*, II, 322.

26. Ibid., p. 321. The drawing of the canoe is described as being on "leaf 43," whereas the list (p. 324) gives the reference as leaf 46.

27. Ibid., p. 323.

28. Sir Richard Hawkins, *The Observations of Sir Richard Hawkins Knight, in his voyage into the South Sea, Anno Domini 1593* (London, 1622), p. 95.

29. B.L. Sloane MS 61, fol. 37v.

30. Ibid., fol. 36r.

31. Helen Wallis, "English Enterprise in the Region of the Strait of Magellan," in John Parker, ed., *Merchants and Scholars* (Minneapolis, 1965), p. 204.

32. The atlas of 1575, e.g., B.L. Additional MS 31317, in "Sir Francis Drake an Exhibition," p. 26, item 13.

33. Nuttall, *New Light on Drake*, p. 308.

34. Ibid., pp. 113, 308.

35. Ibid., p. 318.

36. C.S.P., Spain, vol. III, item 77, p. 95.

37. Donno, *An Elizabethan in 1582*, p. 23.

38. C.S.P., Spain, vol. III, item 248, p. 341. Mendoza was misinformed in the suggestion that Winter also had discovered the insular character of Tierra del Fuego.

39. Donno, *An Elizabethan in 1582*, pp. 239–240.

40. Ibid., p. 96.

41. J. G. Kohl, *Descriptive Catalogue of those Maps, Charts and Surveys relating to America which are mentioned in Vol. III of Hakluyt's Great Work* (Washington, D.C., 1857), pp. 79–80. Quoted from Hakluyt, *Principal Navigations*, vol. XI (1904), pp. 169–170.

42. Edmund Howes, *The Annales, or Generall Chronicle of England, begun first by maister Iohn Stow and after him continued . . . unto the end of this present yeere 1614 . . .* (London, 1615), p. 807.

43. Nicholas Breton, *A Discourse in commendation of the valiant as vertuous minded Gentleman, Maister Frauncis Drake, with a reioysing of his happy adventures* (London, 1581), sig. Avii, Aviii, pp. 9–10.

44. William Borough, *A Discours of the Variation of the Cumpas,* (London, 1581), sig. ivᵛ.

45. H. P. Kraus, *Sir Francis Drake: A Pictorial Biography* (Amsterdam, 1970), p. 86. The letter is transcribed in J. H. Hessels, *Abrahami Ortelii . . . et ad Jacobum Colum Ortellianum . . . epistulae* (Cambridge, Eng., 1887), p. 238.

46. Lancelot Voisin, Seigneur de la Popellinière, *Les Trois Mondes* (1582), bk. 3. 38v.

47. The map is discussed in letters of Jean Groute, a Parisian friend of Hakluyt, and Jaques Noel of St. Malo. See Hakluyt, *Principal Navigations*, vol. III (1600), pp. 236–7; vol. VIII (1904), pp. 272–4; also David B. Quinn, *New American World* (New York, 1979), pp. 304–305.

48. C.S.P., Foreign, Elizabeth, vol. XIX (1916), p. 18.

49. In translation: A true description of the naval expedition of Francis Drake, Englishman and Knight, who with five ships departed from the western part of England on 13 December 1577, circumnavigated the globe and returned on 26 September 1580 with one ship remaining, the others having been destroyed by waves or fire.

50. As noted earlier, the Huth manuscript shows a picture of the chief of Ternate's canoe.

51. This map was of a kind made for an "Album Amicorum." An example of the map is preserved in the "Album Amicorum" of Petrus Hondius.

52. Published by the Royal Geographical Society, London, with a memoir by Edward Heawood, in 1927.

53. Published as a facsimile with text by E. L. Stevenson and Joseph Fischer, S.J., New York, 1907.

54. Miller Christy, *The Silver Map of the World* . . . (London, 1900), pp. 44–45.

55. H. P. Kraus, *Sir Francis Drake,* pp. 104–105, 218–220.

56. B.L., Department of Printed Books, Harley 5957 (Bagford Collection, no. 19).

57. *Sir Francis Drake: An Exhibition,* item 96, p. 94. The discovery and investigation of the counter-impression was made by my colleague Sarah Tyacke of the B.L. Map Library.

58. British Museum, Department of Coins and Medals, M. 6793. This information is provided by Peter Barber, Department of Manuscripts, B.L. The question of whether Michael Mercator's immediate descendants were medal-makers and had English connections has now been resolved.

59. Helen Wallis, "The First English Globe: A Recent Discovery," *Geographical Journal* 117 (1951) 275–290.

60. Sir Walter Raleigh, *The History of the World* (London, 1614), I, 574.

61. Peter Heylyn, *Cosmographie in Four Bookes* (London, 1652), bk. 4, p. 196.

62. Sir William Sanderson, *An answer to a scurrilous pamphlet* (London, 1656), sig. A3v.

63. Thomas Blundeville, *M. Blundevile His Exercises* (London, 1594), fol. 243v.

64. Helen Wallis, "Further Light on the Molyneux Globes," *Geographical Journal* 121 (1955) 304–311.

65. R. M. Fisher, "William Crashawe and the Middle Temple Globes, 1605–15," *Geographical Journal* 140 (1974) 106.

66. Wallis, "The First English Globe," pp. 275, 286–287.

67. Lady Eliott-Drake, *The Family and Heirs of Sir Francis Drake,* 2 vols. (London, 1911), p. 50.

68. Donno, *An Elizabethan in 1582,* pp. 239–240.

69. Kohl, *Descriptive Catalogue,* p. 5.

70. Blundeville, *M. Blundevile,* fols. 243–244. In the later editions, published after Drake's death, "Sir Francis" is altered to "some expert Mariner."

71. "Carta particolare dello Stretto di Magellano e di Maire. D'America carta XXIII. L°6°," in Robert Dudley, *Arcano del mare* (Florence, 1647), vol. III.

72. Breton, *A Discourse,* sigs. vi, viii, e.g., makes several references to Drake's feat in "passing the Gulf"; see also Wallis, "English Enterprise," pp. 195–197.

73. Breton, *A Discourse,* sig. A.xiii, p. 15.

The Aftermath: A Summary of British Discovery in the Pacific between Drake and Cook

NORMAN J. W. THROWER

When the Lords of the Admiralty wrote the secret instructions, dated 6 July 1776, for Captain James Cook's third voyage, they recalled Francis Drake's explorations of the California coast nearly two hundred years earlier. Cook was instructed after leaving the islands for the South Pacific to:

> proceed in as direct a course as you can to the coast of New Albion, en-
> deavouring to fall in with it in the latitude of 45°0' North; and taking
> care, in your way thither, not to lose any time in search of new lands. . . .
>   Upon your arrival on the coast of New Albion you are . . . to proceed
> northward along the coast, as far as the latitude of 65°, or farther . . . and
> to explore, such rivers or inlets as may appear to be of a considerable
> extent and pointing towards Hudsons or Baffins Bays.[1]

These passages provide links between Drake, the discoverer of New Albion (Nova Albion, as he named it), and Cook. It was intended that Cook should continue from approximately Drake's farthest point north in the Pacific to discover the Northwest Passage. Cook, like Drake before him, did not find the elusive sea route around (or through) North America, but both contributed remarkably to the art and science of navigation.

Sailors of various nations, including the English, served on Iberian ships in the Pacific before 1578 (see Lessa, ch. 5, above) and, in fact, Drake was not the first Englishman to enter this ocean. John Oxenham, who had been with Drake at the capture of Nombre de Dios in 1572, returned to the Caribbean two years later as captain of a small ship with some seventy men.[2] He anchored his ship and with his party marched across the Isthmus of Panama, where, on the Pacific side, they built a pinnace. In this vessel, they sailed into the South Seas and captured two small Spanish ships carrying gold and silver from Quito to Panama. Upon their return to shore, the English were captured and the treasure recovered by a strong force commanded by Juan de Ortega. Most of the English were executed as pirates in Panama, but Oxenham and the master and the pilot of his ship were taken to Lima, imprisoned, and then hanged. Three years after Oxenham's ill-fated adventure, Drake sailed into the Pacific through the Strait of Magellan on the first stage of his circumnavigation of the globe.

After Drake's expedition, the next English voyage in the Pacific was that of Thomas Cavendish. Cavendish, who came from a well-connected family, first became associated with overseas adventurers in 1584, when Sir Walter Raleigh was planning settlements in Virginia. Cavendish was on the Carolina Outer Banks in the summer of 1585 but wanted to lead his own expedition around the globe in emulation of Sir Francis Drake.[3] He put together a small squadron including the newly built *Desire* and left England in June 1586. Following roughly the route taken by Drake, Cavendish traversed the Strait of Magellan and sailed along the Pacific shore of South and Central America. Off the coast of Baja California he captured the Manila galleon the *Santa Ana* and took most of her treasure and supplies. Having gained intelligence from its crew about the Far East, Cavendish struck across the Pacific. He reached Java in March 1588 and returned to England by way of the Cape of Good Hope in September. For his circumnavigation, accomplished in a little over two years, Cavendish expected the same rewards Drake had received, including knighthood. But his achievement was overshadowed by the recent Armada victory, and he had to be content with the freedoms of Southampton and Portsmouth and the continued support of his prominent patrons toward further adventuring. Thus, in 1590, Cavendish began preparing for a second voyage in which he planned to sail again through the Strait of Magellan and across the Pacific to China, there to initiate commerce with England. A return journey on a route similar to that of his earlier great voyage would have made him the first man to have led two circumnavigations. But the enterprise, which began when a squadron of three ships and 350 men left Plymouth on 26 August 1591, ended tragically the next year. Cavendish died aboard the *Galleon Leicester* on her premature return to England without having reached the Pacific.

John Davis, an experienced Arctic explorer, had joined Cavendish's second voyage as captain of the *Desire* in the hope of finding the Northwest Passage from the Pacific by way of the (mythical) Strait of Anian, about 50°N latitude. After sighting the Southern (later the Falkland) Isles, which became known to the English after this event as Davis' Isles (Davis's Southern Islands), Davis became separated from the main body of Cavendish's squadron. He pressed on through the Strait of Magellan and reached the Pacific. However, through a combination of bad weather, a shortage of supplies, and his crew's lack of cooperation, he soon turned back and reached home in June 1592.

This unsuccessful adventure was followed by another in 1594, when Richard Hawkins led an expedition into the Pacific. Hawkins was the only son of Sir John Hawkins, kinsman and associate of Drake and a member of the West Country family which had been prominent in English overseas enterprises for over a century (see Gill, ch. 6, above). Richard Hawkins had accompanied Drake to the West Indies in 1585, and he had commanded the *Swallow* against the Spanish Armada in 1588. Like Drake and Cavendish, he planned a voyage around the globe, and left the Thames in the *Dainty* in April 1593. A year later, after many vicissitudes, the ship passed through the Strait of Magellan, sailed along the coast of Chile, and successfully attacked Valparaiso. Continuing north, the *Dainty* was intercepted by two well-armed Spanish ships under the command of Don Beltrán de Castro. After a running fight of three days, Hawkins, severely wounded, surrendered. He was taken to Lima and in 1597 sent to Spain, where he was imprisoned. After protracted negotiations Hawkins was released, and when he returned home he was knighted, on 23 July 1603. But his voyage to the Pacific coast of South America was not followed by further English adventures in that region for many decades.[4]

In the late sixteenth and early seventeenth centuries, the English became interested in the East India trade. From 1597 on the Dutch, who eventually displaced the Portuguese in the area, were active in Southeast Asia. The first English expedition to reach the East Indian Archipelago since Drake and Cavendish had visited the area on their circumnavigations was a flotilla commanded by James Lancaster in 1591. Lancaster came by the usual route via the Cape of Good Hope, and he returned to the East Indies by the same passage in 1601 and again in 1603, sponsored by the East India Company (established in 1600). The English founded a trading factory at the Moluccas. Between 1604 and 1615 a succession of English voyages, using the same route to the East Indies by way of southern Africa, were led by Sir Henry Middleton, William Keeling, David Middleton, Antony Hippon, and John Saris. Gradually, the English learned firsthand about the shores of the Pacific from insular Southeast Asia to Japan. Trade was maintained through these contacts until 1623, when the Dutch effectively excluded the English from the area for about a century.

Seventy-five years elapsed between Hawkins's ill-fated penetration of the Pacific along the coast of the Americas and the next English voyage in that direction, that of Sir John Narborough between 1669 and 1671. The Duke of York (later James II) granted a commission to Narborough to command H.M.S. *Sweepstakes,* a vessel of three hundred tons and thirty-six guns with a crew of eighty. She was equipped for twelve months and was accompanied by a hired consort, the *Bachelour,* a pink of seventy tons and four guns, with a crew of twenty and carrying supplies. Narborough, who had previous service in the south Atlantic, was allowed a sum of three hundred pounds for trading in the South Seas. That this was partly a commercial enterprise and partly for exploration, was indicated by Narborough: "The design of this voyage is to make discovery of the seas and coasts of that part of the world [the Pacific coast of the Americas] and to lay the foundation of a trade there."[5] The two ships left England in mid-October 1669 and, sailing by way of Madeira and the Cape Verde Islands, reached Patagonia early the next year. The *Bachelour* was lost sight of by the *Sweepstakes,* which, after wintering at about 48°S, continued alone and traversed the Strait of Magellan by 24 November. The *Bachelour,* believing the *Sweepstakes* to be lost in a storm, returned to England. This loss was crucial because the *Bachelour* carried stores necessary for the voyage. Narborough nevertheless sailed north for Valdivia, which he attained on 21 December. Although Narborough's men were hospitably received at first, the Spaniards soon imprisoned four of them, including a lieutenant. They had not been released by the time Narborough sailed from Valdivia for the Strait of Magellan, which he reached on 6 January 1671. Five weeks later the *Sweepstakes* passed into the Atlantic, and she arrived back in England in May. The voyage was unsuccessful in its major objectives, but Narborough produced a chart of the Strait of Magellan which was used by later explorers. It has been suggested, sardonically, that Narborough's voyage was undertaken to land four Englishmen on the coast of Chile, and that he made no serious attempt to retrieve them. Probably it is fairer to say with Anson that the voyage was "rather an encouragement for future trials of this kind, than any objection against them."[6]

Some two decades after Narborough's voyage, a second expedition was sent from England to follow the same general course. In 1689 Captain John Strong was commissioned to take the *Welfare,* a vessel of 270 tons and with a crew of ninety, on essentially the same mission. The *Welfare* was provided with stores of cloth and ironwork for trade, and she carried letters of marque permitting Strong to engage the French, with whom the English were then at war. She left England in early November 1689, and by January 1690 the Southern Isles sighted by Davis had been reached.[7] Here Strong discovered and sailed through a passage which he called Falkland Sound in honor of Antony Cary, Viscount Falkland, First Lord of the Admiralty. Later the name was applied to the entire island group and its dependencies. It took Strong three months to navigate the Strait of Magellan, so that he reached Valdivia by June 1690. The Spaniards there would not trade with the English. Strong carried on some contraband trade before sailing to Juan Fernandez, where some stranded English buccaneers were picked up. By November the *Welfare* had returned to Chile; at Concepción, in an attempt to sell their goods, eleven of the crew were captured. As on Narborough's voyage, no serious attempt was made to recover the prisoners. Strong learned of the fate of Narborough's lieutenant, who, after having served the Spaniards for sixteen years and helping them build fortifications, was accused of treason and executed. The *Welfare* reached the Strait of Magellan in early December and sailed home by way of the West Indies. Although two prizes were taken, the promoters lost £12,000. Strong's voyage, like Narborough's, was unsuccessful in its main objectives; but it is remembered for the discovery of Falkland Sound.

Narborough and Strong, like Drake and Cook, led officially approved voyages. English pirates, including Richard Sawkins and Bartholomew Sharp, were also active in the last decade of the seventeenth century. Basil Ringrose, who accompanied these pirate leaders, wrote vividly about their exploits in *Bucaniers of America* (1685).[8] Earlier, in 1670, Henry Morgan had gathered a large force of pirates at the Caribbean port of Chagres and marched across the Isthmus (as Oxenham had done nearly a century before) to sack Panama City. That year, a treaty was signed between England and Spain by which English colonies in the New World were recognized by Spain and, in return, England promised to deal with the atrocities of the buccaneers.[9] In an attempt to help enforce this treaty, Morgan was made Deputy Governor of Jamaica and knighted; but the piracy continued. In early 1680, another large group of pirates, including Sawkins, Sharp, and Ringrose, were at Panama, where they captured a number of craft including *La Santissima Trinidad*, which they renamed *Trinity* and in which many of them sailed for the next two years, visiting the Islands of Juan Fernandez and cruising along the shores of Central and South America, attacking towns on the way. A high point of the voyage was the capture of a Spanish *derrotero*, or pilot book, by which the English gained secret cartographic intelligence. By sailing south of the Strait of Magellan, Sharp and his crew became the first Englishmen to round Cape Horn from the Pacific to the Atlantic. Some of those who returned to England were tried, but perhaps because of the capture of the *derrotero*, which was of great potential value to the English, they were exonerated.

The most remarkable of the buccaneers in many respects was William Dampier. Although he was not a great leader, Dampier, like Ringrose, published accounts of his travels; through his first book, *A New Voyage Round the World* (1697), he came to the attention of influential persons in the Royal Society and the Royal Navy. Dampier, born in 1652, the son of a tenant farmer in the West Country of England, had little formal education. He was apprenticed to a master mariner, and in 1671 he sailed to the East Indies; but he was back in England the following year. It was not long before Dampier was overseas again, this time in Jamaica, where he helped manage a plantation. He returned to England and married in 1678 but soon left for Central America, where he was associated with several well-known buccaneers. He was pillaging on the Pacific Coast of the Americas in 1683, and the next year he joined a ship which took him from Baja California to Guam and then to the Philippines. During the following five years, Dampier was on several vessels voyaging in the East Indies and the Indian Ocean, and in 1688 he touched the northern coast of Australia (New Holland)—the first Englishman to do so. He returned to England in 1691, completing his first circumnavigation, with a journal which had been kept under the most difficult circumstances: "I took care before I left the ship to provide my self a large Joint of Bambo [sic], which I stopt at both ends, closing it with Wax, so as to keep out any Water. In this I preserved my journal and other writings from being wet, tho' I was often forced to swim."[10]

The publication of this journal, containing detailed observations on natural history, physical geography, and ethnography, was followed by a second book, *Voyages and Discoveries* (1699), which was as successful as the first. Dampier petitioned the Admiralty to lead an expedition and was given a commission in the Royal Navy to command the *Roebuck,* a remodeled fire ship of 290 tons and twenty-six guns, for the purpose of geographical exploration. A crew of fifty signed on, and the ship made its way by the coast of Brazil and the Cape of Good Hope to the west coast of Australia, which was reached at 25°S latitude. From this point Dampier turned northward, exploring the coast and landing at several places before sailing to Timor. After refitting the ship and replenishing his supplies, he sailed east to the margins of the Pacific, where he made his most important discovery: that New Guinea and New Britain are separated by a body of water now called Dampier Strait. He returned by way of the Cape of Good Hope and Ascension Island, where the *Roebuck,* now rotten through and through, sank at anchor.[11]

Dampier was back in England by the summer of 1701 with his journals, most of which he had managed to save. He wrote a third book based on these, *A Voyage to New Holland,* which was also a great success. Dampier made two more voyages to the Pacific, both circumnavigations. Between 1703 and 1704, he took two merchant ships around the globe from east to west; and when Woodes Rogers circumnavigated the earth in the same direction from 1708 to 1710, during the War of the Spanish Succession, Dampier was pilot, a position well suited to his talents. An interesting event on this last voyage was the liberation from Juan Fernandez of Alexander Selkirk, later immortalized by Defoe as Robinson Crusoe. Dampier's own writings, though important as literary sources, are not essentially adventure or travel stories but factual and detailed accounts of places, people, plants, and animals (many of them new to his readers), as well as of winds, currents, and so on. Dampier's description of breadfruit was recalled later by Captain Cook, who examined the plant and recommended that it be transplanted to the West Indies. This was the reason for the voyage of the *Bounty,* 1787–1789, under Captain William Bligh (who had served with Cook), a voyage which turned mutinous; the mission was later successfully completed by Bligh in a new ship. Dampier became, through his travels and writings, the most influential English explorer of the Pacific between the times of Drake and Cook.

Piracy continued in the Pacific basin in the eighteenth century under such leaders as John Clipperton and George Shelvocke. A man of very different character was Commodore (later Lord) George Anson, who led a squadron of six Royal Navy warships and two small store vessels on an expedition to the Pacific between 1740 and 1744 during the War of the Austrian Succession, with the object of attacking Spanish shipping. Of Anson's ships only one vessel, the *Centurion*, returned to England following the prescribed course of the voyage, laden with great treasure from the Spanish Manila galleon which she had intercepted.[12] Anson gained great official and public recognition, though he made no significant geographical discoveries and lost about one thousand men.

The next British naval explorers in the Pacific were Cook's immediate precursors: Commodore, the Honourable John (Foul-weather Jack, grandfather of the poet) Byron, Lieutenant Samuel Wallis, and Lieutenant Philip Carteret. All were regular Royal Navy officers on officially sponsored voyages, and all were attempting to find the elusive Terra Australis in the South Pacific. The idea of a great southern continent had existed since antiquity, and it was espoused in the eighteenth century, particularly by Alexander Dalrymple of the East India Company, later the first hydrographer of the Royal Navy. Dalrymple had navigated the coasts of southern and eastern Asia on behalf of the East India Company, and he was the Royal Society's choice as leader of the expedition which Lieutenant (later Captain) Cook was appointed to lead in 1768. There was certainly a precedent for Dalrymple to be appointed in the same manner as Dampier had been, but Dampier's poor performance as a commander influenced the Royal Navy to select one of its own personnel to be leader.[13]

At the conclusion of the Seven Years' War, Byron was sent on a peaceful exploring mission (1764–65) in the frigate *Dolphin*, with the sloop *Tamar*.[14] Byron was to attempt to find the Strait of Anian and if possible to sail through it from west to east. Should this not be feasible, he was to try to discover the southern continent by circumnavigating in the latitudes in which land had been reported by sailors of several nations for two hundred years. Once in the Pacific, Byron attempted only the second task. But contrary winds drove him from 25°S latitude on the South American side to 20°N latitude on the Asiatic side of the Pacific and thus thwarted the enterprise. In the mid-Pacific Byron discovered two islands in the Tuamotu Archipelago and one each in the Tokelan group and the Gilbert Islands which had not previously been seen by European sailors. He returned to England by way of Batavia and the Cape of Good Hope with modest additions to geographical knowledge of the Pacific.

Byron's voyage did not discourage the British government from further exploring the area, and in 1767 another expedition was sent out. This voyage was planned for exploration westward from the coast of South America, farther south than had been customary. If land were found, the expedition was to return to England via the same route it had come by (around Cape Horn); if not, it was to continue across the Pacific and return home by way of the East Indies. For this purpose the *Dolphin*, used by Byron in his circumnavigation, was selected, to be accompanied by a sloop, the *Swallow*. Samuel Wallis was appointed commander of the *Dolphin* and of the expedition, and Philip Carteret commanded the *Swallow*.[15] Carteret had sailed around the world with Byron as first lieutenant in the *Tamar* and later the *Dolphin*, whereas Wallis had no previous experience in exploration. The two ships left England in August 1766. It took some four months to clear the Strait of Magellan; at its western exit the two ships were separated in a storm, and they sailed independently across the Pacific. Wallis, driven by the trade winds and taking a generally more northerly course, made discoveries in the Low Archipelago and the Society Islands, including Tahiti, which he called King George Third's Island. The *Dolphin* proceeded from there across the Pacific north of the equator, reaching home by way of the East Indies and southern Africa. Wallis arrived in England on 20 May 1768, when preparations were being made for Cook's first voyage to the Pacific —to Tahiti—to observe the transit of Venus.

Carteret, meanwhile, taking a generally more southerly route as prescribed in the orders, discovered Pitcairn Island, named for the seaman who first saw it. The *Swallow*, now in bad condition, passed through the Tuamotus and reached the Solomon Islands. These islands, which took their name from the presumed location of gold obtained by King Solomon's navy, were a kind of fata morgana which had been pursued since the beginnings of European expansion overseas and which had been seen by the Spanish in the sixteenth century. This was unknown to Carteret at the time; nevertheless, he discovered the strait separating New Britain from New Ireland and thus entered a region visited some eighty years earlier by Dampier. Carteret returned to England via the Celebes, Batavia, and Cape Town. The *Swallow* reached England after Cook had sailed with the botanist Joseph (later Sir, Baronet) Banks, the astronomer Charles Green, and other scientists in the *Endeavor* on his first great voyage to the Pacific.

Any discussion of the considerable British presence in the Pacific between the times of Drake and Cook would not be complete without reference to another captain who never reached this greatest of oceans: Edmond Halley, the astronomer who in 1694 had been given the rank of Captain in the Royal Navy and command of a little ship, the *Paramore*. The purpose of this appointment was to enable Halley to make, in 1698–1701, what have been called the first sea journeys taken for purely scientific purposes. Earlier, Halley had written a paper on the transit of Venus, and after his voyages in the Atlantic he returned to the subject. Halley predicted that the transit of Venus would occur in 1761 and 1769, and he wrote: "I strongly urge diligent searchers of the heavens (for whom when I have ended my days, these sights are being kept in store) to bear in mind this injunction of mine and to apply themselves actively and with all their might to making the necessary observations."[16] He pointed out the practical value of sending expeditions to distant parts of the earth to make observations of the transit of Venus, which might improve the estimate of the distance of the earth from the sun, not known at the time.

Halley's words were remembered many years after his death at the Royal Society, which sponsored Cook's first Pacific voyage, with the official reason of observing the transit of Venus. The success of the voyage led to Cook's second and third (and final) voyages, during which most of the large geographical problems of the Pacific were resolved. George Vancouver, who had been with Cook, and Matthew Flinders, who had served under Bligh who, in turn, had served under Cook, continued the more detailed coastal exploration and charting of northwest America and Australia, respectively. Thus, with Cook a new era of scientific exploration began in the Pacific, an era which had its foundations in two centuries of English voyaging inspired and personified by Sir Francis Drake.

NOTES

1. John C. Beaglehole, ed., *The Journals of Captain James Cook on His Voyages of Discovery: The Voyage of the "Resolution" and "Discovery," 1776–1780,* Hakluyt Society, 2nd ser. (Cambridge, 1967), p. ccxxi.

2. James Burney, *A Chronological History of the Voyages in the South Seas or Pacific Ocean,* vol. I (London, 1803), pp. 292–299. Burney's five volumes (1803–1817) contain descriptions of the important Pacific voyages of Europeans prior to 1764.

3. David B. Quinn, ed., *The Last Voyage of Thomas Cavendish, 1591–1592,* Society for the History of Discoveries (Chicago, 1975), p. 9.

4. Herman R. Friis, ed., *The Pacific Basin: A History of Its Geographical Exploration,* American Geographical Society (New York, 1967), see esp. chap. 12, "Geographical Exploration by the British," pp. 221–255, by Richard I. Ruggles.

5. Burney, *Chronological History,* vol. III (London, 1813), pp. 323–324.

6. Richard Walter, *Anson's Voyage round the World,* ed. G. S. Laird Clowes (London, 1928), p. 89.

7. Burney, *Chronological History,* vol. IV (London, 1816), pp. 329–337.

8. Basil Ringrose, *Bucaniers of America,* vol. II, (London, 1685) and Derek Howse and Norman J. W. Thrower, eds., *A Buccaneer's Atlas: The South Sea Waggoner of Basil Ringrose,* forthcoming.

9. Burney, *Chronological History,* IV, 63–64.

10. William Dampier, *A New Voyage around the World* (London, 1697), p. 16.

11. William Dampier, *A Voyage to New Holland,* ed. James A. Williamson (London, 1939), pp. 245–248.

12. Walter, *Anson's Voyage,* esp. pp. 349–393.

13. Howard T. Fry, *Alexander Dalrymple and the Expansion of British Trade,* British Commonwealth Society Imperial Studies no. 29 (London, 1970), pp. 270–277.

14. John Hawkesworth, *An Account of the Voyages . . . in the Southern Hemisphere,* 3 vols. (London, 1773), I, 3. Volume I deals with the voyages of Byron, Wallis, and Carteret, vols. II and III with Cook's first Pacific voyage in the *Endeavour.*

15. Helen Wallis, ed., *Carteret's Voyage Round the World, 1767–1769,* Hakluyt Society, 2nd ser., 124, 125, 2 vols. (Cambridge, 1965), I, 20; II, 287, 299–300.

16. Norman J. W. Thrower, ed., *The Three Voyages of Edmond Halley in the "Paramore," 1698–1701,* Hakluyt Society, 2nd ser., 156, 157, 2 vols. (Glasgow, 1981), I, 26.

A Collection of Drake

Bibliographic Items, 1569–1659

BENJAMIN P. DRAPER

This collection is a selection and condensation of the extensive "Drake Bibliography, 1569–1979" prepared by Benjamin P. Draper. Manuscript copies of the larger work, which contains close to six hundred entries, have been deposited in the British Library, London; the Bancroft Library at the University of California, Berkeley; the University of California, Los Angeles; and the California State Archives, Sacramento. Scholars interested in Drake, and particularly those concerned with his continuing reputation from the second half of the seventeenth century, will want to consult this more complete work which carries the bibliography forward to the present time. Annotations of entries for the period 1569–1659 are much fuller in the larger manuscript than in this selection. Moreover, for this shorter collection a few entries have been omitted even from the first ninety years of coverage: mainly maps and artifacts covered in the chapters of this volume. In addition to books, manuscripts, maps, and artifacts, the full Draper bibliography includes periodical and newspaper articles and illustrations.*

These entries represent the personal interest of Dr. Draper, yet they form a

---

*There are actually two versions of the larger Draper bibliography: one dated 1977 is chronological, as in the abridged form printed here; another version, dated 1979, is alphabetical by classes of material.

related group of printed and manuscript materials. They extend from the earliest reference by Drake's kinsman Sir John Hawkins to Sir William Davenant's opera *Sir Francis Drake*—that is, from a cursory mention to a full-scale patriotic fantasy. After 1659, most items are derivative. The beginning date, 1569, is the year of Drake's marriage and of Mercator's world map (known to Drake before the Famous Voyage), as well as of the reference by Hawkins.

In his quest for material on Drake, Dr. Draper in most instances followed the bibliographer's rule and actually had each book or manuscript in his hands. His studies took him to the Library of Congress, Morgan Library in New York, New York Public Library, Harvard University, and the University of Chicago; he also spent many hours in the Huntington Library, San Marino, California, the Bancroft Library at the University of California, Berkeley, and the Clark Library at the University of California, Los Angeles. In England, he worked in the British Library and the Public Record Office in London and at Buckland Abbey, Drake's great house, now a museum. On the Continent he visited the Archivo General de Indias, Seville, and the Archivo General, Simancas; the Bibliothèque Nationale, Paris; and libraries in Madrid, Amsterdam, and Rotterdam. In this selection of Drake items, library locations of books and Short Title Catalog numbers are not usually given.

Dr. Draper, who was born in 1907, died in 1980, a few months before the work of the Sir Francis Drake Commission in California had terminated. He was the first vice president of the commission from its beginning, and its true founder. Dr. Draper did not live to put his manuscript into final form; this collection was prepared for publication by Frances Zeitlin, retired Medieval and Renaissance bibliographer at the Research Library, University of California, Los Angeles. Together with the larger "Drake Bibliography, 1569–1979," this remains a testimony to Dr. Draper's diligent dedication to Sir Francis Drake studies.

His Royal Highness Prince Philip, Duke of Edinburgh, wrote the following preface to the original "Drake Bibliography, 1569–1977":

BUCKINGHAM PALACE

Sir Francis Drake was one of those rare people in history whose exploits and personal ties have continued to be just as exciting as they were to their contemporaries. He seemed to be gifted with characteristics which somehow embodied the national taste and spirit of his age.

Perhaps there is a great deal more truth in the words of that well known song "It ain't what you do, it is the way that you do it" than the author realised. Certainly Drake did things in his own daring and spectacular way in an age of daring and spectacle. He was not the first man to circumnavigate the globe, but he certainly invested his journey with a quite remarkable degree of drama and romance.

The author of this book has completed an immense task for which scholars and historians long into the future will have cause to be grateful.

Indeed it fulfills the words of the prayer which Drake himself is reputed to have composed when his fortunes were at a low ebb on the coast of South America:

"When thou givest to thy servants to endeavour any great matter, grant us also to know that it is not the beginning but the continuing of the same unto the end until it be thoroughly finished which yieldeth the true glory."

Philip

We are grateful to Prince Philip for providing this letter, the message reproduced in the front of this volume, and his interest in Drake celebrations worldwide.

N.J.W.T.

USAGES AND ABBREVIATIONS

Accent marks in Spanish: Since accent marks were rarely used in sixteenth-century Spanish, they will usually not be found in this bibliography in direct quotations from early sources.

Except in direct quotations, names of persons have been supplied with accent marks in accordance with modern practice. Geographical names are treated in the same way, unless there is an accepted English usage which omits accentuation, such as "Mexico," "Panama," or "Peru."

Manuscript titles: Titles of manuscripts in their original language which have been taken either from archival catalogs or calendars, or from scholarly editions of the manuscripts, are enclosed in quotation marks. When facsimile copies of manuscripts have been used, titles are given as in the original, without quotation marks. These facsimiles may be in Dr. Draper's files, or found reproduced in printed works. When such sources are not available, a descriptive title in English is supplied.

Chronology: The bibliography is arranged in chronological order according to the date of the original document (in the case of manuscripts) or of original publication (in the case of printed books). Undated manuscripts have been placed in the location where they are thought to belong.

Abbreviations:

A.G.I.*   Archivo General de Indias, Seville (Patronato Real).
A.G.N.   Archivo General de la Nación, Mexico.
A.G.S.   Archivo General, Simancas.
Andrews   Kenneth R. Andrews, ed. *The Last Voyage of Drake & Hawkins* (Hakluyt Society, 2nd ser., 142). Cambridge, 1972.
B.L.   British Library.

*The old A.G.I. locations used by Nuttall, Wagner, et al. are used throughout this bibliography.

C.D.I.   *Colección de documentos inéditos para la historia* de *España.* 113 vols. Madrid, 1842–1899.

Corbett   Julian S. Corbett. *Drake and the Tudor Navy.* 2 vols. London, 1898.

Eliott-Drake   Lady Eliott-Drake [Elizabeth]. *The Family and Heirs of Sir Francis Drake.* 2 vols. London, 1911.

H.H.   David B. Quinn, ed. *The Hakluyt Handbook* (Hakluyt Society, 2nd ser., 144, 145). 2 vols. London, 1974.

Hume   Martin S. Hume, ed. *Calendar of Letters and State Papers Relating to English Affairs . . . in . . . the Archives of Simancas.* Vols. II (1568–1579) and III (1580–1586). London, 1894–1896.

Kraus   Hans P. Kraus. *Sir Francis Drake: A Pictorial Biography.* Amsterdam, 1970.

Navarrete   Madrid. Museo Naval, *Indice de la colección de documentos de Fernández de Navarrete que posee el Museo Naval.* ed. V. Vicente Vela. Madrid, 1946.

Nuttall**   Zelia Nuttall, ed. *New Light on Drake* (Hakluyt Society, 2nd ser., 34). London, 1914. Repr.: New York, 1967.

PN 1589   Richard Hakluyt. *Principall Navigations . . . .* London, 1589.

PN 1600   Richard Hakluyt. *Principal Navigations . . . .* 3 vols. [2nd ed.] London, 1598/99–1600.

P.R.O.   Public Record Office, London.

Penzer   Nicholas M. Penzer, ed. *The World Encompassed and Analogous Contemporary Documents . . .* with an intro. by Sir Richard C. Temple. London, 1926. Repr.: New York, 1969.

Repertorio   *Repertorio de documentos existentes en las colecciones de MSS. del Museo Naval y que se refieren a las empresas del Draque contra España, 1568–1594.* Vol. II of *La Dragontea de Lope de Vega Carpic.* Madrid, 1935.

S.P.12   State Papers Domestic, Reign of Elizabeth I.

Taylor   E. G. R. Taylor, ed. *The Troublesome Voyage of Captain Edward Fenton* (Hakluyt Society, 2nd ser., 113). London, 1959.

Vaux   W. S. W. Vaux, ed. *The World Encompassed by Sir Francis Drake* (Hakluyt Society [16]). London, 1854.

Wagner   Henry R. Wagner. *Sir Francis Drake's Voyage around the World.* San Francisco, 1926.

**Copies of materials used by Nuttall are found in: 1) "Documents relating to Sir Francis Drake's voyage of circumnavigation . . . transcripts made . . . from the originals preserved in South American and Spanish collections." *In Spanish.* Partly typewritten. *B.L. Additional MS 44, 894.* Also, 2) "Materials relating to Sir Francis Drake." Typed manuscripts of the English documents published in pts. 9, 12, 13, and app. of *New Light on Drake. Bancroft Library MS Z-R 14.*

Wallis   British Library. *Sir Francis Drake: An Exhibition to Commemorate Francis Drake's Voyage around the World,
1577–1580.* ed. Helen Wallis. London, 1977.

BIBLIOGRAPHY

1. Sir John Hawkins
*A true declaration of the troublesome voyage of M. John Haukins to the
parties of Guynea and the west Indies, in the yeares of our Lord 1567. and
1568.* London, 1569.

The expedition of 1567–68 under Hawkins' command was Drake's second
recorded voyage. Hawkins recounts that after the disastrous battle with the
Spaniards at San Juan de Ulúa, off the coast of Mexico, in September 1568,
Drake, in command of the *Judith,* "forsoke us in oure great miserie."
    Used as a source in PN 1589, reprinted in PN 1600 III.

2. Draft project of the proposed expedition by Francis Drake to the Pacific.
[ca. 1577.] *B. L. Cotton MS Otho E. VIII, fols. 8–9.*

This three-page memorandum, badly damaged by fire, was first described and
partially reproduced by E. G. R. Taylor, "The Missing Draft Project of Drake's
Voyage of 1577–80," *Geographical Journal* 75 (1930) 44–47. It shows that the
voyage was sponsored by the Navy Board (the Earl of Lincoln, Sir William
Winter, George Winter, and John Hawkins) and by Queen Elizabeth's inner
circle of advisers, the Earl of Leicester, Sir Francis Walsingham, and Sir Christopher Hatton. Drake himself invested £1,000.

3. John Dee
General and Rare Memorials pertayning to the Perfect Arte of Navigation.
London, 1577.

Dee was the counselor of great Elizabethan sea captains, including Hawkins,
and of such principal backers of Drake as Leicester, Walsingham, and Hatton.
Dee's precise role in the circumnavigation is not known.
    The *Memorials* is the first part of what was intended as a four-part work on
the philosophy and history of navigation. Parts 2 and 3 no longer exist; part 4,
"The Great Volume of Famous and Riche Discoveries," remains in manuscript
(*B.L. Cotton MS Vitellius C. VII, fols. 178b, 179*).

4. Thomas Doughty
"The sume of Thomas Doughtie his oration upon the pellica[n] when he
came from [the] price [i.e., prize] to the pellican to Remayne the companie
being called by the Botteswain together." [Undated.] *B. L. Harleian MS
6221, fol. 7.*

Doughty, one of the principals on the voyage of circumnavigation, made this speech after his quarrel with Drake off the Cape Verde Islands. It had a strong bearing on the events which led to Doughty's execution.

Printed in Corbett I, 223–224 and Penzer 168–169. This and the following document are found in *B. L. Harleian MS 6221*, in a collection of manuscripts entitled "Sr Fraunsis Drake's voyage wth his proseeding against Thomas Doughtye."

5. Documents relating to Thomas Doughty. [Undated.] *B. L. Harleian MS 6221, fol. 9.*

Notes of testimony against Doughty by various members of Drake's company in regard to Doughty's attempts to assert his authority as commander in Drake's absence.

Printed in Vaux 165–174.

6. Thomas Doughty
Will signed by Thomas Doughty 11 September 1577 and proved 15 October 1579, together with a codicil. [July? 1578.] *MS P.R.O. PROB. 11/61/40 fol. 313d.*

The codicil was presumably added by Doughty at Port San Julian when he realized he was to be beheaded. The execution took place on 2 July 1578, and the will was probably carried back to England aboard the *Elizabeth*.

7. Declarations of Captain John Oxenham and other Englishmen who were prisoners in the Holy Office of the City of Los Reyes, about what they knew concerning the exploration of the Strait of Magellan. Los Reyes [Lima], 20 February 1579. *MS in Spanish. A.G.I. Patronato. 1/1/4–1, no. 32.*

John Oxenham, John Butler (ship's master), and Thomas "Xervel" or "Xerores" were captured by the Spaniards in the Isthmus of Panama in 1575. Their questioning occurred a week after Drake had reached Callao. Oxenham and Butler were sentenced to serve in the galleys, "Xervel" to life imprisonment (see also no. 53).

Translated, Nuttall 5–12.

8. Benito Díaz Bravo
Letter. Port of Manta [Ecuador], 7 March 1579. *MS in Spanish. A.G.I. Patronato. 2/5/2–21.*

The letter was probably addressed to the president of the Audiencia at Panama. Díaz Bravo, a pilot, was captured near Cojimíes, Ecuador, on 28 February and released the following day. He describes the robbing of his ship, his conversation with Drake, and the simulated hanging to which he and others

of his crew were subjected (see also nos. 13, 21).
    Translated, Wagner 354–356.

9. Fr. Gaspar de Palma
Letter to Juan Pérez Medina. Yauco, 14 March 1579. *MS in Spanish. A.G.I. Patronato. 2/5/2–21.*

    The letter warns that the "Lutherans" are threatening the city of Guayaquil and murdering inhabitants of the coast (see also no. 14).
    Partially translated, Nuttall 153–154.

10. San Juan de Antón
"Relacion que hizo . . . por mandado del Dⁿ. Alonso Criado de Castilla, que . . . presidia aquella Audiencia. . . ." Panama, 16 March 1579. [Certified copy, 15 April 1579.] *MS in Spanish. A.G.I. Patronato. 2/5/2–21.*

    San Juan de Antón was captain and owner of the Spanish vessel *Nuestra Señora de la Concepción*, nicknamed *Cacafuego*, captured by Drake off the coast of Peru on 1 March 1579. He was released on 7 March with a letter of safe-conduct (see no. 27). The deposition exists in several versions: a contemporary copy in *A.G.I. Patronato. 1/1/2–21*; an eighteenth-century copy in Museo Naval, Madrid, *M. SS. 35–3, 6 fols.* (Navarrete no. 897); abstract in *Repertorio* 48–58.
    Contemporary translations in *P.R.O. S.P. 94/1, no. 23A; Lansdowne MS 30, no. 12; Ashmolean MS 830, fol. 19.* Modern translations, Wagner 360–368, Nuttall 163–175.
    Another statement, made by Antón to Pedro de Sarmiento on 31 March 1579, is included in Sarmiento's *Relación* (see no. 33).

11. Nicolás Jorge
Deposition. Before the Audiencia of Panama, 28 March 1579. *MS in Spanish. A.G.I. Patronato. 2/5/2–21.*

    Jorge, a Flemish citizen, gave testimony concerning Drake's seizure of treasure in the port of Arica, Peru, on 5 February. He was captured by Drake and taken with him, then released onto the ship of San Juan de Antón.
    Translated, Nuttall 135–140, Wagner 350–353.

12. Benito Díaz Bravo
Deposition. Before the Audiencia of Panama, 3 April 1579. *MS in Spanish. A.G.I. Patronato. 2/5/2–21.*

    Contains essentially the same information as his letter of 7 March 1579 (see no. 8).
    Translated, Nuttall 146–148.

13. Francisco Jácome
Deposition. Before the Audiencia of Panama, 3 April 1579. *MS in Spanish.*
A.G.I. Patronato. 2/5/2–21.

Jácome, clerk of Díaz Bravo's ship, was captured and released with him and was also a victim of the simulated hanging (cf. no. 8). He testified on Drake's strength in men and artillery.
Translated, Nuttall 149–150; excerpts in Penzer, 226–227.

14. Juan Pérez de Medina
Deposition. Before the Audiencia of Panama, 9 April 1579. *MS in Spanish.*
A.G.I. Patronato. 2/5/2–21.

Medina, a passenger on Díaz Bravo's ship, carried with him the letter of Fr. Gaspar de Palma (see no. 9) and showed it to the court.
Translated, Nuttall 152–154.

15. Domingo de Lizarza
Deposition. Before the Audiencia of Panama, 9 April 1579. *MS in Spanish.*
A.G.I. Patronato. 2/5/2–21.

Lizarza, clerk of San Juan de Antón's ship the *Cacafuego,* was captured and released with his captain. His testimony adds little to that of Antón.
Translated, Nuttall 176–179.

16. Custodio Rodrigues
Deposition. Before the Audiencia of Panama, 13 April 1579. *MS in Spanish.*
A.G.I. Patronato. 2/5/2–21.

Rodrigues, a Portuguese sailor or pilot, was captured in the port of Paita, Peru, sometime in February and released with San Juan de Antón. He witnessed the capture of Díaz Bravo and Antón and testified that Drake planned to rendezvous with his two lost ships in the Moluccas.
Translated, Nuttall 141–144.

17. Gaspar de Vargas
Letter to Don Martín Enríquez, viceroy of New Spain. Guatulco, Mexico, 13 April 1579. *MS in Spanish. A.G.I. Patronato. 2/5/2–21.*

Vargas was the Alcalde of Guatulco, a small town near the coast, whose port was sacked by Drake on 13 April. Drake carried off the curate, the visiting mayor of Suchitepec, and Francisco Gómez Rengifo, the factor of Guatulco. The letter was received by the Viceroy on 23 April and enclosed in a letter he wrote to Philip II the same day.
Translated, Nuttall 213–215, Wagner 379–380.

18. Nuno da Silva*
Log Book. 19 [sic] January 1578 to 13 April 1579. *MS in Portuguese.*
A.G.I. Patronato. 1/1/2–32, no. 30.

Nuno da Silva was the Portuguese pilot captured by Drake off the Cape
Verde Islands on 30 January 1578 and abandoned by him at Guatulco on 13
April 1579. His services were apparently invaluable to Drake, as his accounts
have been to historians. The log begins the day of his capture and ends the day
of his release.

Photographic copy in the collection of Zelia Nuttall transcripts and documents, *B. L. Additional MS 44,894, fols. 250–266.* Translated, Nuttall
276–294.

19. Nuno da Silva
Relacion q̄ dio vn portugues A quien el cosario yngles dexo enel puerto de-
guatulco. [Guatulco] 13 [14?] April 1579. *MS in Spanish. A.G.I. Patronato.*
2/5/2–21, no. 6. (2 copies, with slight variations.)

Nuno da Silva's "First Relation" was enclosed in the letter sent by the Alcalde
Gaspar de Vargas to the Viceroy of New Spain on 14 April 1579 (see no. 20).
Translated by Nuttall 245–252; Wagner, instead of printing his translations

---

*A note on the name of the Portuguese pilot: His name in Portuguese was *Nuno da Silva.* On
a document signed by him in 1583 (photographic reproduction in Nuttall, pl. XV) he used the
form Nuno da Sylva, a common sixteenth-century spelling. The Portuguese form was correctly
used by Jan Huyghen van Linschoten, William Phillip, Richard Hakluyt, Vaux, Eliott-Drake, and
Samuel Eliot Morison (in his *The European Discovery of America,* Oxford University Press,
1974).

In the Spanish-speaking world the name consistently appears, from the earliest documents to
the most recent publications, in a Hispanicized form: Nuño de Silva (with accepted variant
spellings of Sylva, Silba, and Sylba).

Silva's English companions on the voyage (e.g., John Drake, Francis Fletcher) gave him the
name Sylvestre, a sort of English-Latin translation of da Silva.

During the nineteenth century, a bastardized Spanish-Portuguese form was sometimes used by
English-speaking writers: Nuno de Silva, combining the Portuguese given name with the Hispanicized surname. This usage was followed by Barrow and the *Dictionary of National Biography.*

Nuttall was the first to use the bastardized form Nuño da Silva, combining a Spanish given
name with the Portuguese surname. She appears to have been oblivious to the problem; her
facsimile of the document signed Nuno da Sylva shows the filing name used by the Spanish clerk,
Nuño de Silba, but is captioned by her as Nuño da Silva.

Wagner picked up Nuttall's usage, though apparently not without slight misgivings. Note 1
on p. 338 reads: "As Silva was Portuguese, his name no doubt was *da* Silva, although in all the
Spanish documents it is written *de* Silva."

Between them, Nuttall and Wagner seem to have established the usage of twentieth-century
English and American scholars.

Beginning with early documents and continuing over the years, eccentric forms of the given
name appear, such as Nunno, Nonnez (Edward Cliffe), Nunez (Thompson), Nugnos (on a
sixteenth-century map) and the completely unjustifiable Nunho (Kraus).

[F. Z.]

of the various Nuno da Silva documents separately, put together a composite account (338–349).

Photocopies with complete Draper Bibliography.

20. Gaspar de Vargas
Report sent to Viceroy Martín Enríquez. Guatulco, 14 April 1579. *MS in Spanish. A.G.I. Patronato. 2/5/2–21, no. 6.*

The report contains a description of Drake and his ship, as furnished by the three men captured by Drake the day before. Of Nuno da Silva it says: "He carries with him a Portuguese pilot who is very skillful. It seems that it is he who governs and directs this Armada. This Portuguese speaks the English language as though it were his own and he is the General's all in all." A brief report by Nuno da Silva is enclosed (see no. 19), a copy of which was sent by the Viceroy to Don Francisco de Toledo, Viceroy of Peru, on 17 May.

Translated, Nuttall 238–241; extracts in Wagner 380–381.

21. Alonso Sánchez Colchero
Deposition. Before Diego García de Palacios, judge of the Audiencia of Guatemala. Realejo, Nicaragua, 15 April 1579. *MS in Spanish. A.G.I. Patronato. 2/5/2–21.*

Sánchez Colchero, pilot aboard the ship of Rodrigo Tello, was captured off the island of Caño on 20 March 1579. He testified that when he refused to act as pilot for Drake he was subjected to a simulated hanging (cf. nos. 8, 13).

Translated, Nuttall 193–198; excerpts, Penzer 226–227.

22. Don Francisco de Zárate
"Carta . . . al Virrey de Nueva España." Realejo, Nicaragua, 16 April 1579. *MS in Spanish. A.G.I. Patronato. 1/5/2–21, no. 9.*

Don Francisco was captured out of Acapulco by Drake on 4 April 1579 and "held for fifty-five hours." On his release he went to Realejo. He relates: "Drake is a man about 35 years of age, low of stature, with a fair beard and is one of the greatest mariners that sails the sea. . . . He is served on silver dishes with gold borders. . . . He carries painters who paint for him pictures of the coast in its exact colours. . . . He showed me the commission that he received from her [the Queen]." (Nuttall translation.)

The eighteenth-century copy now in Museo Naval, Madrid, *M. SS. 35–6, 4 fols.* (Navarrete no. 900), published in *Repertorio 51–61*, is translated in Eliott-Drake I, 36–41. Translations also in Nuttall 201–210 and Wagner 373–377; extracts from Nuttall in Penzer 215–220.

23. Cornieles Lanberd
Deposition. Before Ventura de Medina, Chief Constable of the Audiencia of

Panama, 8 May 1579. [Certified copy, 17 June 1579.] *MS in Spanish. A.G.I. Patronato. 2/5/2–21.*

Lanberd, a Flemish merchant, was on the ship of Rodrigo Tello and was captured on 20 March off the island of Caño. He was questioned about Drake's strength and his plans, and he reported on the mistreatment of Sánchez Colchero when he refused to act as pilot for Drake (cf. no. 21).

Translated, Nuttall 180–183, Wagner 369–372.

24. Jusepe de Parraces
Deposition. Before the Chief Constable of the Audiencia of Panama, 8 May 1579. [Certified copy, Panama, 17 June 1579.] *MS in Spanish. A.G.I. Patronato. 2/5/2–21.*

Parraces was a passenger on Tello's ship, taken prisoner on 20 March. He testified that Drake gave him and Juan de Espinosa a safe-conduct and that he wrote on the outside the names of the captains "who command the ships of which he and all his men say he is the General."

Printed in Manuel M. Peralta, *Costa Rica, Nicaragua y Panamá en el siglo XVI* (Madrid, 1883). Translated, Nuttall 185–189.

25. Diego de Messa
Deposition. Before the Chief Constable of the Audiencia of Panama, 8 May 1579. [Certified copy, Panama, 17 June 1579.] *MS in Spanish. A.G.I. Patronato. 2/5/2–21.*

Messa was another captive from Tello's ship; his testimony adds little to that of the others.

Translated, Nuttall 190–193.

26. Bernardino López
Deposition. Before Bishop Granero de Avalos. Guatulco, 15 May 1579. *MS in Spanish. A.G.N. Inquisición.*

López, Lieutenant-Governor of the port, testified about the sacking of the town and about his visit to Drake's ship with two other men to ask Drake not to burn the town or the ships in the harbor.

Translated, Nuttall 342–347.

27. Nuno da Silva
Relacion del viaje delcossario Ingles que dio Elpiloto nuno de silua ante susenoria a 20 demayo de 79. yesta nola dio el tan desmenuzada si no que como sele yua preguntando Respondia. Mexico, 20 May 1579. *MS in Spanish. A.G.I. Patronato. 2/5/2–21, no. 8.* (2 copies, with slight variations.)

The "Second Relation" of Nuno da Silva is the best known of his many accounts of Drake's voyage from the Cape Verde Islands to Guatulco. Its fame rests on the fact that an English version, long mistakenly thought to be Hakluyt's own translation of a Spanish document, was published in PN 1600 III, pp. 742–748, and subsequently reprinted a number of times.

There are two almost identical manuscript versions in A.G.I. Other extant manuscripts are the late sixteenth-century "Relacion del viage del cosario yngles que dio el piloto Nuño de Silva ante su excelencia del virrey de Mexico a. 20 de mayo de .79," in "Memoria de la Costa Rica del Mar del Norte," *Library of Congress, Kraus Collection*; and the eighteenth-century transcription in Museo Naval, Madrid, *M. SS. 35–11, 8 fols.* (Navarrete no. 904), abstract in *Repertorio*, pp. 64–65.

The "Second Relation" was first published by Jan Huyghen van Linschoten in a Dutch translation in his *Itinerario*, book III, chap. 55 (see no. 91). An English translation of the *Itinerario* was made by William Phillip and published in 1598. Phillip's version of the Silva "Relation," pp. 416–423, was the one reprinted by Hakluyt and subsequently by Vaux, pp. 254–278, and Penzer, pp. 169–181.

The source of the Silva manuscript used by Linschoten is not known; it was apparently very close to the versions in A.G.I. Nuttall, pp. 256–271, reprinted the version found in Hakluyt. She had compared it with an A.G.I. manuscript which she presumed to be its source, and had made notes of supposed errors and omissions. Since in almost all cases the Dutch version has the same reading as the A.G.I. manuscripts, the errors and omissions must be attributed to Phillip.

The version of the manuscript used by Linschoten was accompanied by a copy of the letter of safe-conduct of 6 March 1579 given by Drake to San Juan de Antón, addressed to Captain Winter; this letter was printed as an adjunct to the Silva "Relation." In printing these two items together, Linschoten was followed by Phillip, Hakluyt, Vaux, and Penzer. Nuttall, unaware of Hakluyt's source and not finding the Drake letter in A.G.I., assumed that Hakluyt had copied, or miscopied, an English original. She found a "better" version in A.G.S. (Inquisición. Peru), in a manuscript copy of the examination of John Butler, an English prisoner of the Inquisition, who was called from prison in Lima on 7 July 1579 to make a Spanish translation of Drake's letter. Nuttall translated this back into English and published it on pp. 16–17.

The photocopies are with the complete Draper Bibliography.

28. Nuno da Silva
Deposition. Before the Inquisition, Mexico, 23 May 1579.
MS in Spanish. A.G.N. Inquisición. vol. 85, pt. 17.

Another detailed account of the voyage. A somewhat different version was sent to the Council of the Inquisition in Spain and is at A.G.S.
Translated, Nuttall 295–322.

29. John Winter
Report sent to George Winter and Sir William Winter. [Plymouth?] 2 June 1579. *B.L. Lansdowne MS 100, no. 2.*

Endorsed by Lord Burghley: "Voyadge of Mr. Wynter with Mr. Drak to ye streyt of Magallanas June 1579." Winter was captain of the *Elizabeth* and Drake's second in command. He was separated from the *Marigold* and the *Pelican* (as it was still called) on 8 October 1578, after passing through the Strait and encountering a great storm. Winter took the *Elizabeth* back through the Strait and reached Plymouth on 2 June 1579. He sent this report of the voyage to his father and uncle, both of whom were members of the Navy Board, on the day of his arrival in England.

This document was discovered by E. G. R. Taylor, who published it in "More Light on Drake," *Mariner's Mirror* 16 (1930) 134–151; reprinted in J. Hampden, *Francis Drake Privateer* (London, 1972), pp. 239–243.

30. David Lewes
Letter of Dr. Lewes, Judge of the Admiralty, to the Lords of the Privy Council. "The Arches," 3 June 1579. *MS P.R.O. S.P. 12/139, no. 5.*

Dr. Lewes wrote for instructions relative to the Portuguese merchandise taken from Nuno da Silva and brought back to England by John Winter. The Ambassador of Portugal was demanding restitution.

Printed in Nuttall 383–384.

31. John Winter
Declaration made before the Court of Admiralty concerning the taking of the *Mary*, and an account of her cargo. June 1579. *MS P.R.O. S.P. 12/139, no. 24/1.*

Winter testified that the taking of Nuno da Silva's ship had been against his wishes and solely on Drake's orders. He lists the items taken from the ship and the disposition of those not still aboard the *Elizabeth*. This document is annexed to the "Commission out of the Court of Admiralty granted to Don Antonio de Castiglio for the recovery of the ship and goods taken at sea by Francis Drake and his company." Signed by the Queen. 17 June 1579. *MS P.R.O. S.P. 12/139, no. 24.*
Printed in Nuttall 385–386.

32. Don Luis de Velasco
Letter to Philip II. Mexico, 18 September 1579. *MS in Spanish. A.G.I. Patronato. 2/5/2-21, no. 7.*

At the time he wrote this letter, Don Luis, son of the second Viceroy of New Spain and later to become Viceroy himself, was the *Regidor* (Prefect) of the City of Mexico. He complains of the dilatory and ineffective measures used by Viceroy Martín Enríquez in attempting to pursue Drake and correctly conjectures that Drake had continued to the north and would not turn toward the Moluccas until summer was over.

Translated, Nuttall 230–237.

33. Pedro Sarmiento de Gamboa
"Relacion de lo que el corsario Francisco hizo y robó en la costa de Chile y
Perú y las diligencias que el Virey Don Francisco de Toledo hizo contra el,"
[1579].

One of the major documents about Drake's voyage, written by one of Spain's
most celebrated sixteenth-century navigators. The original manuscript has been
lost, and the source of knowledge about this "Relation" is the version printed
in C.D.I. XCIV, (1889), pp. 432–458. Sarmiento was sent in pursuit of Drake
sometime between July and October 1579 and actually came close to him. He
learned a great deal about Drake's voyage, and he had an interview with San
Juan de Antón, who recounted the capture of the *Cacafuego* and what he had
learned about Drake.

Nuttall, 59–88, made the first English translation, and Wagner, 385–395,
translated extracts from the C.D.I. version. Penzer, 200-215, printed extracts
from the Nuttall translation.

34. Francisco de Toledo
Relacion de la entrada que hizo por el estrecho el Navio yngles y de lo que
se previno contra. Los Reyes [Lima], 1579. *MS in Spanish. Library of Congress, Kraus Collection.*

Draft of a letter from the Viceroy of Peru to Juan Ortiz de Zárate, Governor
of Rio de la Plata, telling of Drake's passage through the Strait, his depredations, and the measures taken against him.

Translated in C. R. Markham, ed., *Narratives of the Voyages of Pedro
Sarmiento de Gamboa to the Straits of Magellan* (Hakluyt Society 91, London,
1895) pp. 206–208, and Kraus 112–114 (with facsimile reproduction).

35. Edward Cliffe
Account. [Undated.] *B.L. Lansdowne MS 100, fols. 17r–21v.*

Cliffe was a sailor who returned with Winter in 1579. His account of the first
part of the voyage was first printed in PN 1600 III and reprinted in Vaux
269–284 and Penzer 188–200. The account was used by the compiler of *The
World Encompassed* (1628); Wagner 294–302 prints corresponding passages
in parallel columns.

36. Francisco Gómez Rengifo
Deposition. Before Doctor Sancho de Alçorriz. Antequera [Oaxaca], 18 February 1580. *MS in Spanish. A.G.N. Inquisición.*

Gómez Rengifo, a citizen of Guatulco who acted as factor for a number of
Spanish merchants trading with Peru and Honduras, was robbed of everything
of value in his house in the raid of 13 April 1579 and was carried aboard
Drake's ship. He gives an account of his conversations with Drake and reports

that Drake read from a book that is presumably Foxe's *Book of Martyrs*. Gómez had testified on 29 December 1579 concerning the property of Nuno da Silva that had been left in his charge at Guatulco.

Translated, Nuttall 363–364.

37. Juan Pascual

Examination. Before Fr. Andrés de Aguirre. Acapulco, 5 March 1580. *MS in Spanish. A.G.N. Inquisición.*

Juan Pascual, a Portuguese sailor, was captured on 4 April 1579 from the ship on which Don Francisco de Zárate was traveling and was released at Guatulco. He was questioned particularly on the religious behavior of Nuno da Silva.

Translated, Nuttall 323–327.

38. Juan Pascual

Deposition. Before Bishop Granero de Avalos. Guatulco, 13 May 1580. *MS in Spanish. A.G.N. Inquisición. no. 6b.*

Pascual testified more extensively than before on religious practices aboard Drake's ship.

Translated, Nuttall 332–339.

39. Gaspar de Vargas

Deposition. Before Bishop Granero de Avalos. Guatulco, 14 May 1580. *MS. in Spanish. A.G.N. Inquisición.*

Vargas was questioned by the Inquisitor about the raid on Guatulco (see also nos. 17, 20).

Translated, Nuttall 340–342.

40. Simón de Miranda

Deposition. Before Bishop Granero de Avalos. Guatulco, 15 May 1580. *MS in Spanish. A.G.N. Inquisición.*

Miranda was the vicar of the port of Guatulco and one of the three citizens taken aboard Drake's ship. He was released the next day. He testified that Drake spoke evil of the Pope, and that Nuno da Silva was intimate with Drake and joined the English in prayers.

Translated, Nuttall 347–350.

41. Nuno da Silva

Examination. By the Inquisitors. Mexico, 21 May 1580. *MS in Spanish. A.G.N. Inquisición.*

The questioning concerned the safe-conducts given to San Juan de Antón (*see also* no. 27) and to Don Francisco de Zárate. Silva was also questioned as to whether Drake and the other captains had said that their voyage was by order of the Queen; he replied that this was so.

Translated, Nuttall 377–379.

42. Pedro de Rada
Letter to Doctor Gómez de Santillán. Portugalete, Spain, 29 July 1580. *MS in Spanish. A.G.I. Patronato, 2/5/2-21.*

Santillán was President of the Board of Trade in Seville and a member of the Council of the Indies. The letter informs him of the report of two French shipmasters that Drake had landed at Belle Isle, off the entrance to Nantes, and had proceeded from there to La Rochelle. It says that he brought a great quantity of treasure and tells how he passed through the Strait of Magellan to the South Sea, and that he had not dared to go to England because of a noble gentleman whom he had beheaded. A second letter to Santillán of 19 August confirms this report.

Nuttall 407–410 translates both letters.

43. Don Bernardino de Mendoza
Letter to Philip II. London, 16 October 1580. *In Spanish. B.L. Additional MS 28, 420, fol. 30.*

This letter from the Spanish Ambassador reports at length on Drake's long private audience with the Queen after his return from the voyage of circumnavigation. It is not found in A.G.S. with the rest of the official correspondence between the King and Mendoza, having presumably been intercepted by the English.

Translated, Hume III, 54–56. The extensive correspondence between the Ambassador and the King concerning Drake's voyage and the Spanish demands for restitution begins with Mendoza's letter of 8 January 1578. Most of it is published in C.D.I. XCI-XCII (1888) and translated in Hume II and III.

44. Queen Elizabeth I
Letter to Edmund Tremayne. "To assist Francis Drake in sending up certain bullion brought into the realm by him, but to leave so much of it in Drake's hands as shall amount to the sum of 10,000 l., the leaving of which sum in his hands is to be kept most secret to himself alone." Richmond, 24 October 1580. *MS P.R.O. S.O. 12/143 no. 30.*

Printed in Nuttall 429–430.

45. Edmund Tremayne
Letter to Walsingham. Collacombe (Lamerton, Devonshire), 8 November 1580. *MS P.R.O. S.P. 12/144 no. 17.*

"Reports that he has administered interrogatories to the gentlemen and others of Drake's company as to the value of his captures, reputed to the amount of one million and a half. Has left the amount of £10,000 in Drake's hands, selected by himself."

Enclosed are:

I. "The register of such treasure delivered to Chri: Harris, Esq. to be safely conducted and delivered into the Tower. Signed E. Tremayne, Frauncis Drake, and Chri. Harris, 5 November 1580." *MS P.R.O. S.P. 12/144 no. 17, I.*

II. "The answer of Lawrence Elyot, John Chester, and others, the gentlemen, and nearly fifty others of Drake's company, to the interrogatories relative to the value of his prize, conduct during the voyage, and treatment of the Spaniards." *MS P.R.O. S.P. 12/147 no. 17, 11.* Fascimile: Nuttall pl. XVI; Wallis 100 has facsimiles of some of the signatures.

46. Francis Walsingham
"Project . . . for establishing a company of such as shall trade beyond the equinoctial line: and in consideration of the late notable discoveries made by Francis Drake, he to be appointed Governor of the same for life." [November] 1580. *MS [Holograph]. P.R.O. S.P. 12/144, no. 44.*
   Printed in Nuttall 430, Wagner 214.

47. Gerard Mercator
Letter to Master Abraham Ortelius. Antwerp, 12 December 1580. *MS in Latin. Library of Congress, Kraus Collection.*

   Mercator speculates on the motives that inspired Drake's voyage and on the source of the treasure with which he returned.
   Photographic copy and translation, Kraus 85–88.

48. "Detailed account by Alderman Richard Martyn, Francis Drake, and Christopher Harris, of the amount of gold and silver bullion in ingots, brought from Sion, and laid up in a vault under the Jewel House; the silver bullion weighing 22,899 lbs. 5 oz., the coarse silver 512 lbs. 6 oz., and the gold bullion 101 lbs. 10 oz." London, 24 December 1580. [Indorsed by Burghley, *The quantite of bullion brought into y [e] Tower by Fr. Drake.*] *MS P.R.O. S.P. 12/144 no. 60.*
   Wallis 97–98 has facsimiles of portions of this document. (See also no. 69.)

49. John Cooke.
Narrative. [Undated.] *B.L. Harleian MS 540, fols. 93r–110v.*

   This account of the first part of Drake's voyage, from Plymouth to the Strait of Magellan, was one of the principal sources used by Hakluyt for "The Famous Voyage" (1589). Cooke was one of the mariners on the *Elizabeth*, whose captain, John Winter, turned back through the Strait after losing Drake's ship in a storm and reached England on 2 June 1579. Hakluyt omits most of Cooke's narration of the quarrel between Drake and Thomas Doughty.

The manuscript is thought to be in the handwriting of John Stow. First printed in full in Vaux 189–218; reprinted by Penzer 142–168; Wagner 245–262 prints excerpts in parallel columns with corresponding passages of "The Famous Voyage."

50. Nicholas Breton
A Discourse in commendation of the valiant as vertuous minded Gentleman, Maister Frauncis Drake, with a reioysing of his happy aduentures. London, 1581. *Library of Congress, Kraus Collection* (unique copy).

A short eulogy, preceded by a poem of eighteen lines, written apparently before Drake's knighting on 4 April 1581.

Facsimile of title page, Kraus 69, Wallis 95.

51. The Black Book. Plymouth, 1540–1709. *MS Plymouth Guildhall.*

A record of important events in the history of Plymouth. An entry for 1580 records Drake's return from around the world, at Michaelmas, and his knighting by the Queen.

A photographic copy of the entry, and a transcription, are in the Bancroft Library. For the survival of the Black Book see Crispin Gill, *Plymouth, a New History* (Newton Abbot, 1966), p. 234.

52. Grant of arms to Sir Francis Drake. Recorded by Robert Cooke, Clarenceaux King of Arms. 20 June 1581. *MS Plymouth City Museum and Art Gallery.*

An early seventeenth-century transcript is in *Harleian MS 1172, fol. 5b*; another copy is in *Ashmolean MS 858, fols. 38–39.*

For discussions of Drake's coat of arms see Corbett I, app., and Eliott-Drake I, 52–54.

53. Account of the auto-da-fé of 29 October 1581. Lima. [Undated.] *MS in Spanish. A.G.S.*

Report sent to the Inquisitor General at Seville regarding the questioning of "Joan Oxnem," "Jhoan Butlar" and "Thomas Xervel." The three were hanged, but "Enrique Butlar," supposedly John Butler's younger brother, was sentenced to the galleys (see also no. 7).

Published in José Toribio Medina, *Historia del Tribunal del Santo Oficio de Lima* (1569–1820), 2 vols. (Santiago, 1887; repr. Santiago, 1956) I, 156–157. Translated, Nuttall 2–3.

54. Robert Commaundre
"The Booke of Heraldrye and other things together with the Order of Coronacions . . . ." [Undated.] *B.L. Egerton MS 2642.*

A commonplace book. Contains: "In laudem Francisci Drake, Militis. T.N. Cicestrensis scripsit," fol. 224b; "In commendacion of Sir Frauncys Drake, Knight, the Renowned": a note of his circumnavigation, fol. 381b.

55. Robert Norman
The newe Attractive, Containing a short discourse of the Magnes or Lodestone: . . . Hereunto are annexed certaine necessarie rules for the arte of Navigation. . . . London, 1581.
Published in the same volume with William Borough, *A Discovrs of the Variation of the Cumpas, or Magneticall Needle. . . to be annexed to The newe Attractive of R.N.* [London] 1581.

Norman dedicates his book to William Borough, Comptroller of the Queen's Navy; Borough dedicates his to the travelers, seamen, and mariners of England. The purpose of both men was to advance the art of navigation and to end foreign supremacy in that field; in his preface Borough rejoices that "now at length our Countrieman Sir Francis Drake for valorous attempt, prudent proceading, & fortunate performyng his voiage about the worlde, is not onely become equall to any of them, but in fame farre surmounteth them all."

Many editions. Facsimile reprint: Amsterdam and Norwood, N.J., 1974.

56. Queen Elizabeth I
Warrant for the grant of the manor of Sherford in the county of Devon to Francis Drake, knight, and to his heirs. Westminster, 12 January 1582. *MS in Latin. P.R.O. Warrants for the Great Seal Series II (c. 82) bundle 1380.*
Photographic copy (reduced), Wallis 104.

57. Francisco de Dueñas
Report of an expedition to the Moluccas. Manila, May/June 1582. *MS in Spanish. A.G.I. Patronato. 1/21/13, no. 14. 37 fols.*

Dueñas was sent to the Moluccas in autumn 1581 by Gonzalo Ronquillo de Peñalosa, Governor of the Philippines, to report on the reaction of the Portuguese to the news of Philip II's succession to the throne of Portugal. A good deal of information on Drake is included in this report.

Extracts translated in Wagner 173–182 *passim.*

58. Charles de L'Ecluse
Caroli Clvsii Atreb. aliqvot notae in Garciae Aromatum Historiam. Eiusdem descriptiones nonnullarum Stirpium, & aliarum exoticarum rerum, que à Generoso vir Francisco Drake . . . obseruatae sunt . . . . Antwerp, 1582.

This little handbook of the aromatic plants collected on Drake's voyage is the first published scientific account of the circumnavigation. Clusius, the famous professor of botany at the University of Leiden, obtained botanical specimens personally from Winter and Eliot in 1581.

59. Henri Lancelot Voisin, Sieur de La Popelinière
Les trois mondes.... Paris, 1582.

The French historian states that Queen Elizabeth retained possession of the log of Drake's voyage, so that it could not be published (p. 36).

60. Fr. Juan de Rivadeneyra
Letter to the Governor of Tucumán, 19 March 1583. *MS in Spanish. A.G.I. Patronato. 2/5/2–21.*

Fray Juan was captured by Fenton from the same little bark as Richard Carter (see no. 62) but was released immediately. He writes about Drake's successes and gives information about Fenton's fleet.
Excerpts translated in Wagner 401–402, reprinted in Taylor 236–237.

61. Richard Madox
Diary. 1582–83. *B. L. Cotton MSS app. XLVII, 49 fols.; continued in Titus B. VIII, fols. 179–221.*

Richard Madox was the official registrar of the Edward Fenton voyage of 1582–83 and one of its chaplains. In addition to his official narrative of the voyage (*Cotton MS Otho E. VIII, fols. 140–143, 173*) he surreptitiously kept a private diary, in which he commented freely on the events of the trip and the shipboard gossip. To insure secrecy, he wrote much of it in cipher, or in Latin or Greek.
About one-quarter of this diary was transcribed in Taylor 150–198. The complete text was first published in E. S. Donno, *An Elizabethan in 1582: The Diary of Richard Madox, Fellow of All Souls* (Hakluyt Society, 2nd ser., 147; London, 1976).

62. Richard Carter, alias Juan Pérez
"Relacion que dio Juan Perez vecino del Rio dela Plata en la Capitania del Espiritu Santo." [Buenos Aires?] 1583. *MS in Spanish. A.G.I. Patronato. 2/5/2–21.*

Carter's capture is described in the account of the Fenton voyage by Luke Ward, printed in PN 1589. "We found an Englishman named Richard Carter, borne in Limehouse, who had bene out of England foure and twentie years." Carter had been living for the past twelve years at "Ascencion, up the River of Plate." He was captured off the Brazilian coast late in 1582 and carried to the

Rio de la Plata, where he was released. He later acted as interpreter for John Drake during his questioning at Santa Fe in 1584 (see no. 66).

Eighteenth-century copy listed in Navarrete no. 915. Translation of excerpts, Wagner 398–400; reprinted in Taylor 234–236.

63. Memoranda, apparently relating to the Drake voyage. [Undated.]
B. L. Harleian MS 280, fols. 81–82.

This group of notes immediately precedes the "Anonymous Narrative" (see no. 64) in the Harleian manuscript and is written in the same hand. It records amounts of gold and silver taken, tells of Nuno da Silva being left at Guatulco and subsequently being taken to Spain in 1582, and recounts the excommunication by Drake of Francis Fletcher.

Printed in Vaux 175–177.

64. Anonymous Narrative. "A discourse of Sir Francis Drakes iorney and exploytes after hee had past ye Straytes of Magellan into Mare de Sur, and through the rest of his voyadge afterward till hee arived in England. 1580 Anno." [Undated.] *B. L. Harleian MS 280, fols. 83–90.*

This document is one of the two principal sources used by Hakluyt for "The Famous Voyage" (see no. 76); the other was John Cooke's "Narrative" (no. 49). The "Anonymous Narrative" covers the second part of the voyage, beginning with the landfall at the island of Mocha, off the coast of Chile. Camden also used this source. Corbett II, app. E attributes the document to William Legge.

Printed in Vaux 178–186. Wagner 264–285, prints most of the document in parallel columns with corresponding passages of "The Famous Voyage."

65. William Gager
"Verses to Francis Drake." [Undated.] *B. L. Additional MS 22, 583. fol. 84.*

Part of a group of poems in Latin and English dedicated to a number of people, including Nicholas Breton and Queen Elizabeth. At fol. 62 begins a series of poems written September 1583 and dedicated to a group of senior members of Christ Church, Oxford, of which Gager was one and Richard Hakluyt another.

66. John Drake
"Relacion circunstanciada del viage que hizo Francisco Drak Ingles al Mar del Sur por el Estre[c]ho de Magallanes con todo lo ocurrido...desde el año de 1577 que salio del Puerto de Plemua en Inglaterra hasta su regreso al mismo Reyno. ..." Santa Fe, Provincia del Rio de La Plata, 24 March 1584. *MS in Spanish. A. G. I. Patronato. 2/5/2–21.*

John Drake, Francis Drake's young cousin, who completed the circumnavigation with him, commanded the bark *Francis* on the Fenton expedition of 1582. He was captured on the Rio de la Plata, imprisoned by Indians for thirteen months, and escaped to Buenos Aires. Richard Carter, alias Juan Pérez, revealed his identity to the Spaniards and acted as interpreter at this questioning before the authorities. (See also nos. 62, 70.)

An eighteenth-century copy in Museo Naval, Madrid, *M. SS. 35–18, 7 fols.* (Navarrete no. 921) is transcribed in *Repertorio* 74–88 and is transcribed and translated in Eliott-Drake II, 343–359. Extracts translated in Nuttall 18–34.

67. Richard Hakluyt

"A particuler discourse concerninge the greate necessitie and manifolde comodyties that are like to growe to this Realme of Englande by the Westerne discoveries lately attempted, Written in the yere 1584...." 1585 [copy]. *MS New York Public Library. Harkness Collection.*

This confidential report, prepared for Sir Walter Raleigh's presentation to the Queen, survives only in this manuscript.

It was first published under the title *A Discourse on Western Planting*, ed. Charles Deane with intro. by Leonard Woods (Cambridge, Mass., 1877), and simultaneously as *Documentary History of the State of Maine*, vol. II (Collections of the Maine Historical Society, 2nd series, 1877). A second edition, entitled "Discourse of Western Planting," appeared in *The Original Writings and Correspondence of the Two Richard Hakluyts*, ed. E. G. R. Taylor (Hakluyt Society, 2nd ser., 77; London, 1935), II, 213–326. The history of the manuscript and its publication is in H.H. II, 284–286.

68. Henry Robarts (Roberts)

A most friendly farewell, Giuen by a wellwiller to Sir Frauncis Drake . . . and the rest of the fleete bound to the Southward, and to all the gentlemen . . . who set sale from Wolwich the XV. day of Iuly, 1585. London [1585].

A pamphlet in verse.

Reprinted with an introduction by E. M. Blackie (Cambridge, Mass. 1924).

69. William Cecil, Lord Burghley

"A briefe note of all such silver bullion as was brought into the Tower by Sir Fras. Drake, Knight, and laid in the vaute under the Jewel-House, as also what hath been taken out, and what remaineth," 26 December 1585. *Hatfield House, Herts. Cecil Manuscripts.*

Refers to the treasure brought back from the voyage of circumnavigation. (cf. no. 48)

70. John Drake

"Discurso y Relacion dela causa del capitan Juan Drac Ingles." Ciudad de los Reyes [Lima], 8, 9, and 10 January 1587. *MS in Spanish. A.G.I. Patronato. 2/5/2-21.*

Having been imprisoned since his questioning in Santa Fe (see no. 66), John Drake was examined again before the Tribunal of the Inquisition in regard to both the Drake and Fenton expeditions. His ultimate fate is unknown.

An eighteenth-century copy in the Museo Naval, Madrid, *M. SS. 35–22, 15 fols.* (Navarrete no. 1876) is abstracted in *Repertorio* 98–99 and transcribed and translated in Eliott-Drake II, 360–401.

71. Robert Leng
"The true Discripcion of the last voiage of that worthy Captayne, Sir Fraun-cis Drake, knight, with his service done against the Spanyardes" 1587. [Holograph.] *B.L. Additional MS 21, 620.*

An account of the Cadiz expedition of 1587.
Published as *Sir Francis Drake's Memorable Service done against the Span-iards in 1587, Written by Robert Leng, Gentleman, one of his co-adventurers and fellow-soldiers. Now first edited, from the original ms. in the British Mu-seum, together with an appendix of illustrative papers, by Clarence Hopper* (Camden Society 87, Miscellany 5, London, 1863).

72. Thomas Greepe
The Trewe and Perfect Newes of the Woorthy and Valiant Exploytes, per-formed and doone by that Valiant Knight Syr Frauncis Drake.
London, 1587.

Facsimile edition, with introduction, notes, and bibliography by David W. Waters (Hartford, 1955).

73. Joannes Hercusanus, Danus
Magnifico ac strenvo viro D. Francisco Draco Anglo Eqviti avrato. London, 1587.

A broadside poem.
Translated with the title "To the magnificent and valiant man, Sir Francis Drake, the English Knight," *The Western Antiquary* 8 (1888) 27.

74. Raphael Holinshed
The Third volume of Chronicles, beginning at duke William the Norman, commonlie called the Conqueror. . . . First compiled by Raphael Holinshed and by him extended to the year 1577. Now newlie recognized, augmented, and continued . . . to the yeare 1586. London, 1587.

The first edition of the *Chronicles*, published in 1577, was the work of Holinshed, William Harrison, and Richard Stanyhurst. The greatly enlarged edition of 1587 appeared after Holinshed's death under the direction of John Vowell, alias Hooker, assisted by Francis Thynne, Abraham Fleming, and John Stow. This is apparently the first account published in English of Drake's voyage that gives any geographical details, even though these have been somewhat garbled. The name Nova Albion appears on p. 1555 of volume III, and the crowning of Drake by the Indians is mentioned.

75. Juan Suárez de Peralta

"Tratado del descubrimiento de las Yndias y su conquista, y los ritos y sacrificios, y costumbres de los yndios; y de los virreyes y gobernadores, que las han gobernado, especialmente en la Nueva España, y del suceso del Marqués del Valle, segundo, Don Martin Cortes: del[a] rebelion que se le ynputó y de las justicias y muertes que hizieron en Mexico los Juezes comisarios que para ello fueron por su magestad; y del rompimiento de los yngleses, y del principio que tuvo Francisco Draque para ser declarado enemigo" 1589. [Holograph.] *Toledo, Biblioteca Pública Provincial. MS 302 (Colección Borbón-Lorenzana). 179 fols.*

Although the battle of San Juan de Ulúa of 1568 is described in detail, this manuscript has no information about Drake; his name is introduced in two places (pp. 272, 274) apparently because of his notoriety.

First published by Justo Zaragoza, *Noticias históricas de la Nueva España* (Madrid, 1878). Second edition: *Tratado del descubrimiento de las Indias (Noticias históricas de la Nueva España), compuesto en 1589, nota preliminar de Federico Gómez de Orozco* (Mexico City, 1949).

76. Richard Hakluyt

The Principall Navigations, Voiages and Discoveries of the English nation, made by Sea or ouer Land . . . London, 1589.

A pioneering work, bringing together for the first time the scattered records of English voyages and travels. Hakluyt used both printed texts and unpublished manuscripts, the latter usually reproduced in their entirety and in translation. In most extant copies of the work, six unnumbered folio leaves have been inserted between pp. 643 and 644, printed on the same paper and in the same typeface as the rest of the volume, entitled: "The famous voyage of Sir Francis Drake into the South Sea, and there hence about the whole of the Globe of the Earth, begun in the yeere of our Lord, 1577." This is the first detailed account to be published of Drake's circumnavigation. Among the sources that can be identified are John Cooke's narrative and the "Anonymous Narrative." There are indications that Francis Fletcher's narrative was also used.

Wagner 245–285 reprinted "The Famous Voyage" in parallel columns with the pertinent passages of the Cooke narrative (first part of the voyage) and the "Anonymous Narrative" (second part). A photolithographic facsimile of the 1589 PN has been published in two volumes with an introduction by D. B.

Quinn and R. A. Skelton, and a new index by A. Quinn (Hakluyt Society, extra ser. 39, Cambridge, 1965).

The second, greatly enlarged edition is entitled: *The Principal Navigations, Voiages, Traffiqves and Discoueries of the English Nation, made by Sea or ouer-land.* . . . 3 vols. London, 1598/99–1600.

Vol. III contains voyages to "all parts of the *Newfound* world of *America,* or the *West Indies.*" "The Famous Voyage" is reprinted with some changes (pp. 730–742); and a separate account of the northwest coast, taken from the full account, appears on pp. 440–442. Three additional accounts relating to the circumnavigation are printed for the first time: the "relation" of 20 May 1579 of Nuno da Silva (pp. 742–748); Edward Cliffe's account of the voyage of John Winter (pp. 748–753); and "A discourse of the West Indies and South Sea," by López Vaz (pp. 778–802).

A number of editions of PN 1600 have been published; the best is the twelve-volume set published as the Hakluyt Society Extra Series 1–12, Glasgow, 1903–1905: a slightly modified reprint of the original edition, with contemporary maps, plans, and charts in facsimile, an essay on Hakluyt by Walter Raleigh, and a full index. For printing history and sources, see H. H.

77. López Vaz

"A discourse of the West Indies and South Sea, written by Lopez Vaz a Portugall, conteining diuers memorable matters not to be found in any other writers, and continued vnto the yere 1587." In Richard Hakluyt, *Principal Navigations* 1600 III 778–802.

López Vaz was captured in January 1587 in the Rio de la Plata by the Earl of Cumberland's fleet. His discourse (ms now lost) covers the years 1572–1586 and contains an account of Drake's circumnavigation which Vaz said he had obtained in writing from Nuno da Silva.

Parts of this translation, relating to Nombre de Dios, were originally published in PN 1589.

78. John Stow

A Svmmarie of the Chronicles of England, from the first arriving of Brute in this Island, vnto this present yeare of Christ, 1590. London, 1590.

Stow began publishing his Chronicles at least as early as 1565. The first collected edition appeared in 1580. The 1590 edition has a brief notice of the knighting of Drake aboard his ship at Deptford on 4 April 1579. The 1592 edition, entitled *The Annales of England,* gives a short account of Drake's voyage around the world. Stow's information about the first part of the voyage came from John Cooke's narrative, the same source used by Hakluyt for "The Famous Voyage." Hakluyt used a number of items from Stow's collection of manuscripts, many of which were copied by Stow himself, as was the Cooke narrative. In 1615, after Stow's death, Edmund Howe published a continuation of the *Annales* which included a new chapter, "The life & death of Sir Francis Drake."

Wagner 303–307 reprints in full Stow's account of the voyage, taken from the edition of 1635 which has the same text Stow printed in 1592. He also reprints "The life & death of Sir Francis Drake" from Howe's edition of 1615.

79. A declaration of the trve cavses of the great trovbles, presvpposed to be intended against the realme of England. n.p., 1592.

This rare pamphlet, which was perhaps surreptitiously printed on the Continent, attacks English policy and gives a brief account of Drake's marauding expedition to the "back-syde of America, where no pirates had been before him."

80. Thomas Blundeville
M. Blvndevile His Exercises; containing sixe Treatises. London, 1594.

These treatises were intended for the instruction of young gentlemen. Part II is entitled: "A plaine description of Mercator his two Globes. . . . Whereunto is added a briefe description of the two great Globes lately set foorth by M. Molinaxe: and of Sir Frances Drake his first voyage into the Indies." This account of the voyages of circumnavigation of Drake and Cavendish is little more than a description of their routes as shown on the famous Molyneux terrestrial globe of 1592. It concludes with the wish that "it might please Sir Frances to write a perfect Diarie of his whole voyage" and expresses the author's conviction that he has already written such an account "and will publish the same when he shall think most meete."

A number of editions of this work were published. The description of the two voyages is reprinted in Wagner 311–313.

81. Henry Robarts (Roberts)
The Trumpet of Fame: or Sir Frances Drakes and Sir John Hawkins Farewell. . . . London, 1595.

A verse salute to the departure of the two generals on their last voyage. Second edition, ed. Thomas Park. (Lee Priory, Kent, 1818).

82. "Relazion de lo sucedido en San Juan de Puerto Rico de las Yndias, con la armada Ynglesa del cargo de Francesco Draque y Juan Aquines, á los 23 de Noviembre, de 1595." [Undated] *B.L. Additional MS 13, 964.*

An account of the attack on the defenses of San Juan, undertaken by Drake after Hawkins' death, and its repulse.

There are two versions of the official report of this action. The document cited above was transcribed and translated in Hakluyt Society [4] (London,

1849) by W. D. Cooley (see no. 88). The other manuscript copy, supposedly in the Biblioteca de la Real Academia de la Historia, Madrid, but not found there, was printed in Alejandro Tapia y Rivera, *Biblioteca histórica de Puerto Rico* (Puerto Rico, 1854; 2nd ed., San Juan de Puerto Rico, 1945). Andrews 161–178 has collated the two available Spanish texts and made a new translation.

83. John Davis
Worldes Hydrographical Discription. London, 1595.

The famous navigator John Davis commanded three expeditions in search of the Northwest Passage in 1585, 1586, and 1587. His unpublished letters were used as sources for PN 1589; subsequently, the work cited above was used as the source for the three voyages in PN 1600 III. The short account of Drake's voyage deals mainly with the Strait of Magellan, through which Davis himself passed three times in the course of Cavendish's last voyage of 1591.

The *Hydrographical Description* was reprinted in *The Voyages and Works of John Davis, the Navigator,* ed. A. H. Markham (Hakluyt Society 59[a]; London, 1880). Wagner 314–315 printed the section on Drake.

84. George Peele
The Olde Wives Tale. A Pleasant Conceited Comedie, played by the Queenes Maiesties Players. London, 1595.

Contains topical references to Drake's circumnavigation. Peele had earlier written a poem in blank verse, *A Farewell. Entituled to the famous and fortunate generalls of our English forces: Iohn Norris & Syr Frauncis Drake* (London, 1589).

85. Sir Francis Drake
Last will and testament. August 1595. With a codicil dated 27 January 1596. Proved at London, 17 May 1596. *MS P.R.O. PROB 11/87 fol. 1.*

Drake drew up his will in England and carried it, unsigned, on his last voyage. The day before his death he signed it and had it witnessed by Charles Manners, Jonas Bodenham, Thomas Webbes, Roger Langsford, George Watkins, and William Maynarde. He dictated a codicil, which he signed and had witnessed by the same men, bequeathing his manor of Yarcombe to his cousin Francis Drake on condition of the payment of £2,000 to his brother Thomas Drake, and leaving his manor of Samford Spiney to Jonas Bodenham. (See also no. 86)

The text of the will and codicil are printed in full in *Wills from Doctors' Commons. A Selection from the Wills of Eminent Persons Proved in the Prerogative Court of Canterbury, 1495–1695,* ed. John G. Nichols and John Bruce (Camden Society 83, London, 1863, pp. 72–79). Full discussions of the litigation over the will are found in Eliott-Drake I, 137ff, and G. M. Thomson, *Sir Francis Drake* (London, 1972) pp. 339–340.

86. Sir Francis Drake
Indenture (Deed of Settlement). 27 January 1596. *MS Plymouth Central Public Library.*

This document, separate from the will and codicil signed by Drake on the same day (see no. 85), was dictated and signed aboard the *Defiance.* It entails all Drake's estates excepting the manor of Samford Spiney upon Drake's brother Thomas and his heirs.
See Eliott-Drake I, 125–126; Andrews 102.

87. Paris Profiles. 1595–1596. *Paris. Bibliothèque Nationale. Manuscrit Anglais 51. 22 fols.*

A series of sketches in color, drawn by someone aboard the *Defiance,* of Drake's principal landfalls on his last voyage, identifying coastal elevations and noting hydrographical features. On fol. 17, which depicts Portobelo, the artist records the death of Drake "this morninge…the 28 of Januarie 1595," [i.e. 1596 new style].
The manuscript was first described by Charles de la Roncière, "Un atlas inconnu de la dernière expédition de Drake (vues prises de son bord)," *Bulletin de géographie historique et descriptive,* no. 3 (1909), 396–404, with plates of fols. 1–17. Andrews pl. V–X reproduces fols. 13, 15, 17–19.

88. Thomas Maynarde
"Sir Fr. Drake his voyage 1595." [Undated.] *B. L. Additional MS 5209.*

A narrative by a young kinsman of Drake's who accompanied him as a seaman on the last voyage and who briefly describes his death.
First printed in *Sir Francis Drake, His Voyage, 1595,…Together with the Spanish Account of Drake's attack on Puerto Rico,* ed. W. D. Cooley (Hakluyt Society [4]; London, 1849). (See also no. 82.) Reprinted with corrections, Andrews 85–107.

89. Charles Fitzgeffrey
Sir Francis Drake, His Honorable lifes commendation, and his Tragicall Deathes lamentation. Oxford, 1596.

An epic poem praising the exploits of the English adventurers and explorers of the sixteenth century. The author made free use of Hakluyt's *Principal Navigations.* The poem has appeared in many editions, including one of collected works of Fitzgeffrey in 1881 and a facsimile of 1928.

90. *Franciscus Dracus Redivivus. Das ist/ Kurtze Beschreibung/ aller vornehmbsten Reysen/ Schiffarten vnnd Wasserschlachten/ So…Franciscus Dracus…vollbracht. Item von der jetzigen Englischen Admiraln vnnd Schiffobersten bey Calis Malis verrichten vnd Abzug.…Amsterdam, 1596.*

A tract depicting Drake and Cavendish as heroes of the Protestant struggle against Spain. Published in Cologne the same year.

91. Jan Huyghen van Linschoten

Itinerario, Voyage ofte Schipvaert...naer Ooste ofte Portugaels Indien, 1579–1592. 3 vols. in 4. Amsterdam, 1595–96.

A major compilation of voyages, chiefly to the East Indies, based partly on the author's own experiences and partly on unpublished personal accounts of others, which he translated into Dutch. Most of the material on the Americas is found in Book III, first published separately in 1595 with the title *Reysgeschrift*. This volume contains translations of many Portuguese and Spanish documents, including the first published version of Nuno da Silva's "Second Relation" and of Francis Drake's letter of safe-conduct for San Juan de Antón (see no. 27).

The complete work was translated into English by William Phillip at the instigation of Richard Hakluyt and published as *Discours of Voyages into ye Easte & West Indies* (London, 1598; facsimile reprint, Amsterdam, 1974). The two-volume edition by A. C. Burnell and P. A. Tiele (Hakluyt Society 70–71; London, 1885) is taken from the Phillip translation of books I and II only and does not include the *Reysgeschrift* with its Drake material.

A modern edition of the *Itinerario* has been published by Linschoten-Vereeniging in 5 vols.:| The Hague, 1910–1939; rev. 1955– in progress.

92. Francis Pretty

Beschryvinge vande overtreffelijcke ende wijdtervermaerde zeevaerdt vanden Edelen Heer ende Meester Thomas Candish.... Hier noch byghevoecht de voyagie van Sire Francoys Draeck, en Sire Jan Haukens ridderen.... Anno 1595. Amsterdam, 1598.

Emanuel Van Meteren translated into Dutch Pretty's manuscript account of Cavendish's circumnavigation, in which Pretty had participated. The English manuscript was given to Van Meteren for this purpose by Richard Hakluyt in 1595. The Dutch translation was published in 1598, together with an account of the Drake and Hawkins voyage of 1595, and was then translated from Dutch into Latin for Theodor de Bry's *America*, pt. VIII (1599), before it appeared in English, for the first time, in PN 1600 III (see H. H. 307, 311).

93. Lope Félix de Vega Carpio

La Dragontea. Valencia, 1598.

Lope de Vega wrote this epic poem to celebrate Drake's final defeat and death. He reviews Drake's career in some detail, making use of contemporary documents as well as of his own experiences in the Armada. The ten cantos are a mixture of fact and fantasy, in which real events and people appear together with the imaginary and allegorical. Drake is portrayed as dragon and devil, motivated by greed; and the Queen, the English, and Lutheranism are violently attacked. Drake dies in agony, poisoned by his own men, and the Christian religion gives thanks to God.

A modern edition was published by the Museo Naval of Madrid in 1935: vol. I contains the poem; vol. II is entitled *Repertorio de documentos existentes en las colecciones de Mss. del Museo Naval y que se refieren a las empresas del Draque contra España, 1568–1594.*

94. Theodor de Bry
Americae pars VIII:| *Continens primo, descriptionem trivm itinervm . . . Francisci Draken . . . secvndo, iter . . . Thomae Candisch . . . tertio, duo itinera . . . Gvaltheri Ralegh.* Frankfurt, 1599.

De Bry's richly illustrated collection of *Grands Voyages,* originally suggested by Richard Hakluyt, appeared from 1590 to 1601 in Latin and German. The account of Drake's circumnavigation is the first Latin translation (abridged) of "The Famous Voyage." The translator was Gotthard Arthus.

95. Thomas Westcote
"Pedigree of Devon." [Undated.] *Oxford. Bodleian Library. MS 22, 767.*

Westcote also wrote *Pedigrees of Most of our Devonshire Families* (Exeter, 1845).

96. Antonio Herrera y Tordesillas
Descripcion de las Indias occidentales. Madrid, 1601.

Volume I of Herrera's *Historia general de los hechos de los castellanos en las islas i tierra firme del mar oceano.* 4 vols. (Madrid, 1601–1615).Translations into Latin, French, and Dutch published in 1622 had a small title page map showing California as an island, the first known printed depiction of this error, which was in part disseminated by information from N. de Morena, one of Drake's Portuguese pilots left behind in Nova Albion.

97. Levinus Hulsius
Sammlung von Sechs und Zwanzig Schiffarten in verschiedene fremde Lander. 26 vols. Nuremberg; Frankfurt, 1598–1659.

Sechste Theil Kurtze Warhafftige Relation vnd beschreibung der Wunder-barsten vier Schiffarten so jemals verricht worden (Nuremberg, 1603): contains the first German translation of "The Famous Voyage" in a much-condensed version.

98. Antonio Herrera y Tordesillas
Historia General del Mundo de tiempo del señor Rey don Felipe II el Prudente. 3 vols. Valladolid, 1606–1612.

The account of Drake's circumnavigation in volume II, book IX, copied almost literally from John Drake's "Relation" of 1584 (see no. 66), is translated in Wagner 330–334. A great deal of information on Drake's various expeditions, mostly from Spanish sources, is found throughout the work.

99. Bartolomé Leonardo de Argensola
Conqvista de las Islas Malvcas. Madrid, 1609.

The account of Drake at the island of Ternate relies heavily on Herrera (see no. 96) and on the Francisco de Dueñas report of 1582 (see no. 57), as well as on another Dueñas report.
    English translation: *The Discovery and Conquest of the Molucco and Philippine Islands* (London, 1708).

100. Giuseppe Rosaccio
Discorso... Nel quale si tratta brevemente della Nobilita, & Eccellenza della Terra rispetto à Cieli, & altri Elementi. Florence (n.d.).

A rare geographical pamphlet, written probably around 1610. Drake's circumnavigation is described.
    Copy in Library of Congress, Kraus Collection.

101. François de Louvencourt
Le Voyage De L'Illvstre Seignevr Et Cheualier François Drach, Admiral d'Angleterre, alentour du monde. Paris, 1613.

The first French version of "The Famous Voyage" is the most complete of the early translations. The 1589 text was used. Subsequent editions in 1627 and 1641 appeared with a second part, "Des Singvlaritez Remarqvees Aux Isles & terres-fermes du Midy, & des Indes Orientales; par l'Illustre Seigneur & Chevalier François Drach, Admiral d'Angleterre." It is with the 1641 edition, *Le Voyage Cvrievx...*, that almost all known copies of the Nicola van Sype Drake map have been found.

102. William Camden
Annales Rervm Anglicarvm, et Hibernicarvm, Regnante Elizabeth, ad Annvm Salvtis M. D. LXXXIX. London, 1615.

Contains books I–III. Camden is the source for most of what is known of Drake's early life. For his account of the circumnavigation he used the "Anonymous Narrative," supplemented by "The Famous Voyage" and other sources. First English translation: *Annales, the True and Royall History of the famous Empress Elizabeth,* by Abraham Darcie, from the 1624 French translation of Paul de Bellegent.
    Book IV, completed in 1617, published in Latin (Leiden, 1625; London, 1627), was included in the first complete translation into English by Robert

Norton: *The Historie of the Most Renowned and Victorious Princesse Elizabeth, Late Queen of England* (London, 1630).

Wagner 317–323 reprints the account of Drake's life from Darcie.

103. Luis Cabrera de Córdova
Filipe Secvndo rey de España. Madrid, 1619.

Only part I, which covers 1527–1583, appeared in 1619; the rest of the work remained unpublished until a second edition was produced from a manuscript in the Bibliothèque National: *Filipe Segundo, rey de España,* 4 vols. (Madrid, 1876–77). The early volume includes the battle of San Juan de Ulúa and Drake's voyage around the world.

104. Henry Holland
Heroologia Anglica. 2 vols. Arnhem, 1620.

A biographical work on famous English men and women, with 67 full-page portraits engraved by Willem and Magdalena van der Passe.

105. Samuel Purchas
Pvrchas His Pilgrimes. 4 vols. London, 1625.

After Hakluyt's death in 1617, his manuscripts passed to the Reverend Samuel Purchas and became the nucleus of a new work. On the engraved added title page of Purchas's first volume appears the catch title "Haklvytvs Posthumous." Purchas summarized much of what Hakluyt had already published and added a great deal of new material. "The Famous Voyage" is reprinted with only minor changes. The "Relation" of Peter Carder (who was separated from Drake's expedition in 1578 and captured but survived to return to England in 1586) is printed for the first time in volume IV.

The best edition is *Hakluytus Posthumous*...(Hakluyt Society, Extra Series [14–33], 20 vols. Glasgow, 1905–1907), a slightly modified reprint of the 1625 edition, with index in vol. XX.

106. Sir Francis Drake Reviued: Calling vpon this Dull or Effeminate Age, to folowe his Noble Steps for Golde & Siluer, By this Memorable Relation, of the Rare Occurrances (neuer yet declared to the World) in a Third Voyage, made by him into the West-Indies, in the Yeares 72. & 73. when Nombre de Dios was... surprised. Faithfully taken out of the Reporte of Mr. Christofer Ceely, Ellis Hixon, and others...By Philip Nichols, Preacher. Reviewed also by Sr Francis Drake himselfe before his Death...Set forth by Sr Francis Drake Baronet (his Nephew) now liuing. London, 1626.

The "Dedicatorie Epistle" to Queen Elizabeth is signed "Francis Drake, Jan. 1, 1592." The authenticity of this work has been questioned, but its conformity to the facts seems to be supported by contemporary Spanish documents, many of which are published in *Documents Concerning English Voyages to the*

Spanish Main, *1569–1580* ed. I. A. Wright (Hakluyt Society, 2nd ser., 70; London, 1932), where a reprint of the 1628 edition also appears. This work is related to *Sloane MS 301,* "A Relation of the rare occurrences in a third voyage made by Sir Francis Drake into the West Indies in the years 72 and 73...by Phillip Nicholls Preacher." (See Wallis 38–39.)

107. The World Encompassed By Sir Francis Drake, Being his next voyage to that to Nombre de Dios formerly imprinted; carefully collected out of the notes of Master Francis Fletcher Preacher in this imployment, and diuers others his followers in the same....London, 1628.

The first full-length account of Drake's circumnavigation. The original manuscript of Fletcher's journal is lost; there remains only a manuscript copy of the first part, which breaks off with the arrival at the island of Mocha. This copy by John Conyers, dated 1677 (*Sloane MS 61*), reproduces many of Fletcher's drawings.

Vaux prints extracts from Fletcher as footnotes to the text and other sources of the work in appendices: "Documents relating to Mr. Thomas Doughty" (*Harleian MS 6221;* see no. 5); "Memoranda, apparently relating to this voyage" (*Harleian MS 280;* see no. 63); "Short abstract of the present voyage, in handwriting of the time"; John Cooke's narrative (see no. 49); and five pertinent extracts from PN 1600 III.

Penzer transcribes Fletcher's journal and prints it in full for the first time; six extracts from Nuttall not found in Vaux are also printed. Wagner 294–302 prints passages in parallel columns with corresponding passages of the Cliffe narrative (see no. 35). A facsimile was published (Cleveland, 1966) with a historical introduction by A. L. Rowse and bibliographical notes by R. O. Dougan.

108. Sir James Whitelocke
"Liber Famelicus." 18 April 1609–27 December 1631.

A family history. Sir James recounts that his older brother William Whitelocke served with Drake on many voyages and was with him at his death, putting his armor on him a little before the end.

At the time of the publication of *Liber Famelicus,* ed. John Bruce (Camden Society 70; London, 1858), the manuscript, in Sir James's hand, was in the possession of a descendant of his son Bulstrode Whitelocke. Andrews 45–46 reprints the part about Drake from the Camden publication.

109. Thomas Fuller
The Holy State. Cambridge (Eng.), 1642.

Extra title page: *The Profane State.* Chapter 21, "The Life of Sir Francis Drake," has marginal references to a now lost manuscript by George Fortescue, a member of Drake's expedition of 1577–1580.

110. Sir Francis Drake Revived. Who is or may be a Pattern to stirre up all Heroicke and active Spirits of these times.... Being a Summary and true Relation of foure severall VOYAGES made by the said Sir Francis Drake to the West Indies. London, 1653.

The first collection of Drake's voyages, each printed with a separate title page, containing: *Sir Francis Drake Revived*, [London], 1653; *The World Encompassed*, London, 1652; *A Summarie and True Discourse of Sir Francis Drake's West Indian Voyage* [of 1585–86, by Walter Bigges and Lieutenant Crofts], London, 1652; and *A Full Relation of Another Voyage made by Sir Francis Drake and others to the West Indies; who set forth from Plimouth the 28. of August, 1595,* London, 1652.

The author of the last work is unknown; it was first published, together with Bigges's *Summarie and True Discourse*, in 1652, and no manuscript or earlier printing has been traced (Andrews 79–80). Bigges's work was first published in Latin as *Expeditio Francisci Draki Equitis* (Leiden, 1588) and in French the same year. It was published in English in 1589 and reprinted with *A Full Relation* in 1652 and again in the present work.

111. Sir William D'Avenant
The History of Sr. Francis Drake: Exprest by Instrumentall and Vocall Musick, and by Art of Perspective in Scenes, &c. The First Part. London, 1659.

This is a patriotic opera written at a time when Cromwell's government was at war with Spain and English forces were involved in the West Indies. It was performed at the Cockpit in Drury Lane during the winter of 1658–59 and consists of six "entries" or acts, three set in Peru and three in the vicinity of Panama. The story is based on Drake's successful West Indian voyage of 1572. It includes a scene in which Drake climbs to the top of a tall tree to observe both the Atlantic and Pacific Oceans and contains the prophecy that Drake will be the first Englishman to take a ship into the Pacific. Although it lacks many features of Italian opera of the period, the use of sung dialogue, recitative, choruses, and dancing makes it important in the development of opera in England. No second part is extant.

The History of Sir Francis Drake was revived in 1663 at D'Avenant's own theater, the Duke's Playhouse, as act III of an entertainment called *The Playhouse to be Let.* That play was first printed in D'Avenant's collected *Works* (London, 1673; facsimile ed. New York, 1968). A collection of D'Avenant's *Dramatic Works* was edited by J. Maidment and W. H. Logan (London, 1872–1874; repr., New York, 1964).

INDEX

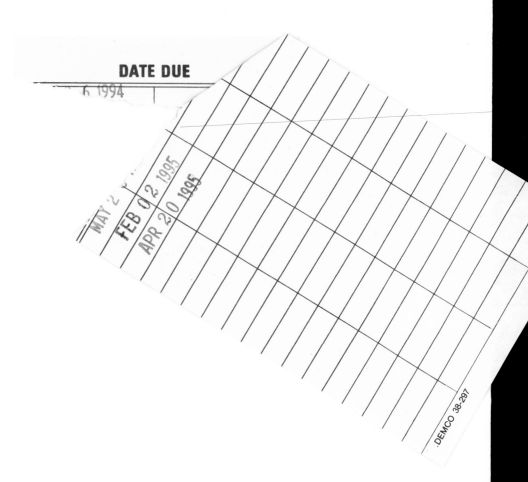